THE
OPTIONS
APPLICATIONS
HANDBOOK

THE
OPTIONS
APPLICATIONS
HANDBOOK

HEDGING AND SPECULATING
TECHNIQUES FOR PROFESSIONAL INVESTORS

ERIK BANKS AND PAUL SIEGEL

McGraw-Hill

New York   Chicago   San Francisco
Lisbon   London   Madrid   Mexico City
Milan   New Delhi   San Juan   Seoul
Singapore   Sydney   Toronto

The *McGraw-Hill* Companies

1 2 3 4 5 6 7 8 9 0   FGR/FGR   0 9 8 7 6

ISBN-13 978-0-07-145315-8
ISBN-10   0-07-145315-6

This publication is designed to provide accurate and authoritative information in regard to the subject matter covered. It is sold with the understanding that neither the author nor the publisher is engaged in rendering legal, accounting, or other professional service. If legal advice or other expert assistance is required, the services of a competent professional person should be sought.

—From a Declaration of Principles jointly adopted by Committee of the American Bar Association and a Committee of Publishers

McGraw-Hill books are available at special quantity discounts to use as premiums and sales promotions, or for use in corporate training programs. For more information, please write to the Director of Special Sales, McGraw-Hill Professional, Two Penn Plaza, New York, NY 10121-2298. Or contact your local bookstore.

DEDICATION

This book is dedicated to our friends and families. Without their continued patience and support, this book would not have been possible. We also dedicate this book to the many corporate and investment bankers who work with options. They all know too well the Yogi Berra caution: "The future ain't what it used to be."

C O N T E N T S

THE
OPTIONS
APPLICATIONS
HANDBOOK

Option Products and Applications

An Introduction to Options Markets

INTRODUCTION

Options, or financial contracts that derive their value from an underlying reference asset, have become an essential component of the global financial markets. Growth over the past few decades has been significant, largely because these derivatives provide participants with valuable risk management, speculating, and investing opportunities. The global options market, which amounts to several trillion dollars of notional value, includes both exchange-traded (listed) and customized over-the-counter (OTC) contracts on a broad range of assets, including equities and indexes, interest rates, currencies, commodities, credit spreads, and other specialized references.

In this introductory chapter we will explore general issues regarding the options market, including common option terminology, option trading marketplaces, option asset classes, and general uses of options. We will expand on each of these introductory topics at various points in the text. We shall also review, in outline form, the material appearing in the balance of the book in order to properly frame our discussion. The reader will note that each of the chapters in the book features a series of exercises that are designed to test and reinforce the key points; an answer key is located at the end of the text.

OPTION TERMINOLOGY

We begin our discussion with a simple definition: an option is a financial instrument that gives the holder (or buyer) the right, but not the obligation, to buy or sell a reference asset at a specific price within a specific time frame. In exchange for receipt of an up-front payment, or premium, from the buyer, the seller is obliged to honor the terms of the contract. Since the option derives its value from a reference asset, it comprises part of the class of financial instruments known as derivatives, which also includes swaps, forwards, and futures.[1]

Options are defined by certain common terms:

- Call option: a contract giving the buyer the right to buy a specific asset at a defined price.
- Put option: a contract giving the buyer the right to sell a specific asset at a defined price.
- Holder or buyer: the party (whether an individual or institution) that purchases the option, so gaining the right, but not the obligation, to exercise the option. A holder or buyer purchasing a call or put option is "long" the option.
- Writer or seller: the party that sells the option and thus legally commits to perform should the buyer exercise the right to buy or sell the specified asset. The writer selling a call or put option is "short" the option.
- Strike price: the price at which the buyer of the option can buy the specified asset from, or sell it to, the seller.
- Contract size: the amount of the specified asset that can be bought or sold at the strike price; this may be defined in terms of a notional amount (e.g., $100m) or a physical amount (e.g., 25,000 barrels of oil).
- Expiration date: the last date on which an option can be exercised. If an option expires without being exercised it

---

1 A *swap* is a customized contract that calls for the exchange of flows between two parties, based on a defined notional principal amount. Interest rate swaps can be based on the exchange of fixed and floating rates or two different floating rates; currency swaps can be based on fixed/fixed, fixed/floating, or floating/floating rates in two different currencies. A *forward* is a customized contract where one party agrees to buy, and another to sell, a particular amount of an asset, at some predetermined forward price, for settlement in the future. A *futures* contract is similar to a forward, except that it is traded on a formal exchange in standardized terms, and is marked-to-market daily (and not only on the future settlement date).

ceases to exist; the buyer no longer has the right to buy or sell and the seller no longer has any obligations to perform under the contract.

- Exercise date: the date on which an option can be exercised.
- Exercise style: the timing of possible exercise, which may be American, European, or Bermudan.

  □ American exercise: the option can be exercised on any date up to, and including, the expiration date.

  □ European exercise: the option can be exercised only on the expiration date.

  □ Bermudan exercise: the option can be exercised periodically up to, and including, the expiration date.

- Premium: the amount the buyer pays the seller for the option. The premium is nonrefundable, meaning the seller keeps the amount paid whether or not the option is ever exercised. An up-front payment of cash is the most common form of premium payment, though in some instances it can be amortized and paid over time.

- Settlement: The manner in which the option is settled on exercise; this may be in physical or financial terms, depending on market convention or the specific agreement negotiated between buyer and seller. Physical settlement results in delivery of physical goods (e.g., oil, corn), while financial settlement results only in a net exchange of cash.

OPTION MARKETPLACES

Options can be bought and sold through two marketplaces: the listed, or exchange-traded market, and the OTC market. Each market features particular advantages and disadvantages.

Exchange-Traded Markets

The exchange-traded market is comprised of all regulated futures/options exchanges. Formal exchanges—such as the Chicago Mercantile Exchange, Euronext, Eurex, New York Mercantile Exchange, Tokyo Commodity Exchange, and others— list and trade derivative contracts on a multitude of references. The primary contracts include futures, options, and futures options;

we shall focus our discussion on the latter two, as the futures contract, which is simply a derivative obliging the buyer to purchase from the seller a reference asset at a stated price for future delivery, is out of scope. Nevertheless, the same structure and characteristics apply to all listed products described below.

Each exchange sets standard terms for the options/futures options it lists, including contract size, tick value, expiry date, exercise style, strike price, settlement type/process. Standardized characteristics mean that participants cannot create their own "customized" terms—they can only buy and sell the exchange's defined contracts. While this reduces flexibility, it also means that a greater mass of liquidity can build in a given product because all participants trade the same instrument; this can lead to narrower bid-offer spreads. Options and futures options are generally available on standard or serial cycles. Standard contract dates tend to match those of an exchange's futures offerings (which are often quarterly), while serial contracts are sequential short-term contracts that cover nonstandard months.

Buyers and sellers of exchange-traded options deal directly through an exchange's clearinghouse, which is an entity that accommodates all execution and settlement. In fact, the exchange clearinghouse is a party to all trades, meaning that the option buyer purchases a contract from the clearinghouse while the option seller sells a contract to the exchange. At no time do buyers and sellers face each other directly.[2] In order to eliminate counterparty credit risks—or the risk of loss due to counterparty failure—the clearinghouse requires every participant to post initial margin (e.g., a security deposit in the form of cash or high-quality government securities) to cover the potential exposure of the contract(s). The clearinghouse revalues open positions every day, and calls for additional margin (variation margin) if a participant's position has generated a loss, or returns margin if the position has resulted in a gain.

---

2 For instance, all options listed on U.S. exchanges are issued and cleared by The Options Clearing Corporation (OCC). The OCC assures performance to the selling and purchasing clearing members. The Chicago Board Options Exchange (CBOE) created the OCC in 1973. Since then, it has become an entity owned jointly by four U.S. option exchanges, the CBOE, the American Stock Exchange (ASE), the Pacific Exchange (PE), and the Philadelphia Stock Exchange (PSE). Standard & Poor's has granted the OCC an "AAA" credit rating based on the OCC's three-tiered backup system and the collateralization which stands behind OCC's obligations to its clearing members.

FIGURE 1.1

Exercise of a Futures Option on Crude Oil Futures

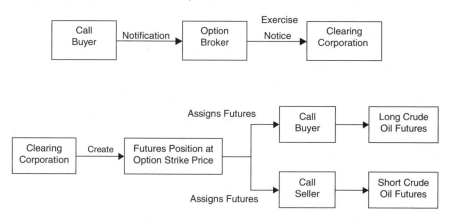

Listed options and futures options can be terminated in three ways: offset, expiration, and exercise. For instance, an institution that has purchased an option or futures option can close out the position by selling the same option—this creates an offsetting position. To be a true offset the position must be of the same type (call or put) and have the same strike price and expiry date as the original position. Similarly, an institution that has sold an option must buy back the same option in order to close out the position. Expiration is a second form of termination and occurs when the contract ends without value; in this case the seller has no further obligations. Exercise is the third form of termination and involves actual exercise and delivery of cash or the reference asset/futures contract; this strategy is employed when the option has value and has not been offset. For instance, when a listed option is exercised, the clearinghouse will deliver the cash or asset to the option buyer and demand the same from the seller. When a futures option is exercised, the buyer and seller are assigned futures positions by the exchange clearinghouse, as noted in the example of crude oil futures options in Figure 1.1.[3]

---

3 Note that if the futures position itself is not offset, the underlying physical asset will be delivered to the buyer by the seller (e.g., in this case, crude oil); such physical settlement is rare (e.g., 1%–5% of all contracts, depending on exchange).

OTC Markets

The OTC market is a largely unregulated forum where options (and other derivatives) are traded on a customized basis between two parties, without the use of centralized exchanges or their clearinghouses. Dealing is arranged telephonically or via electronic communications networks and transactions are documented via individual confirmations and other supporting legal documentation. The OTC derivatives market, which developed in the early 1980s through the introduction of currency and interest rate swaps, has become the single largest forum for options trading, with notional amounts now extending into the trillions of dollars.

Parities involved in the OTC market negotiate specific details regarding each transaction, which stands in contrast to the standardized listed market. This difference gives rise to two characteristics: the OTC market supports complete customization of characteristics such as strike price, tick value, expiry date, settlement process, and exercise style, meaning participants can create "tailor-made" risk management or investment solutions; and, customization leads to the creation of unique contracts, meaning the same critical mass of liquidity that can be found in many standardized option contracts is often lacking. That said, the OTC market quotes certain standard structures, so liquidity can build in a particular group of contracts; indeed, some OTC interest rate, currency, and equity options are very liquid. Like listed options, OTC contracts can be terminated by establishing an offsetting OTC position, by allowing the contract to expire (if out-of-the-money), or by exercising/selling the contract (if in-the-money).

While most activity is centered in conventional (or vanilla) options, the market also supports activity in exotic or complex options with payoff parameters that are different from those found in conventional markets. In fact, the exotic options sector has become one of the fastest-growing components of the derivatives market, precisely because it is tailored to the very specific risk and investment management needs of intermediaries and end users. We shall discuss exotic options at greater length in Chapter 3, and demonstrate their practical use in Chapter 7.

Because participants in the OTC market do not deal through exchange clearinghouses, they do not receive the credit risk mitigation benefits that arise from the margin/clearinghouse structure. Counterparty credit risks can therefore appear. In fact, credit risks arise when an institution buys an option, becoming exposed to counterparty performance as the contract moves in-the-money. We shall consider aspects of credit risk in Chapter 11.

OPTION ASSET CLASSES

One of the most powerful features of the global options markets is that contracts can be bought and sold on a very broad range of assets and markets. Options trades are routinely arranged on references from the equity markets (including single stock, baskets, and indexes, equity volatility), fixed income markets (including short- and long-term interest rates, interest rate volatility, credit spreads, credit defaults), currency markets, commodity markets (including energy, softs, metals, agriculturals), and other noncommodity markets (including weather, inflation, catastrophe).

Equities

Equity-related options comprise one of the most popular segments of the option market, with intermediaries and end users actively dealing in puts and calls on individual stocks, baskets, industry sectors, and market indexes. The market has become global, with contracts arranged on equity references in both developed and emerging equity markets; activity in options of large capitalization stocks and major market indexes is particularly significant. Equity options, which can be arranged to settle in either physical or financial form, are routinely used to hedge underlying equity portfolio exposures or express a leveraged view of equity market direction and/or volatility.

Interest Rates

The interest rate option market is also very active, with OTC and listed options dealt on a range of interest rate references, including money market and government rates from both developed and emerging markets. Dealing in interest rate contracts such as U.S. Treasuries, gilts, bunds, Japanese Government Bonds, as well as interbank deposits is exceptionally active; the contacts can be used to efficiently establish a speculative or hedge position with physical or financial settlement. Caps and floors are also an important component of the sector: caps (which are strips of individual options that establish a maximum interest rate) and floors (strips of options that set a minimum interest rate) are used for funding, investment, and risk management purposes. Caps and floors generally reference an actively traded floating rate benchmark such as London Interbank Offered Rate (LIBOR), Euro Interbank Offered Rate (EURIBOR), Tokyo Interbank Offered Rate (TIBOR), Treasury bill rates, bank bill rates, or commercial paper (CP) rates.

Currencies

Currency options are traded frequently in both the listed and OTC markets. Activity in currency options dates back to the early 1970s when the fixed exchange rate regime covering most of the world's major currencies was abandoned in favor of freely floating rates. This ushered in an era of currency volatility, which caused demand for currency contracts to increase sharply. The same process continues to the present time: institutions take positions to hedge underlying currency exposures generated by international cash flows, or to speculate on currency direction or volatility. Most volume is centered in vanilla puts and calls on major currency pairs, including $/¥, $/€, $/£, $/C$, $/SFr, as well as various cross rates, including €/£, €/¥, and €/Sfr. Some activity also takes place in second-tier and emerging market currencies, though such business tends to be more opportunistic.

Commodities

Listed commodity options on energy products (crude oil, natural gas), industrial metals (copper, aluminum), precious metals (gold, silver, platinum, palladium), and agricultural goods (corn, wheat, soybeans, pork bellies) have been popular with hedgers and speculators for decades; new contracts, such as those on electricity, have also emerged in recent years with changes in market dynamics (e.g., deregulation, increased competition and volatility). OTC options on the same references (as well as broader commodity baskets and indexes) have also proven appealing. It is important to note that while significant turnover occurs in commodity options, the majority of contracts bought and sold are closed out prior to maturity (or are arranged to settle on a financial, rather than physical, basis). Physical acceptance and delivery of gold, oil, wheat, and other commodities via the options mechanism is relatively uncommon.

Credits

Options on credit risks—including credits spreads and credit defaults—are relatively new to the marketplace. Trading in such credit derivatives, which is still conducted exclusively on an OTC basis, commenced with the introduction of default swaps in the mid-1990s. As intermediaries and end users gained comfort with the basic default swap product, they expanded into options on defaults and credit spreads (e.g., the differential between a risky credit's spread and a risk-free benchmark, such as U.S. Treasuries or U.K. gilts). Credit-related options can be settled physically or financially, though the trend towards financial settlement has become stronger in recent years.

Other References

Given the creative powers of intermediaries and the demands of end users, it comes as no surprise that the financial marketplace features options on other types of references. For instance, OTC and/or listed options have been introduced on inflation indexes, macro-economic indexes (e.g., GDP), real estate indexes, weather risk (e.g., temperature), catastrophe risk (e.g., hurricane, earthquake), and so forth. Since many of these references are nondeliverable (e.g., temperature, GDP), settlement is financial, rather than physical.

Table 1.1 summarizes key listed and OTC option references.

TABLE 1.1

Listed and OTC Option References

Asset Class	Key References
Equities	Individual stocks, baskets, industry sectors, country sectors, broad market indexes
Interests	Money market rates, government bond rates
Currencies	G10 currencies, 2d tier/regional currencies, emerging currencies
Commodities	Energy products, industrial metals, precious metals, agricultural goods
Credits	Defaults, credit spread movements
Others	Inflation, economic growth, catastrophe, weather

GENERAL USES OF OPTIONS

The use of options goes well beyond the profit-motivated trading that is most visible to the public. Sophisticated institutions use options for a variety of purposes, including hedging, speculating, arbitraging/monetizing. Though we will explore option applications in greater detail in Chapter 7, we introduce the topic in general terms in this section. We begin with a simple explanation of each motivating factor in the context of options:

- Hedging: creating an option position in order to protect an input or output that might otherwise generate a loss. An option hedge is intended to be a zero-sum game: a gain on the input or output should be offset by a loss on the option, and vice versa.
- Speculating: creating an option position or strategy in order to take advantage of price or volatility moves in the reference asset. The speculative position is intended to generate a profit but also exposes the participant to limited or unlimited losses in the process.
- Arbitraging/monetizing: creating a low-risk or riskless option strategy that generates modest profit with only limited downside. A pure arbitrage is riskless; a market arbitrage position has very modest amounts of risk. Monetizing, a subset of this process, is based on creating an option position that crystallizes value on some underlying asset.

For instance, an institution holding a large portfolio of equities can protect itself from a market downturn by buying put options on individual stocks or a broad market index. The institution continues to hold its underlying stock portfolio but effectively insures the downside by paying a premium in exchange for a compensatory payment should the price of the stocks fall. If the stock prices rally, the institution gains on its portfolio and sacrifices only the cost of the option premium.

If the institution is actually seeking exposure to the portfolio of stocks (i.e., it does not already own them), it can create a speculative, and highly leveraged, position by buying a call option on the portfolio it seeks. Again, by paying a premium, the institution gains upside to the portfolio of stocks and suffers no downside (apart from the premium it paid to secure the option). Since the payment of premium is small in relation to the value of the portfolio commanded by the option, the position is said to have leverage. It is also speculative, as the institution is expressing a specific view on the market and/or volatility.

OUTLINE OF THE BOOK

Our focus in this book is on the practical issues and applications surrounding options. In order to achieve our goal we divide the book into two sections: Option Products and Applications, and Valuation, Hedging, and Control.

In the balance of Part I we examine products and applications in greater detail:

- Chapter 2, Conventional Options, focuses on the mechanics of call and put options, basic option payoff profiles, and the creation of synthetic options/assets. This introductory topic contains examples from different markets to help illustrate the flexibility of the contracts.

- Chapter 3, Exotic Options, discusses second generation option contracts that build on the basic structure of conventional options. This chapter considers major types of path dependent options—contracts whose terminal value depends on the actual path of the reference asset over time—including barrier options, Asian (average) options, lookback options, and ladder/cliquet/shout options. It also examines path independent derivatives, or those whose terminal value depends only on the value of the reference asset at maturity. This class includes digital options, multivariate options (comprising best/worst of options, multiple strike options, spread/basket options), compound options, chooser options, and power options.

- Chapter 4, Option-Embedded Securities, demonstrates the flexibility of options by discussing how they can be embedded in securities to provide customized funding/risk/investment management tools. Key structured instruments covered in this section include convertible bonds/variations, callable and puttable bonds, mortgage-backed securities, and structured notes.

- Chapter 5, Option-Embedded Derivatives, continues the theme introduced in Chapter 4 by illustrating how options

can be combined with other derivatives to create
customized risk and investment products, including
swaptions, callable and puttable swaps, and callable
and puttable asset swap packages.

- Chapter 6, Option Strategies, expands the product
  focus by considering how options can be used in
  combinations to create risk management and speculative
  views on a particular reference asset. The chapter
  examines key directional strategies, including bullish/
  bearish price spreads, and volatility strategies, including
  straddles, strangles, butterflies, condors, and calendar
  spreads.
- Chapter 7, Corporate and Investor Applications, concludes
  Part I by examining how end users and intermediaries can
  use options to fulfill a variety of goals, including hedging,
  speculating, arbitraging, and value monetization.

In Part II, Valuation Tools, we present four chapters that focus
on pricing and risk management issues. Though aspects of option
pricing can quickly become quite quantitative, we opt for a practical
approach to the topic.

- Chapter 8, An Overview of Option Pricing, examines
  fundamental pricing matters in an intuitive light by
  considering elements related to intrinsic and time value,
  moneyness, and pricing inputs.
- Chapter 9, Option Pricing Models, considers the fundamental
  elements of commonly used option pricing frameworks,
  including the Black-Scholes process and the binomial model.
  Models used to price foreign currency options and interest
  rate options supplement these. Once again, our emphasis is
  on the practical mechanics behind these models.
- Chapter 10, Hedging Option Portfolios, extends the
  pricing discussion by considering how marketmakers
  and dealers manage risk in their portfolios in practice. The
  chapter considers the nature and use of the option "Greek"
  risk sensitivities (delta, gamma, vega, theta, rho), and
  demonstrates methods of hedging these sensitivities in
  a portfolio setting.
- Chapter 11, Risk and Control Issues, considers key topics
  related to option risk control, including credit and market

portfolio risk management and internal financial and audit processes. This is supplemented by a review of legal, regulatory, and accounting controls.

With this background in hand we are prepared to explore options in detail.

CHAPTER EXERCISES

1. The buyer of a put option has the:
    a. Obligation to sell an asset
    b. Right to sell an asset
    c. Obligation to buy an asset
    d. Right to buy an asset
    e. None of the above

2. The seller of a call option has the:
    a. Obligation to sell an asset
    b. Right to sell an asset
    c. Obligation to buy an asset
    d. Right to buy an asset
    e. None of the above

3. Which of the following is/are true?
    a. A European option can be exercised only at maturity
    b. An American option can be exercised at any time
    c. A Bermudan option can be exercised at any time
    d. a and b
    e. a and c

4. Which of the following is/are true of exchange-traded options?
    a. Contracts are generally less liquid than OTC options
    b. Contracts are not customizable
    c. Contracts carry more credit risk than OTC options
    d. a and c
    e. b and c

5. Which of the following represent advantages of the OTC options market over the exchange-traded options market?
   a. OTC contracts are standardized and therefore more liquid than exchange contracts
   b. OTC contracts feature less counterparty risk than exchange contracts
   c. OTC contracts are customizable and therefore more flexible than exchange contracts
   d. OTC contracts have more price transparency than exchange contracts
   e. All of the above

6. Options are available on which of the following asset classes?
   a. Inflation
   b. Wheat
   c. Equity baskets
   d. Credit spreads
   e. All of the above

7. Options can be used to:
   a. Generate a speculative profit
   b. Hedge an existing or anticipated risk position
   c. Monetize value in an underlying asset position
   d. All of the above
   e. None of the above

8. If the seller of an exchange-traded futures call option is exercised against, the seller must:
   a. Accept cash
   b. Deliver cash
   c. Accept a futures contract
   d. Deliver a futures contract
   e. None of the above

CHAPTER 2

Conventional Options

INTRODUCTION

Conventional, or vanilla, options are the cornerstone of the options marketplace. Standard puts and calls represent the essential building blocks of any option-based risk management or investment strategy. While many institutions use them individually, they can also be used in combinations (as we shall discuss in Chapter 6), or embedded in other financial assets (as we will see in Chapters 4 and 5). In this chapter we explore the essential characteristics of conventional options by considering the structure and function of call and put options, option payoff profiles, and the creation of synthetic option/asset positions. We shall revisit the use of conventional options in a series of applications at various points in Part I.

THE STRUCTURE AND FUNCTION OF CONVENTIONAL OPTIONS

As we have noted in Chapter 1, a call option is a unilateral contract that gives the buyer the right, but not the obligation, to purchase from the seller a specified asset at a predetermined strike price. In order to secure this right, the buyer pays the seller an option premium. The right may be exercised at any time until maturity (American option), at maturity only (European option) or at specified points up until maturity (Bermudan option). If the buyer exercises the option (e.g., the price of the underlying reference asset is above the strike price), the buyer delivers the required amount of cash, which is defined by strike price * number of units, and receives the underlying asset; the buyer may then liquidate the asset in the marketplace at the higher prevailing market price, hold the asset for future use, or use it to fulfill current obligations. The seller must deliver the specified asset if exercise occurs. If the seller does not own the asset, the seller must purchase the relevant amount from the marketplace at the prevailing market price (this process is know as naked, or uncovered, call writing). If the seller owns the asset, it simply delivers the required amount upon exercise (this is known as covered call writing). If the buyer does not exercise the option—meaning the price of the underlying reference asset is below the strike price—the contract expires and the seller has no further performance obligation.

A put option functions in a similar manner, giving the buyer the right, but not the obligation, to sell a specified asset at a predetermined strike price. The buyer will exercise the put option when the market price is below the strike price, delivering the specified asset to the seller in exchange for the required amount of cash. The buyer will obviously not exercise the contract when the market price is above the strike price; the buyer will simply allow it to expire. The seller, in turn, is obliged to acquire the asset upon exercise by delivering cash; if the seller possesses the cash he or she is essentially writing covered puts, and if not he or she is writing naked puts.

These basic option relationships are shown as:

- Payoff of call = max (0, asset price − strike price)
- Payoff of put = max (0, strike price − asset price)

Because the seller of an option must perform if the price of the reference moves above/below the strike price, it requires risk compensation from the buyer in the form of an option premium. The price of an option is obtained through the option valuation process, which we shall discuss in Part II of the book. For now we note that premium is comprised of two elements: intrinsic value and time value. Intrinsic value is the difference between the strike price and the current market price and indicates a contract's degree of "moneyness"; a contract that is "in-the-money" can be exercised or sold for immediate gain. A call option has intrinsic value when the market price is above the strike price; a put option has intrinsic value when the market price is below the strike price. Options where the market and strike prices are precisely equal are considered to be "at-the-money" and have no intrinsic value. Similarly, those where the market price is below (calls) or above (puts) the strike price are "out-of-the-money" and have no intrinsic value. Options with intrinsic value are more valuable than those that without intrinsic value, meaning the option premium the seller charges the buyer is greater. For example, if an institution wants to buy a call option on a stock with a strike of $20 when the current price is $22, it will be buying a contract with $2 of intrinsic value; if the current price is $19, it will be buying a contract with no intrinsic value. The former is clearly more valuable than the latter, suggesting it carries a greater premium.

Time value is the second major element of option premium. Time is an essential component of the option contract as it gives the buyer more opportunity to achieve a positive result. That is, as the maturity of the contract is lengthened, there is more time for the reference asset to move and cause the option to migrate in-the-money (or deeper in-the-money). Accordingly, options with long maturities have greater time value and command a higher premium; those with short maturities have less time value and are thus cheaper. Time must also be considered a wasting asset: with each passing day, the time value component of the contract erodes; this "time decay" works in favor of the option seller, who stands to benefit by preserving more premium as maturity draws nearer. In fact, time decay accelerates as maturity draws nearer; very short-term options lose value more rapidly than longer-term options.

We can summarize the discussion above by noting:

$$Premium = Intrinsic\ value + Time\ value$$

Let us consider a few simple examples to illustrate how conventional calls and puts work.

Example 1: Long Call

An investment fund, which is bullish on U.S. stocks, is interested in gaining broad exposure to the stock market but does not want to purchase individual stocks. Accordingly, it decides to buy a 12-month European, at-the-money call option on the S&P 500 Index, with a strike price of 650 and a payoff of $10,000 for each point that the S&P 500 rises above the strike. We can consider two possible scenarios in 12 months:

- Scenario 1: The S&P 500 Index ends at 695. The payoff to the investment fund is equal to $450,000 [(695 – 650) * $10,0000], less the amount of premium paid for the option.

■ Scenario 2: The S&P 500 Index ends at 645. Because the call option ends out-of-the-money, the investment fund receives no payoff and the contract expires worthless. The fund's net loss on the position is equal to the premium paid for the option.

Example 2: Short Call

A bank believes that U.S. Treasury bond prices will start to fall over the next six months as a period of rising interest rates takes hold. In order to capitalize on this view, the bank decides to sell a six-month, American call option on the benchmark 10-year U.S. Treasury bond, with an at-the-money strike of 101 and a payoff to the buyer of $100,000 per point (note that the bank does not currently own the bond). If the bank's view proves correct and prices fall, it will not have to make a payoff to the option buyer; it will simply retain the premium it receives for selling the option. The following scenarios occur in six months:

■ Scenario 1: The 10-year U.S. Treasury bond rallies to 104.50 as the anticipated interest rate rise fails to materialize. The call option buyer exercises the contract, requiring the bank to deliver the benchmark bond in exchange for $10.1 m of cash ($100,000 * 101). Because the bank does not own the bond it must purchase it in the market for a total of $10.45 m ($100,000 * 104.5), meaning that it loses $350,000, less the premium received from selling the option.

■ Scenario 2: Interest rates rise and the 10-year bond declines in value. The terminal price of the bond at contract expiry is 99.50, meaning the buyer's contract is worthless. The bank preserves the full amount of the premium received and has no further obligations under the trade.

Example 3: Long Put

A U.S. based multinational company, which generates a portion of its revenues in Japanese yen, is very concerned that the dollar will depreciate against the yen over the next year, meaning that any yen profits will appear smaller when translated back to the home currency. The yen is currently trading at ¥115/$. To protect itself against dollar depreciation the company purchases a 12-month, European, at-the-money dollar put/yen call, which pays off

$100,000 per each currency point below ¥115. We can imagine two scenarios:

- Scenario 1: The dollar rallies over the next 12 months on the back of positive macroeconomic news related to the U.S. economy and trade balance. The exchange rate moves to ¥125/$, meaning that the put option the company purchased expires worthless. Nevertheless, the yen-based profits generated by the local operation are translated back into dollars at a more favorable rate.
- Scenario 2: The dollar continues to weaken during the 12-month period, to a terminal price of ¥100/$. This means that the translation of profits back into dollars will be done at the lower rate, which is detrimental to the company's financial position. However, this is partly offset by the gain generated by the long put, which provides a compensatory payment of $1.15 m (i.e., [115 − 105] * $100,000).

Example 4: Short Put

A speculator in crude oil believes that oil supplies are likely to remain tight over the next three months, meaning that prices will be floored near their current level of $60/barrel. In order to profit from this viewpoint the speculator can take an outright view of rising prices by purchasing a call option. However, preferring not to pay any option premium, the speculator chooses to sell a put option struck slightly out-of-the-money ($58/barrel), earning premium income in the process. The payoff on the option is equal to $100,000 per each dollar below the strike price of $58, and the transaction is settled in financial, rather than physical, terms. In three months the following scenarios appear:

- Scenario 1: The price of oil continues to rally as a result of short supplies and high demand. Oil reaches a high of $65/barrel, meaning that the option the speculator sold expires worthless. The speculator preserves the premium generated from the sale and has no further obligations under the contract.
- Scenario 2: Forecasts prove incorrect and the price of oil declines to $55/barrel. Under this scenario the speculator is obliged to make a net cash payment of $300,000.

([$58 − $55] * $100,000); the speculator's net loss is equal
to $300,000 less the amount of the premium originally
received for selling the put.

These simple examples illustrate the practical use of the four
different "simple" positions that can be created with conventional
options; they also demonstrate that options can be easily applied
to a range of asset classes (e.g., equity, fixed income, currency,
commodity).

OPTION PAYOFF PROFILES

Payoff profiles, which plot the profit and loss (P&L) outcome of an
option position as the price of the underlying reference rises or
falls, are very helpful in the study of conventional option positions.
In fact, we shall use them at various points throughout the text to
reinforce key points related to option strategies. In this section we
explore general construction of payoff profiles, and apply them to
detailed examples involving currency options and caps/floors.

General Payoff Profiles

A payoff profile is constructed by taking account of three variables:
premium paid/received, the strike price of the option, and the
price of the underlying reference asset. The combination yields a
profile that indicates the P&L on a position. Intuitively we know
that the buyer of an option that is currently out-of-the-money or
at-the-money starts with a loss position equal to the premium paid
to the seller. The maximum amount of loss is, of course, dictated by
the amount of the premium paid—it can never be greater. The
seller of the option faces the reverse scenario: as long as the option
is out-of-the-money or at-the-money, it begins with a profit position
equal to the amount of premium received.

Thereafter the P&L positions depend on whether the market
increases or decreases: the buyer of the call receives increasing
profits once the market moves above the strike (and the cost of the
premium is fully defrayed); the buyer of the put similarly receives
increasing profits as the market moves below the strike (and the
cost of the premium is defrayed). The seller of the call faces increasing losses as the market price rises, while the seller of the put faces
increasing losses as the market price falls. These scenarios reflect

the fact that the options are moving in-the-money; if they remain at- or out-of-the-money, the buyer continues to remain in a net loss position (equal to premium paid) and the seller continues to hold a net profit position (equal to premium received).

The intuition behind these payoff profiles is illustrated in Figures 2.1 through 2.4.

We can draw certain conclusions about the four basic positions by examining the figures above:

- Buyers of options have limited potential for loss (i.e., premium paid) and virtually unlimited potential for gains.
- Sellers of options have limited potential for gains (i.e., premium received) and virtually unlimited risk of losses.
- Option buying strategies are less risky than option selling strategies, though they involve an up-front cost.
- Option selling strategies are riskier than option buying strategies, though some of the risk is defrayed by the up-front income (and more risk can be mitigated through hedging).
- Those who anticipate rising values in the underlying asset should buy calls or sell puts.

FIGURE 2.1

Long Call Option

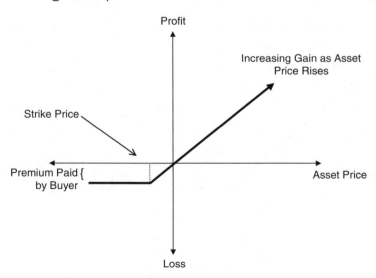

F I G U R E 2.2

Short Call Option

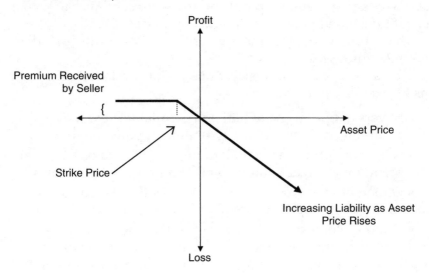

F I G U R E 2.3

Long Put Option

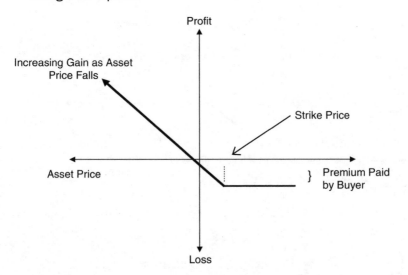

F I G U R E 2.4

Short Put Option

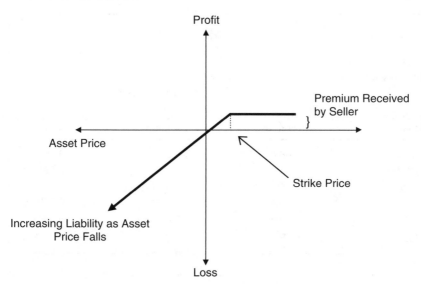

- Those who anticipate falling values in the underlying asset should buy puts or sell calls.

We will build on these concepts and strategies in subsequent chapters.

Option Payoff Profiles I: Currency Options

Let us examine option payoffs in the context of currency options. Consider the data in Table 2.1 which depicts volatility and strikes for a € call/$ put, along with associated spot and three-month forward €/$ levels, and premiums. It is important to note that in the case of currency options, one "half" of the option is a call and the other "half" is a put—this is in keeping with the fact that currency options are quoted as one currency versus another currency. In this example, a €/$ call is a call on € and a put on $; thus, if the call is exercised the buyer will buy € and sell $.

Premiums are quoted as a percentage of the fixed currency amount, which in this example is €. Thus, a €10 m at-the-money three-month option with a volatility at 10% carries a premium of €201,000 (2.01%). The premium declines significantly if a strike

T A B L E 2.1

€/$ Option Data

Currencies		€/$	
Spot		1.1930	
3-m Forward		1.1900	
		As a % of €	
Volatility	**10%**	**13%**	**7%**
Strike	**Premium**	**Premium**	**Premium**
1.1500	4.08%	4.58%	3.65%
1.1700	2.94%	3.52%	2.39%
1.1900	2.01%	2.62%	1.41%
1.2100	1.30%	1.89%	0.74%
1.2300	0.80%	1.32%	0.34%
1.2500	0.46%	0.89%	0.14%

higher than 1.1900 is selected (e.g., the € call leg is further out-of-the-money). The table also shows changes in price for different volatilities, which we will discuss in more detail later. For now we note that the higher the volatility quote, the higher the option premium.

Consider a situation where a bank believes €/$ is going to strengthen from its current level and decides to monetize the view by buying a €10 m call with an out-of-the-money strike of 1.2100 for 1.30% (€130,000) based on 10% volatility. The bank hopes the rate will rise above 1.2100 so that it can exercise and buy € for 1.2100; it will then sell the position in the spot market for some rate above 1.2100. At a spot rate of €/$ 1.1900, the premium of €130,000 equates to $154,700. If this is added to the dollars received upon exercise of the option, the effective breakeven amounts to $12.254 m ($12.1 m + $154,700), or a rate of 1.2255. In other words, in order for the bank to generate a profit through the purchase of the option €/$ must exceed 1.2255.

We can express the bank's position in terms of a payoff profile, as in Figure 2.5. The diagram illustrates both the core position and the position based on the effective rate.

If the bank buys a € put/$ call instead of a € call/$ put it creates a payoff profile that reflects increasing gains as € weakens/$

€/$ Call Payoff Profile

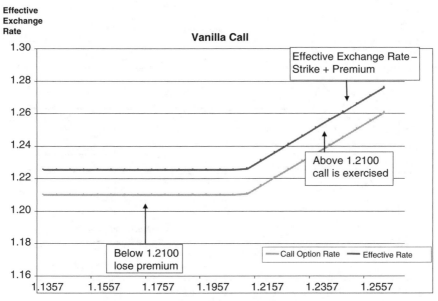

EUR / USD Rate in Three Months

strengthens. If the bank buys an out-of-the-money put struck at 1.1700 for premium of €130,000 ($154,700) with spot at 1.1900 and volatility at 10%, it creates a breakeven rate of 1.1545. Figure 2.6 highlights the payoff profile of the put from the seller's perspective.

Option Payoff Profiles II: Caps and Floors

We extend our discussion by considering several examples using caps and floors, fundamental options of the interest rate market. Caps and floors are closely related to interest rate swaps, allowing borrowers and investors to fix the amount of interest payable or receivable. Unlike swaps, however, they do not lock in a borrower to an unfavorable rate or limit an investor's participation in a favorable rate. This flexibility comes at a price, of course: the cap or floor buyer must pay a premium for the contract, and the premium cost must be incorporated into the overall interest rate paid or received.

F I G U R E 2.6

€Put/$Call Payoff Profile

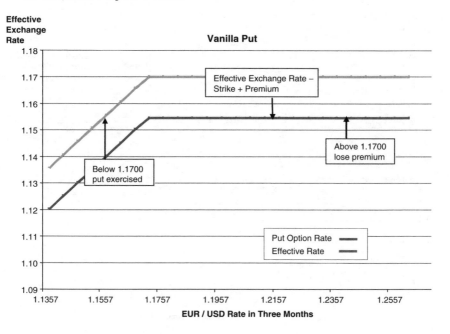

Caps and floors are different from standard options on equities, bonds, or currencies because they do not have a single exercise date. Rather, they feature a series of exercise dates, one for each interest rate reset period (e.g., every month, quarter, or six months). Caps and floors can therefore be viewed as a series of individual options (caplets or floorlets) over an agreed maturity period. Though any floating-rate reference can be used for a cap or floor, interbank rates such as LIBOR, EURIBOR, and TIBOR tend to be most common. For example, a five-year cap based on six-month resets features nine exercise dates at six-month intervals (starting in six month's time); there is no reset for the first period as the rate is set at trade date. The five-year cap thus has nine caplets.

A cap provides a borrower with a maximum interest rate payable during each reset period. Assume a company that borrows on a LIBOR basis wants to fix its borrowing costs at 5%. It buys a $10 m, five-year, six-month LIBOR cap with a 5% strike. If, at the beginning of any six-month period LIBOR sets above 5%, the company receives the differential between the LIBOR set and the 5%

Long LIBOR Cap

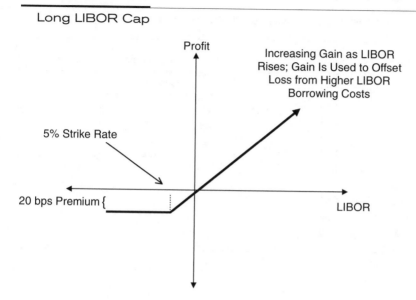

strike (times the notional amount of the cap); this essentially fixes costs at 5%. Let us assume that the first fixing, in six-month's time, is at 4.50%. In this case the first caplet is out-of-the-money, and expires worthless. However, if LIBOR rises to 5.25% by the second fixing date (12 months from trade date), the company receives a compensatory payment of 25 basis points (bps) times the notional (adjusted for the six-month reset period). The company effectively caps its borrowing costs at 5.00% for the six-month period. The effective cost must, of course, take account of the premium paid to secure the cap; if the company pays 20 bps running for the option, its effective annualized borrowing cost is 5.20%. Figure 2.7 illustrates the long LIBOR cap payoff profile. Note that the seller of the LIBOR cap faces the reverse payoff profile.

The cap buyer can select from among any number of strikes. The premium the buyer will pay will, of course, relate to the degree of moneyness characterizing the cap. An at-the-money cap strike is equal to the current swap rate for the same tenor. Thus a five-year swap rate is the at-the-money strike for the cap, suggesting that all cap strikes below this level will be in-the-money and any strike above will be out-of-the-money. Table 2.2 summarizes sample swap rates, cap strikes, and bp premiums.

T A B L E   2.2

Swap Rates, Cap Strikes, and Premiums

Years	Swap	Premiums			
		Cap Strikes			
0.5	3.30				
1.0	3.55	Years	4%	5%	6%	7%
1.5	3.74	2	48	17		
2.0	3.93	3	126	43	17	
2.5	4.07	5	413	196	85	36
3.0	4.22				
3.5	4.36				
4.0	4.51				
4.5	4.65				
5.0	4.80				

For instance, the 3 swap rate and equivalent at-the-money cap strike is 4.22%. The three-year 4.00% strike cap is 22 bps in-the-money, and costs 126 bps. By way of contrast, the 5.00% cap is 78 bps out-of-the-money, and therefore only costs 43 bps.

While a cap limits a borrower's exposure to rising interest rates and is useful for hedging floating rate borrowings, a floor limits the impact of loss impact arising from falling rates. Investors seeking to establish a minimum asset return over some investment horizon often purchase floors. Like a cap, a floor is made up of individual floorlet options that cover each of the relevant forward periods.

Consider an investment fund holding a portfolio of LIBOR-based floating rate securities with maturities out to five years. The fund is concerned that LIBOR may fall from its current 5% level. Accordingly, it buys a five-year out-of-the-money floor with a strike of 4.50%. At the first exercise date, LIBOR sets at 4.75%. This is above the floor's strike price, so the floorlet expires out-of-the-money. At the next fixing in six months (12 months from trade date), LIBOR sets at 4.25%. The current period floorlet is now 25 bps in-the-money. Though the fund receives a lower LIBOR yield on its portfolio of securities, it receives a compensatory payment of 25 bps on the floor, creating a net return of 4.50%. Once again, this example does not take into account the effect of

F I G U R E 2.8

Long LIBOR Floor

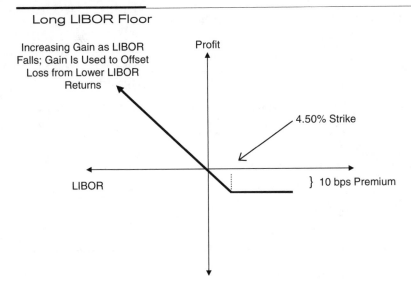

Increasing Gain as LIBOR
Falls; Gain Is Used to Offset
Loss from Lower LIBOR
Returns

Profit

4.50% Strike

LIBOR

} 10 bps Premium

the premium paid by the fund. A premium of 10 bps running, for instance, lowers the effective LIBOR return to 4.40%. Figure 2.8 illustrates the payoff profile of a long LIBOR floor. Again, the seller of the LIBOR floor faces the reverse payoff profile.

As previously mentioned, the at-the-money strike price for a floor is equal to the swap price for the period in question. Table 2.3 contains sample data. The higher the strike, the greater the intrinsic value of the option and the higher the corresponding premium.

It is important to note that caps and floors are quite flexible. Though standard structures feature fixed, or constant, strike levels, customized structures allow each caplet/floorlet to have its own strike. This allows development of more precise risk/investment strategies that relate to a user's view of the forward curve. For instance, in a positive yield curve environment caplets on forward rates at the short end of the curve are likely to be out-of-the-money and those at the long end of the curve are likely to be in-the-money. By choosing individual strikes for each caplet the buyer can create a more precise risk solution. Thus, if the buyer chooses to create a cap structure where all the strikes are set out-of-the-money, the premium cost declines. Figure 2.9 illustrates a cap with varying caplet strikes.

T A B L E 2.3

Swap Rates, Floor Strikes, and Premiums

Years	Swap	Premiums		
		Floor Strikes		
0.5	3.30			
1.0	3.55	Years	4%	5%	6%
1.5	3.74	2	61	132	217
2.0	3.93	3	69	153	267
2.5	4.07	5	84	169	298
3.0	4.22				
3.5	4.36				
4.0	4.51				
4.5	4.65				
5.0	4.80				

F I G U R E 2.9

Cap with Varying Caplet Strikes

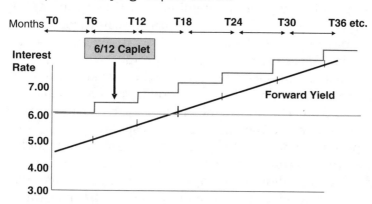

SYNTHETIC LONG AND SHORT OPTION POSITIONS

With some background of basic options and payoff profiles, we now examine the process of creating synthetic option and asset positions. Conventional option contracts can be combined to produce synthetic long and short positions, synthetic put or call positions,

F I G U R E   2.10

Payoff Profile of Long Asset Position

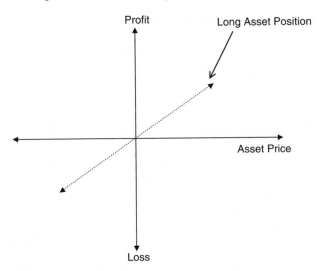

and other exotic profiles. A synthetic position is one that is created (synthesized) from two or more instruments (in this case, options). This is a very powerful characteristic that expands investment and risk management horizons for intermediaries and end users.

To demonstrate the process of synthetic asset creation, we consider the payoff profile of a standard long asset position, which is illustrated in Figure 2.10. We see from this diagram that as the price of the underlying asset increases, the profit attributable to the position rises, and as the price falls, the loss increases.

We know from the payoff profiles above that a long call position generates a profit as the price of the underlying asset moves above the strike price. If we overlay the call option payoff profile on Figure 2.11 (with the strike set at the origin and premium paid ignored for simplicity), we note that the profit components of the two positions are identical. This leads us to conclude that half of the long asset position is comprised of a long call option position.

We can extend the discussion by considering an option position that generates a loss as the price of the underlying asset declines. A short put option, which yields an increasing liability as the price of the asset falls, features just such a characteristic. If we overlay the short put option payoff profile on the long asset

FIGURE 2.11

Payoff Profile of Long Asset Position and Long Call Position

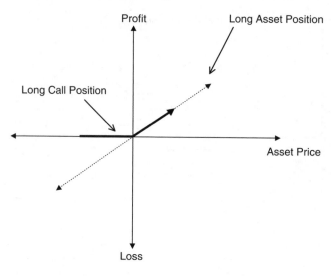

FIGURE 2.12

Payoff Profile of Long Asset Position and Short Put Position

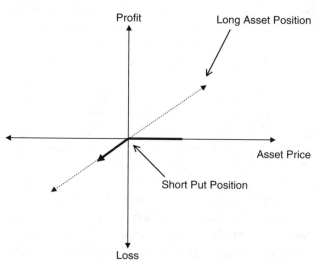

position, as in Figure 2.12 (with the strike again set at the origin and premium received ignored), we obtain an identical payoff profile. This again leads us to believe that the second half of the long asset position is comprised of a short put option. In fact, if we

F I G U R E 2.13

Payoff Profile of Long Asset Position and Long Call/Short Put
Positions

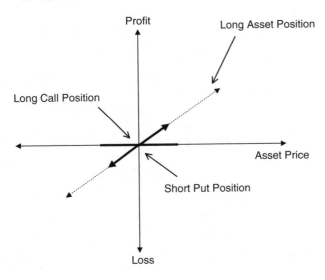

combine the two options together in a single diagram, as in
Figure 2.13, we can see this quite clearly.

This exercise demonstrates how a long call and a short put can
be paired to create a synthetic long asset position. We stress again
that, in order for the proper position to be obtained, the strike
prices and the maturities of the two options must be identical; if
they are not, a mismatch occurs.

We can extend this process by considering the opposite
scenario: the short asset position. The payoff profile of the short
asset position, depicted in Figure 2.14, reflects an increasing profit
as the price of the underlying asset falls, and a loss as it rises.

We next select option positions that generate profits as the
market declines and losses as the market rises. This can be accomplished with a long put option and a short call option (again, struck
at the same price and expiring at the same time). The combined
payoff profiles of the short asset, long put, and short call are
depicted in Figure 2.15.

Long and short option positions can also be used to create
synthetic forward contracts, because the long forward is equivalent
to a long asset position, while the short forward is equal to a short
asset position. In a synthetic forward the strike price, rather than

F I G U R E 2.14

Payoff Profile of Short Asset Position

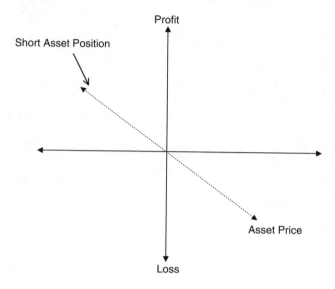

F I G U R E 2.15

Payoff Profile of Short Asset Position, Long Put/Short Call Positions

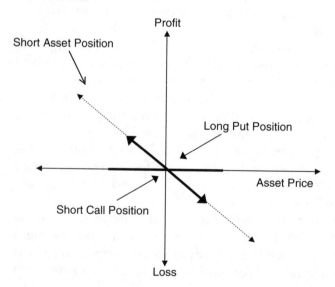

the forward price, becomes the relevant indicator of value; depending on the level of the market in relation to the option strike there may be a net premium payment (this would suggest the creation of a synthetic off-market forward).[1]

The relationships described above can be extended to other investment/arbitrage positions. For instance, buying an asset, selling a call, and buying a put are equivalent to buying an asset and short selling a synthetic asset; there is no market risk in the transaction, indicating that this is equal to the creation of a synthetic Treasury bill position (or some other risk-free asset).

Table 2.4 summarizes the positions described above.

Given these relationships it comes as no surprise that synthetic option positions can be created using assets and options. For instance, a long call option can be synthesized from a long asset and a long put, while a long put option can be created from a long call and a short asset. These positions make intuitive, as well as theoretical, sense: if a company owns an asset and the price rises, it will post a gain; if it also owns a put it will lose on the asset if the

T A B L E 2.4

Synthetic Asset Positions

Option Position	+ Option Position	= Synthetic Asset Position
Long Call	Short Put	Long Asset
Long Put	Short Call	Short Asset

---

1 For instance, to create a long synthetic forward in stock S we note that the payoff at maturity T is:

$$S_T - F_{0,T}$$

This position can be purchased on a dividend discounted basis for

$$S_0 e^{-\delta T}$$

This will provide a share of stock at time T. However, in order not to generate an initial investment in the position (e.g., to create a synthetic prepaid, rather than conventional, forward), we assume that the entire amount can be borrowed at a rate of r. At maturity, we take delivery of the stock and sell it for S_T, repaying:

$$S_0 e^{(r - \delta)T}$$

This is equivalent to borrowing to buy a stock position equal to the expiration payoff of the forward. In simplified terms this means that the forward is simply a package of long stock and a short zero coupon bond (representing the borrowing). We can extend this by rearranging the terms, e.g., a long position in the stock is simply a long forward and a long position in the zero coupon bond, and so forth.

T A B L E   2.5

Synthetic Option Positions

Asset Position	+ Option Position	= Synthetic Option Position
Long asset	Long put	Long Call
Short asset	Long call	Long Put
Short asset	Short put	Short Call
Long asset	Short call	Short Put

price falls, but will gain on the put—this is precisely equal to the payoff profile of a long call. Short call and put options can also be synthesized from combinations of options and assets. For instance, a short call can be created from a short asset and a short put, while a short put can be created from a long asset and a short call. These synthetic option positions are summarized in Table 2.5. Note that our discussion is not limited to combinations of conventional options and assets. Certain other exotic options, such as those described in Chapters 3 and 4, can also be created by combining one or more contracts.

CHAPTER EXERCISES

1. In a positive yield curve environment, caplets priced at the long end of the yield curve will be:
    a. Cheaper than caplets at the short end of the curve
    b. Equally priced
    c. More expensive than caplets at the short end of the curve
    d. More out-of-the-money than caplets at the short end of the curve
    e. None of the above
2. The payoff of a call option is equal to:
    a. Max (0, asset price − strike price)
    b. Max (0, strike price − asset price)
    c. Max (asset price − strike price, strike price − asset price)

   d. Max (0, asset price – strike price)
   e. None of the above
3. In covered call writing, the option seller:
   a. Never owns the asset
   b. May own the asset
   c. Always owns the asset
   d. Owns the call
   e. None of the above
4. The payoff of a put option is equal to:
   a. Max (0, asset price – strike price)
   b. Max (0, strike price – asset price)
   c. Max (asset price – strike price, strike price – asset price)
   d. Max (0, asset price – strike price)
   e. None of the above
5. As an option's time to expiry increases:
   a. Time value increases
   b. Time value decreases
   c. Intrinsic value increases
   d. Intrinsic value decreases
   e. Time value and intrinsic value increase
6. An option that is in-the-money and has not yet reached its expiry date:
   a. Has no intrinsic value
   b. Has no time value
   c. Has intrinsic value
   d. Has time value
   e. Has intrinsic value and time value
7. If the NASDAQ equity index is at 2,000 when an institution buys a 2,100 strike call struck what is the payoff of the call if the NASDAQ ends at 2,050 at option expiration?
   a. 2,000 – 2,100 = –100
   b. 2,100 – 2,000 = 100
   c. 2,100 – 2,050 = 50
   d. 2,050 – 2,100 = –50
   e. None of the above

8. Given a put on Japanese Government Bonds (JGB) struck at 100.5, which of the following is/are true?
    a. The seller's liability commences as soon as JGB prices fall below 100.5
    b. The seller's liability commences as soon as JGB prices rise above 100.5
    c. The buyer's price commences as soon as JGB prices rise above 100.5
    d. None of the above
    e. All of the above

9. The maximum loss on a long call is equal to:
    a. The maximum downside price of the asset
    b. The maximum upside price of the asset
    c. The premium received
    d. The premium paid
    e. None of the above

10. Which is/are false?
    a. Buyers of options have limited potential for loss (i.e., premium paid) and virtually unlimited potential for gains.
    b. Sellers of options have limited potential for gains (i.e., premium received) and virtually unlimited risk of losses.
    c. Option buying strategies are less risky than option selling strategies, though they involve an up-front cost.
    d. Option selling strategies are riskier than option buying strategies, though some of the risk is defrayed by the up-front income (and more risk can be mitigated through hedging).
    e. Those who anticipate rising values in the underlying asset should buy puts or sell calls.

11. If a company buys a two-year LIBOR cap struck at 6.00%, the three caplets pay off how many bps if LIBOR sets at 6.00%, 6.25%, and 5.75% during each sequential period?
    a. 0 bps, 25 bps, 25 bps
    b. 0 bps, 25 bps, −25 bps

     c. 0 bps, 25 bps, 0 bps

     d. 0 bps, 0 bps, 25 bps

     e. 25 bps, 0 bps, 0 bps

12. A synthetic long asset position is created from:

     a. Long call and long put

     b. Long call and short put

     c. Short call and long put

     d. Short call and short put

     e. Short call and long call

Exotic Options

INTRODUCTION

In the last chapter we introduced conventional options and demonstrated, in basic terms, how they can be used. In this chapter we extend our product discussion by considering a series of exotic options, which we define to include contracts that feature nonstandard payoff profiles, or those that cannot be obtained from standard puts and calls. Our focus in this chapter is on path-dependent options, or contracts whose terminal value depends on the price path taken by the reference asset, and path independent options, or contracts whose terminal value depends only on the price of the reference asset at termination.

Through the innovative efforts of financial intermediaries with derivatives expertise, the path-dependent exotic options sector has grown at a rapid rate. Indeed, new "variations on the theme" appear on a fairly regular basis to meet the increasingly specific needs of both end users and other intermediaries. However, for purposes of our discussion in this chapter we can condense the list of relevant products into a core set of contracts that appear to have gained acceptance by the market at large, and which are regularly traded. These include barrier options, Asian options, lookback options, the broad family of ladder, cliquet, and shout options, multivariate (rainbow) options, compound options, chooser options, power (leveraged) options, and digital options. We shall provide a basic description of the instruments and simple examples that demonstrate how each one works in sections that follow; we shall consider them in further detail when we discuss corporate/investor applications in Chapter 7.

BARRIER OPTIONS

Barrier options (also known as knock-in, knock-out options) are path dependent derivatives that create, or extinguish, an underlying option when the reference price or rate reaches a predetermined barrier level. The barrier, which has become the single most popular type of exotic option, comes in various classes and variations. Those with barriers that are set out-of-the-money (e.g., barrier < strike for a call, barrier > strike for a put) are considered "regular" knock-ins and knock-outs; those with barriers that are set in –the-money (e.g., barrier > strike for a call, barrier < strike for a put) options are considered "reverse" knock-ins and knock-outs. The combinations and effects are summarized in Table 3.1.

From an option buyer's perspective, the primary drawback of a standard option is that it may provide more protection (and therefore sell at a higher premium) than is actually needed. Standard options remain actionable up until expiration, regardless of the market price of the underlying asset. In other words, the buyer is paying for protection no matter what happens to the price

T A B L E   3.1

Barrier Option Classes

Option	Class	Effect
Down and out call	Regular knock-out	Out-of-the money option extinguished
Up and out put	Regular knock-out	Out-of-the money option extinguished
Down and in call	Regular knock-in	Out-of-the-money option created
Up and in put	Regular knock-in	Out-of the-money option created
Up and out call	Reverse knock-out	In-the-money option extinguished
Down and out put	Reverse knock-out	In-the-money option extinguished
Up and in call	Reverse knock-in	In-the-money option created
Down and in put	Reverse knock-in	In-the-money option created

of the underlying asset during the time leading up to expiration. However, the option buyer may have a view as to how the underlying asset will perform in the market and may only want protection if the asset's price moves in a certain range. Because the standard option cannot be tailored to reflect the buyer's market view, it offers more protection than the buyer wants. The barrier option seeks to overcome this problem. Note that barrier options have properties of both American- and European-style options: they can be exercised only on the expiration date (European); and, they can cross the barrier and be created or extinguished on any date (American).

Barrier options allow the option buyer to pay only for a specific payoff profile, provided that the buyer is willing to lose the option if the underlying asset passes a "barrier" level. Because there is at least some probability that the underlying option will not be created (i.e., the barrier is not reached), or will be extinguished (i.e., the barrier is reached) during the life of the trade, the premium cost on a barrier is lower than that of a comparable vanilla European option. The seller is assuming less risk than on a standard option, while the buyer is taking on relatively more risk, meaning that the option price must be lower. This has made the derivative popular among a large group of intermediaries and end users.

Consider an example of a bank that believes the 10-year benchmark U.S. Treasury bond will trade higher, but in a relatively narrow range; the current market price for the 10-year on-the-run is 101 and the bank's target price is 102.50. In order to take a leveraged position based on this view, the bank can purchase a call option on the bond price (or a put option on rates). The premium for a vanilla call option struck at-the-money is 50 bps; the premium for an up and out call option struck at-the-money, with a barrier at 102.75, is 40 bps—the 10 bp differential arises from the fact that there is a chance that the option will be extinguished (i.e., if the bond price rises above 102.75). Because the bank believes the upside is capped, it purchases the cheaper option. If the bond price exceeds its target of 102.50 it can sell the option or reverse the transaction in order to realize profit; naturally, if the bond prices breach the barrier before the bank has an opportunity to crystallize profit, it will lose its premium and sacrifice the accumulated intrinsic value. Figure 3.1 illustrates the general flows of an up and out call.

FIGURE 3.1

Up and out call option

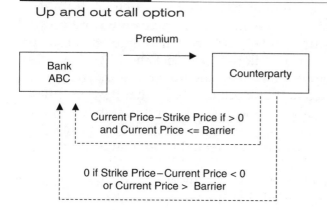

Certain variations on the barrier structure also exist. The partial barrier option (or discrete barrier option) is identical to the conventional barrier, except for the fact that the barrier condition only exists for a specified period of time (e.g., the last 3 months of a 12-month trade). The point barrier option is an extreme version of the partial barrier option, where the trigger exists only on one specific date. Partial and point barriers that lead to the creation of an option are cheaper than regular knock-ins because the probability of creation is lower; partial and point barriers that lead to cancellation of an option are more expensive than regular knock-outs because the probability of cancellation is lower. An outside barrier option is a multivariate (correlation-based) derivative that creates or extinguishes an underlying option based on another reference asset (e.g., an up and in call on a U.S. Treasury bond that creates an underlying call on U.S. Treasury bonds if the price of crude oil exceeds $70/ barrel). Such multivariate structures must incorporate the correlation of the two assets in order to yield an accurate price.

ASIAN OPTIONS

Asian options (average options) are path-dependent derivatives that provide the buyer with a payoff based on the average price/rate or strike of the contract during a set averaging period (commonly known as the tail). The averaging mechanism allows the purchaser to reduce some of the uncertainty related to the terminal price of the option reference, making the contract suitable for both hedging and investment management applications. Asian options can be structured as an average price (rate) option, providing a payoff based on the differential between a fixed strike price and the average price/rate recorded during the tail period, and an average strike option, providing a payoff based on the differential between the terminal price/rate and an average strike recorded during the tail period. Averages can be computed on an arithmetic or geometric basis; tails generally run from the final days to final weeks of a multimonth contract, though longer tails are possible.

Consider the following example: a portfolio manager investing in 10-year bunds wishes to reduce the impact of terminal prices on the portfolio and decides to purchase an Asian call option. The portfolio manager purchases a six-month arithmetic average price call on the 10-year bund, struck at-the-money (101), with a 30-day tail. The following two scenarios occur in six months:

- Scenario 1: The terminal price of the bond is 99 and the tail price is 102. Based on this outcome the portfolio manager thus earns a profit on the position equal to (102-101-premium) * notional. If the portfolio manager had purchased a European call with the same strike, its position would have expired worthless, and if the portfolio manager had purchased an American call, the result would have been uncertain (i.e., dependent on when the portfolio manager exercised or sold the call).

- Scenario 2: The terminal price is 102 and the tail price is 100.9. The option expires worthless, with the portfolio manager losing the premium paid for the option. Though the terminal price was in-the-money, the average price of the bunds was below the target strike during the tail, so the portfolio manager was unable to generate a profit.

LOOKBACK OPTIONS

Lookback options are path-dependent derivative contracts that provide the buyer with a payoff by "looking back" over the price path of the reference asset during the life of the trade and awarding the maximum gain. The option is available in floating strike and fixed strike form. In the floating strike lookback the strike is set by selecting the lowest purchase price (for calls), or highest selling price (for puts) and then comparing it against the terminal price to generate payoff. Using a lookback put as an example, if the highest

F I G U R E 3.2

Floating Strike Lookback Call Option

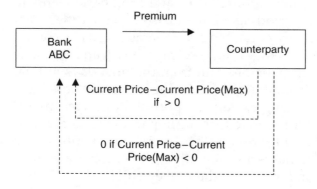

selling price for a bond is 105 and the terminal price is 102, the pay-off to the buyer is 3 (e.g., 105 (strike) – 102 (terminal price)). In the fixed strike lookback (or call on the maximum, put on the minimum) the strike is set in advance and the payoff is generated by selecting the highest selling price (for calls) or lowest selling price (for puts). Thus, if a bond put is set with a strike of 105 and the bond reaches a low of 101 and a terminal price of 102, the payoff to the buyer is 4 (e.g., 105 (strike) – 101 (lowest price achieved)). While lookback options provide greater certainty of maximizing potential gains, the options are more expensive than vanilla structures and are typically used only when a maximum gain is essential. Figure 3.2 illustrates the flows of a floating strike lookback call option.

LADDER, CLIQUET, AND SHOUT OPTIONS

The family of ladder, cliquet, and shout options includes path-dependent contracts that allow intrinsic value gains to be "locked in" at particular intervals prior to expiry. If the market subsequently retraces, the buyer does not lose the gains that have accumulated to that point; this is equivalent to a "monetization" mechanism embedded in the derivative. The general class includes three variations:

- Ladder option, which locks in gains once prespecified market levels (known as rungs) are reached
- Cliquet option (also known as a ratchet option), which locks in gains at predefined time horizons, such as every month of a multiyear transaction

- Shout option, which locks in gains every time the option buyer "shouts" (e.g., declares a lock-in event).

As we might expect, the more rungs, time horizons, or shout opportunities, the more expensive the option; in the extreme, an infinite number of lock-in opportunities translates into a lookback option. Ladders, cliquets, and shouts are most suitable for risk-adverse institutions that do not want to be exposed to the possibility that unrealized gains will be lost in a market retracement.

Consider the example of a bank that buys an at-the-money par strike six-month cliquet put on a 30-year U.S. Treasury, with monthly evaluation periods. The option contains monthly evaluations and payoff is based on the price differential $*$ $100,000. Assume, next, that the 30-year U.S. Treasury bond posts the following end of month prices over the next six months: 100, 100, 100, 98.5, 98, 100. The cliquet generates a gain of $200,000, less premium paid, based on the monthly evaluation path; gains in month four (98.5) are eventually exceeded by gains in month five. If the bond price had declined to 96 during the trade—but not on an evaluation date—the payoff would still have been $200,000; however, if the bank had purchased a more expensive lookback instead of a cliquet, the payoff would have been $400,000. Figure 3.3 illustrates the flows of a cliquet option.

FIGURE 3.3

Cliquet Option

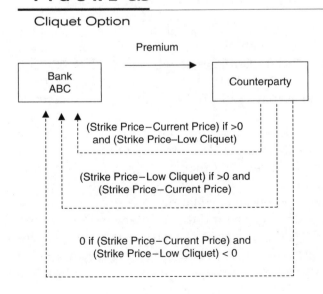

RAINBOW OPTIONS

Rainbow options (or multivariate options, multi-index options) are path-independent derivative contracts that provide the buyer with a payoff based on the performance of more than one reference asset (from the same, or different, asset classes). This derivative structure provides multiple exposure/hedging opportunities through a single contract, suggesting that asset correlations, or comovements, must be considered in the valuation process. In fact, a portfolio of uncorrelated or loosely correlated assets included in a single contract can result in cheaper exposure or protection than the sum of the constituent options. We examine pricing implications of basket and spread options in Appendix II.

Though rainbow options are available in many varieties, the most common structures include:

- Option on the best/worst, which provides a payoff based on the best or worst performing of a series of reference assets (the call on the best, and put on the worst are the two most popular)
- Basket option, which provides a payoff based on the total performance of an entire basket of similar or different references
- Spread option, which provides a payoff based on the spread, or difference, between two similar or different references (e.g., yield curve options are a popular version)

When options reference assets from different markets they may include a quanto feature, which neutralizes the effects of currency risk. Thus, an option that references assets in the UK (£) and Germany (€) may convert all gains back into £ at a fixed rate so that there is no additional impact related to changing £/€ currency rates.

Multivariate derivatives are an efficient way for investment managers to gain exposure to more than one asset through a single transaction. They can, however, be difficult to value, as any pricing model must take account of the direction and volatility of two or more assets, along with potential correlation.

Consider the case of a hedge fund that is interested in expressing a view on the U.S. yield curve and wants to do so through a single transaction. In this instance the fund may be expecting short rates to come under pressure over the next six months, leading to a flattening of the curve between 1 year and 10 years. The current 1–10-year spread is 55 bps, and the fund expects a tightening to at least 30 bps. Accordingly, it buys a six-month yield curve call option struck at-the-money with a spread sensitivity of $10,000/bp.

The following two scenarios occur in six months:

- Scenario 1: One-year rates rise by 20 bps, while 10-year rates remain constant; the spread option is in-the-money (35 bps), meaning the bank earns $200,000 (less premium).
- Scenario 2: One-year rates rise by 10 bps, but 10-year rates climb by 15 bps, leaving the terminal spread at 60 bps; the option expires out-of-the-money.

If the hedge fund had not been able to use a spread option, it would have had to arrange separate options on both the 1- and 10-year bonds.

Spread options are often used in the equity markets. For example, an investment fund might be interested in capturing the differential between the DAX German equity index (current level of 3,000) and the CAC French index (current level of 2,400) and thus purchase a DAX – CAC spread option that pays off once a particular strike spread (e.g., 200 index points) is breached. The payoff of the option is thus defined as max (0, (DAX – CAC – 200)). This suggests the fund is bullish on the DAX and bearish on the CAC and wants to combine the view in a single transaction. Consider the following two scenarios:

- Scenario 1: The DAX rises to 3,250 at option expiry, while the CAC remains unchanged at 2,400. The payoff to the investment fund is thus equal to 650 points (i.e., 3,250 – 2,400 –200), times the index multiplier, less the premium paid.
- Scenario 2: The DAX falls to 2,800, while the CAC increases to 2,600. The investment fund will abandon the option as it has no value (e.g., 2,800 – 2,600 – 200). The fund loses the premium paid to buy the option.

COMPOUND OPTIONS

Compound options (also known as nested options) are path-independent derivatives that grant the buyer the right to buy or sell an underlying option. The contract provides additional flexibility for institutions facing events, outcomes, or cash flows that are uncertain (or may never occur) by allowing an underlying option position to be taken only if needed. The broad class of compounds includes four variations:

- Call on a call, which is an option giving the buyer the right to buy a call option
- Call on a put, which is an option giving the buyer the right to buy a put option
- Put on a call, which is an option giving the buyer the right to sell a call option
- Put on a put, which is an option giving the buyer the right to sell a put option

If the underlying option is in-the-money when the compound expires, the buyer can exercise and forward the seller an additional premium. Alternatively, if the underlying option is out-of-the-money when the compound expires, or the buyer no longer requires the protection, it simply allows the contract to expire.

Options on caps/floors (captions/floortions) are very popular in the fixed-income market. Consider a company that may be issuing $500 million of debt in the future, though its decision depends on a potential acquisition opportunity that will be known in six-months time. Depending on the need and state of the market, the company may wish to hedge the funding level on a forward basis; it can do so with a forward swap (though this represents a commitment), a swaption, or a compound cap option. Based on cost, the company opts to purchase a call on a cap, giving it the right to buy a cap on rates in six-month's time. The following scenarios may arise in six months:

- Scenario 1: The company learns that the acquisition opportunity will not materialize, so it allows the option to expire.
- Scenario 2: The company decides to move ahead with the acquisition and prepares for a $500 million debt issue; it exercises the call option to buy a cap to lock in a maximum rate on its debt issue.

CHOOSER OPTIONS

Chooser options (or preference options, choice options) are path independent derivative contracts that permit the buyer to choose between one of two different options on a defined "choice date." The chooser allows deferral of key details until future events are clarified or contingencies become known, and is thus a flexible instrument. The option is available in two forms: the regular chooser, which allows the buyer to choose between a put and a call with identical strike and maturity parameters; and the complex chooser, which permits the buyer to select between two different options: a call with particular strike and maturity parameters, and a put with different strike and maturity parameters.

Assume an investment fund wishes to take a position on Euro rates but is reluctant to do so until the results of an economic indicator are released. Because the data is likely to have significant market implications, the fund contracts to buy a regular chooser on five-year Euro rates; the put and the call are struck at 3.00% and the maturity of the option is set at 12 months. The economic data is released in two months (on choice date) and appears bullish for rates (e.g., potential easing in the next year); the fund chooses to convert the option into a put on rates (call on prices). Figure 3.4 summarizes the flows of a regular chooser.

POWER OPTIONS

Power options (leveraged options, turbo options) are path-independent derivative contacts that provide the buyer with a

F I G U R E 3.4

Chooser Option

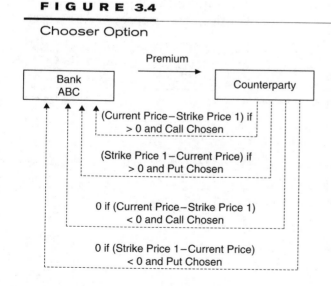

leveraged payoff once the option moves in-the-money. As with other leveraged swap structures, the leverage factor may be created in any manner, though squared options and cubed options are most common. Not surprisingly, power options are generally intended for speculative, rather than hedge, purposes. Consider an example of a securities dealer who has a strong view on the direction of five-year U.S. Treasury prices, and decides to take a leveraged view by buying a squared call option. The current price of the five-year bond is 100, meaning the square is 10,000; the strike is set at-the-money and the maturity is set at six months. The following scenarios occur in six months:

- Scenario 1: The price of the 5 year U.S. Treasury rallies to 105; the payoff on the position is thus $105^2 - 10,000 = 1,025$ (* the bp value of the contract)
- Scenario 2: The price of the bond falls to 99; the position ends out-of-the-money, with the securities dealer losing premium paid for the option.

Figure 3.5 illustrates the squared power call option.

DIGITAL OPTIONS

Digital options (also known as binary options, all or nothing options) are path-independent derivatives that provide the buyer with a discontinuous payoff or protection profile based on a constant cash or asset amount, i.e., no continuum of payoffs based on moneyness, as in a conventional option. The exercise style on digital options is always European.

F I G U R E 3.5

Squared Power Call Option

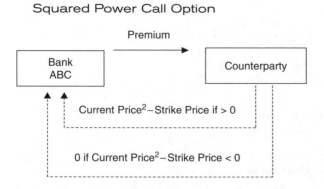

FIGURE 3.6

Payoff Profiles of Digital Call and Regular Call

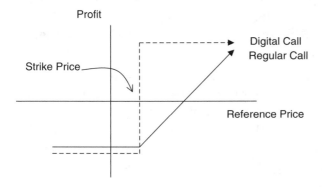

If the digital option is in-the-money at expiry, the buyer receives a fixed cash or asset payout that is unrelated to the degree of moneyness. The payoff differences between a long position in a digital call and a regular call are illustrated in Figure 3.6; we can easily imagine creating the same payoff profiles for long digital puts and short digital positions.

The digital structure is available in various forms, including the "cash or nothing option," which provides a fixed cash payout if the strike is breached (e.g., a ¥10 million cash payment if an option based on the Japanese Government Bond (JGB) prices moves above or below a particular strike) and the "asset or nothing option," which provides a fixed asset payout (e.g., a ¥10 million JGB if the JGB strike is breached). Digitals can also be combined with the barrier options we described in the last chapter to create products known as binary-barriers (also known as one-touch, or American binary, options). These contracts provide a fixed cash or asset payoff when the reference touches the barrier; the payoff is then locked in and paid off immediately (for "at hit" options), or at maturity (for "at expiry" options).

Digitals can be used when an institution is interested only in ensuring that it obtains a fixed amount once the strike is breached on the upside/downside. Depending on the magnitude of the fixed payout, the contract may be more or less expensive than a conventional option. Digitals are also widely used in the creation of structured notes and other embedded derivatives (e.g., index-amortizing rate swaps, range floaters), including those we describe in greater detail in Chapter 4.

Let us consider an example of an investment manager who requires, for asset-liability management purposes, a fixed payout of £1.5 million if the price of the long gilt rises above 101.50. It contracts with a bank to buy a 180-day digital call struck at 101.50 in a current market of 99.70, paying a premium of £250,000. Assume the following two scenarios:

- Scenario 1: In six months the long gilt ends at a price of 100.90; the digital call expires worthless and the investment manager's net loss is premium of £250,000.
- Scenario 2: In six months the long gilt rallies and reaches 102. The investment manager's net gain is £1.25 million (i.e., the fixed payment of £1.5m less the premium paid).

Figure 3.7 illustrates the flows of a digital call option.

MULTIDERIVATIVE PACKAGES

Many of the exotics described above (and in the previous chapter) can be assembled into multiple packages (or embedded in notes or swaps) to provide even more specific risk management or speculative profiles. Although the potential combinations are virtually limitless, some examples include:

- Multiple barrier options (e.g., twin-ins)
- Power barrier options
- Average price barrier options
- Basket shout options

F I G U R E   3.7

Digital Call Option

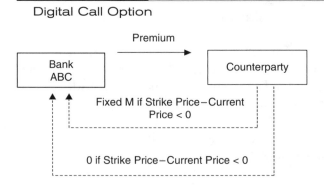

- Compound power options
- Quanto (currency protected) lookback options

Consider an example of a twin-in, where a bank buys a reverse €/$ knock-in call option with a strike at 1.1900 and a trigger at 1.2200 and sells a reverse knock-in put with a strike of 1.1900 and a trigger at 1.1600. If the €/$ rate goes up or down to a significant degree, either the put or the call will be triggered, giving the buyer an in-the-money option. Double knock-outs can also be structured, where a premium is earned as long as the rate stays within a range. If the underlying rate touches a trigger, up or down, the structure knocks out.

Regardless of the structure or complexity, the key is to decompose the derivatives into separate parts in order to undertake proper analysis and valuation.

CHAPTER EXERCISES

1. Which of the following is/are true? Given a current bond price of 105, a strike price of 103, and a barrier of 102, a down and in put option:
   a. Is created without intrinsic value when the barrier is triggered.
   b. Is extinguished without intrinsic value when the barrier is triggered.
   c. Is created with intrinsic value when the barrier is triggered.
   d. Is created without intrinsic value when the barrier is triggered.
   e. None of the above.

2. Given a ladder call on Japanese Government Bonds (JGBs) with a strike of 100 and rungs at 102, 104, and 106, what will the final payoff be if the price path during the life of the option reaches a maximum of 105 and a minimum of 99?
   a. $106 - 105 = 1$
   b. $105 - 100 = 5$
   c. $104 - 100 = 4$
   d. $104 - 99 = 5$
   e. $105 - 99 = 6$

3. Given a strike price of 100, a current bond price of 98, a sensitivity of $10,000 per bond point and a digital payoff $150,000, what is the payoff on a digital option if bond price at maturity is 104?
   a. $40,000
   b. $60,000
   c. $120,000
   d. $150,000
   e. None of the above.

4. Which of the following instruments can help reduce uncertainty regarding the terminal price/rate of a reference bond?
   a. Up and in call option
   b. Digital put option
   c. Power put option
   d. Average price call option
   e. None of the above

5. What are the major advantages of barrier options?
   a. The specific control the user has in incorporating a market view
   b. The relative ease with which they can be hedged
   c. The greater liquidity they feature versus European options
   d. The relatively cheap cost compared to European options
   e. a and d

6. All of the following are true of barrier options except:
   a. Barriers can more accurately take a customer's view and specific risk management needs into account.
   b. The seller of a barrier option assumes less risk than the seller of a standard option.
   c. As the spot price of an asset approaches the barrier, a knock-in option premium approaches the standard European option premium.
   d. As the spot price of an asset approaches the barrier, the knock-out option approaches the standard European option premium.

e. As the spot price of an asset approaches the barrier, the knock-out option approaches the standard American option premium.

7. Speculators use barrier options because:

   a. They do not have strong opinions about future market prices and can use barrier options as an inexpensive means of "guessing."

   b. They can gain greater leverage.

   c. They can set barriers at significant support or resistance levels.

   d. a and b

   e. b and c

Option-Embedded Securities

INTRODUCTION

We have noted in the last 2 chapters that OTC options are extremely flexible. Not only can the contracts be used to create very specific risk and investment management profiles, they can also be incorporated into other financial instruments in order to generate specific end user solutions. In fact, the widespread development of structured and synthetic financial assets over the past three decades owes a great deal to the flexibility of OTC options.

The process of embedding options into capital markets securities has become prevalent. In this chapter we consider some of the most popular option-embedded securities, including convertible bonds and convertible bond variations, callable and puttable bonds, mortgage-backed securities, and structured notes. We shall extend our discussion by examining option-embedded derivatives in the next chapter.

CONVERTIBLE BONDS AND VARIATIONS

Convertible bonds are among the most widely used option-embedded securities in the financial markets, with issuers around the world regularly structuring and floating offerings to meet significant (and generally growing) investor demand. In this section we consider the practical construction and use of convertible bonds, convertible bond variations, and bonds with warrants.

Convertible Bonds

A conventional convertible bond is a debt/equity hybrid that allows the investor to convert a fixed income instrument into a specified number of shares once a particular conversion price is reached; this is precisely equal to a bond and a long investor equity call option. Issuance and conversion flows of the convertible bond are illustrated in Figure 4.1. If conversion occurs, the investor presents the bond for redemption (so forfeiting the right to future coupons, credit spread appreciation, and principal redemption) and receives shares that generally pay a dividend and allow for further capital appreciation. The issuer can generate an attractive cost of funds and minimize the impact of share dilution, while the investor may be able to earn a minimum interest-rate return while preserving potential upside via capital appreciation. The option to convert is, of course, valuable. Since the investor is long a call option, the investor must pay the issuer a premium; this can be done by establishing a below-market coupon or setting a higher market premium over investment value (which we discuss below).

While the standard convertible bond can provide an issuer with important equity funding and deleveraging opportunities, it also carries potential disadvantages. In particular, although new equity may ultimately result from the flotation of a convertible, there is no guarantee of conversion, unless the conversion price is set at artificially low levels, which increases the level of dilution for a given target

FIGURE 4.1

Convertible Bond: At Issuance and Conversion

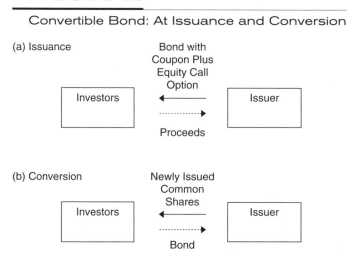

level of equity financing. In addition, and unlike the flotation of common stock via a standard rights issue or public offering, the issuer has no control over the timing of the conversion/issuance. Furthermore, if conversion does not ultimately occur (i.e., the stock price never reaches the appropriate conversion level), the issuer must arrange for refinancing when the convertible is presented for redemption at maturity. It is also important to note that if conversion does not occur the effective cost of funding may compare unfavorably with that of a standard straight bond; yield-to-maturity will increase as maturity draws closer, particularly for zero coupon and puttable structures. Accordingly, in order for the funding advantages to be fully realized, an issuer must be relatively confident that conversion will occur over the medium term. Note also that in some jurisdictions issuers may benefit from favorable tax treatment that can lower all-in funding costs: coupon payments on convertibles that have not been converted into common equity are often tax deductible, while dividend payments on common equity may not be.

Convertible issuers must determine ex-ante an appropriate conversion price and strategy to manage balance sheet leverage should conversion not occur. Establishing a conversion price is a balancing process: the higher the conversion price (i.e., the farther out-of-the-money the equity option), the cheaper the funding and the lower the eventual dilution, but the lower the probability of conversion; the lower the conversion price (i.e., the closer-to-the-money the equity option), the more expensive the funding and the higher the eventual dilution, but the higher the probability of conversion. Naturally, most convertible issuers seek to have their bonds converted at some point, for at least two reasons: the act of converting lowers leverage through the retirement of the fixed income portion of the bond and the issuance of new equity; and, a convertible that remains unconverted for a long period of time (i.e., a so-called "busted" or "broken" convertible) can create uncertainty and stock price pressure for the issuer.[1]

A convertible bond is defined by a number of parameters that help crystallize issuer and investor value. Consider the convertible bond listed in Table 4.1, issued in sterling by U.K.-based Company ABC.

---

1 Although this can occur gradually as an issuer's stock price drifts lower over months or years, it can also happen at the launch of a new issue if the underwriter fails to price the deal properly. If this occurs, the failed new issue can weigh on the issuer's stock price and may require refinancing.

T A B L E 4.1

ABC Convertible Bond Terms

Issuer/rating	ABC plc
Coupon	5.25%
Maturity	5 years
Price	180.25
Nominal (par) value	£1,000
Conversion price	£3.25
Conversion ratio	307.69
Parity	164.77
Premium	9.40%
Current equity price	£5.355
Equity price at issue	£2.56

Let us consider some of the key features of the security based on the terms in the table.

- Nominal value (par value): The value received by the investor at maturity, assuming no conversion takes place. In the example above, each bond has nominal value of £1,000.
- Price: The current price of the bond, quoted as a percentage of nominal value. In the example, ABC's convertible has a current price of 180.25, meaning that the price is 180.25% of the nominal value, or £1802.50.
- Conversion price. The price per share utilized to determine the conversion ratio is set at the time the convertible is issued. If the current market price of the underlying equity is greater than the conversion price, the bond can be converted at a profit. In ABC's case, the current share price is £5.355 and the conversion price is £3.25.
- Conversion ratio: The number of shares of common stock an investor will receive for each bond that is converted. It is calculated using the following formula:

$$\text{conversion ratio} = \frac{\text{nominal value}}{\text{conversion price}} \qquad (4.1)$$

In the ABC example, the conversion ratio is 307.6923 [1,000/3.25], meaning the investor will receive approximately 308 shares for each bond tendered.

- Conversion premium: The percentage by which the conversion price exceeds the underlying stock price at issuance. It is computed as:

$$\text{conversion premium} = \left(\frac{\text{conversion price}}{\text{stock price at issuance}} \right) - 1 \qquad (4.2)$$

In ABC's case the conversion price is £3.25 and the stock price at issuance is £2.56, so the conversion premium is 26.95% [(3.25/2.56) – 1].

- Conversion value: The current value of the underlying equity embedded in the bond, calculated as:

conversion value = conversion ratio * current share price (4.3)

The current conversion value of the ABC bond is £1,647.69 [307.6923 * 5.355].

- Parity: The bond equivalent value of the equity, calculated as:

$$\text{parity} = \frac{\text{conversion ratio} * \text{current stock price}}{\text{nominal value}} * 100 \qquad (4.4)$$

In the ABC example parity is 164.77 [307.6923 * 5.355 * 100/1,000].

- Premium: The amount by which the price of the bond exceeds parity. In other words, it is the percentage amount an investor must pay for the option to convert, and is determined through:

$$\text{premium} = \left(\frac{\text{current bond market price}}{\text{parity}} \right) - 1 \qquad (4.5)$$

The premium on the ABC bond, based on current prices, is 9.40% [(180.25/164.77) – 1].

A typical convertible paying a regular coupon features the essential characteristics of a standard bond, meaning that certain minimum values can be ascribed to the security. For instance, the

T A B L E 4.2

XYZ Convertible Bond Terms

Issuer/rating	XYZ Inc., rated A+
Maturity	5 years
Coupon (semiannual)	3.25%
Nominal (par) value	$1,000
Conversion ratio	14.467
Current price	$1,000
Current equity price	$54
Common dividend per share	$0.25
Initial yield to maturity	3.25%

minimum price of a bond must equal either the conversion value or the bond floor (i.e., straight bond value, or a nonconvertible bond with the same coupon and maturity). Since the convertible bond contains the embedded equity option, it cannot sell for less than a straight bond; arbitrageurs will ensure this remains true by purchasing the undervalued convertible bond and converting it for a riskless profit.

Let us consider a further example by focusing on both bond floor and conversion premium, two essential components of any convertible pricing exercise. Assume Company XYZ is issuing a convertible with the terms noted in Table 4.2.

The bond floor, or the price at which the convertible bond and a comparable straight bond share the same yield, provides information on the minimum value of XYZ's convertible. As the value of the embedded equity option moves further out-of-the-money (e.g., the issuer's stock price falls), the value of the convertible approaches the bond floor.

To compute the bond floor we must first determine the yield on a comparable straight bond. This can be estimated by adding the issuer's credit spread to the appropriate risk-free bond benchmark (e.g., Treasury bond). Assume that the five-year spread for an A+ security is 35 bps over the five-year Treasury yield; at a current yield of 6.25% this generates a comparable straight bond yield of 6.60%. The bond floor is now simply a function of the convertible's maturity, coupon, and the comparable straight debt yield.

T A B L E   4.3

Bond Value Results

	Time Value of Money Key	Value
Number of payments	[n]	5 * 2 = 10
Payment	[PMT]	32.5/2 = 16.25
Yield	[i]	6.60/2 = 3.30
Face (future) value	[FV]	1,000
Solve for price	[PV]	859.28

Using a financial calculator or spreadsheet we obtain the results noted in Table 4.3.

The maximum downside to the investor, assuming market interest rates remain unchanged, is a 14% decline, from par to $859.28. As rates rise, the bond floor will drop further.

We can use the formulas noted above in order to compute the conversion premium. However, if we did not know the value of XYZ's stock at the time of issuance, we can still compute the conversion premium, via the following:

$$\text{conversion price} = \frac{\text{market price of convertible bond}}{\text{conversion ratio}} \qquad (4.6)$$

This is equal to 69.23 [1,000/14.467]. We can then compute conversion premium via:

$$\text{conversion premium} = \frac{\text{conversion price} - \text{market price of common stock}}{\text{market price of common stock}} \qquad (4.7)$$

This amounts to 28% [(69.12 – 54.00)/54.00]. Again, this ratio is important because it indicates the likelihood of conversion. Furthermore, since the premium is a function of market prices, it reflects investor expectations of growth in the issuer's share price. In this example, XYZ's stock price must rise by more than 28% in order for investors to realize gains from the conversion option. If the bond appreciates in value, with the share price remaining unchanged (or increasing by less than the bond), the conversion

F I G U R E 4.2

Convertible Bond Payoff Profile

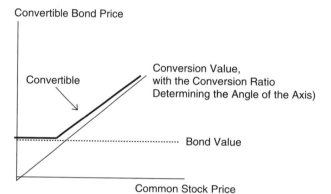

Convertible Bond Price

Conversion Value,
with the Conversion Ratio
Determining the Angle of the Axis)

Convertible

Bond Value

Common Stock Price

premium rises. This may happen if the volatility of the stock increases or if interest rates fall.

Since the convertible has an embedded call option, we can view the payoff profile of the security, from the investor's perspective, using a version of the option payoff diagram introduced in Chapter 2. Knowing that the conversion value is simply the product of the conversion ratio and the price of the common stock, it follows that conversion value increases as the value of the stock increases; the angle of the axis emanating from the origin is a direct function of the conversion ratio. Note further that the bond value acts as a floor in establishing a minimum price. This relationship is illustrated in Figure 4.2.

The value of a convertible increases with rising stock prices, rising volatility, tightening credit spreads, falling rates, lengthening call protection and declining dividend yields. Conversely, it decreases with falling stock prices and volatility, rising rates, widening credit spreads, rising dividend yields and shortening call protection. These relationships, summarized in Table 4.4, can be supported intuitively and quantitatively.

There is no ex-ante way of determining whether a convertible bond will offer a superior investment/funding return over common stock or straight bond alternatives: a convertible can increase investor returns if the common stock price rises and provide downside yield protection if the common stock price falls. As noted, if a convertible is out-of-the-money its value becomes less sensitive to

TABLE 4.4

Convertible Bond Valuation Variables

Convertible Bond Value Increases with...	Convertible Bond Value Decreases with...
Rising stock price	Falling stock price
Rising volatility	Falling volatility
Declining dividend yield	Rising dividend yield
Falling interest rates	Rising interest rates
Tightening credit spreads	Widening credit spreads
Lengthening call protection	Shortening call protection

the common stock price, but quite sensitive to rates and spreads; it will trade as a bond equivalent, making it more appealing to pure fixed-income investors. This characteristic changes once the stock price approaches, and ultimately exceeds, the conversion price: when the conversion value is well above straight value (i.e., the embedded option is in-the-money), the convertible will then trade as an equity equivalent (i.e., the market conversion premium per share becomes increasingly small). However, it is important to note that if a convertible is well in-the-money investors will not pay much of a premium to own the bond; as the common stock continues to rise, the premium will continue to compress and the bond will actually underperform the stock in value terms. The obvious disadvantage of a convertible bond is that the investor sacrifices some upside potential as a result of the market premium; the clear advantage is that the investor mitigates some downside equity risk through the bond floor.

From a basic perspective a noncallable/nonputtable convertible has a single investor equity call option, meaning that the value of the security can be decomposed into two components: straight bond value and call option value. Straight bond value can be derived from any standard fixed-income valuation model that accounts for both interest rates and credit spreads. The call option value can be modeled via a standard Black-Scholes or binomial process, such as we discuss in Part II of the book. If the convertible is callable by the issuer (and in practice many of them are), or if it is puttable by the investor (which is rather less common), then additional embedded options are inserted into the structure and a binomial framework is required.[2]

Though a convertible may be callable or noncallable, it must have a defined maturity date that forces repayment of investor proceeds (generally at par) if conversion has not occurred. While pricing of convertibles depends heavily on the creditworthiness of the issuer and the state of the overall market, standard structures typically feature conversion premiums of 15–25% and final maturities of 10–15 years; coupons are generally set well above the common stock's current dividend yield for the reasons noted above. Low premium convertibles, which are less common, are priced with premiums of approximately 5% in order to promote rapid conversion; coupons on such structures are only slightly higher than the issuer's current dividends.

Convertible Bond Variations

In addition to conventional convertible bonds, companies often issue securities representing slight variations on the basic structure, including exchangeable bonds, zero-coupon convertible bonds, reverse convertible bonds, and mandatory convertible

---

2 A callable convertible may feature hard call protection, soft call protection, or both. Hard call protection is designed to protect the convertible investor by prohibiting issuer calls for a set period of time, generally three to five years. Soft call protection, in turn, protects the investor until the issuer's common stock price reaches a certain percentage of the conversion price (e.g., 130–150%). When a convertible is called, investors can accept the call price or convert into shares. The optimal action is based on whether the call price plus accrued interest is above or below conversion value; if conversion value is above the call price, investors should convert into the underlying shares. Since issuers hope to have their bonds converted, they typically call when the conversion price is at least 5% above the sum of the call price and accrued interest. There are, however, instances when issuers will call when conversion value is well below the call price; this occurs when interest rates have declined markedly and it becomes cheaper to refinance with debt.

Some convertibles are issued on a puttable basis, obligating issuers to redeem the bond on one or more put dates. This feature gives investors the right to redeem the bond in cash terms (a so-called hard put) or shares (a soft put). Since the investor purchases a put option from the issuer through this structure, the coupon it receives on the bond is lower than it would be on an otherwise comparable nonputtable convertible. Puttable convertibles can be put back to the issuer at face value (par put) or at a premium to face value (premium put) on a specific date (or dates). The single premium put structure allows only a single exercise opportunity, while the rolling premium put structure permits multiple put opportunities, with the put premium typically rising on each subsequent put date.

bonds. Each of these is comprised of a fixed income security and one (or more) options.

The exchangeable bond functions just as any conventional convertible bond, except that exercise by the investor of the embedded equity option results in conversion into the shares of an issuer's affiliate rather than the shares of the issuer itself. Thus, if Company ABC floats an exchangeable bond that is convertible into shares of affiliated Subsidiary XYZ, investors receive XYZ shares upon conversion (surrendering the ABC bond in the process). Such transactions are not particularly common, but they do appear. They are typically arranged for listed companies and their affiliates, but may also be floated on behalf of those in the preinitial public offering stage.

The zero-coupon convertible is a deep-discount convertible security issued primarily in the U.S. markets. Like conventional convertibles, zero-coupon versions of the security are generally priced with conversion premia of 15–25% and final maturities ranging from 10 to 30 years. The typical structure is a package comprised of a zero coupon bond, an investor call option on the issuer's stock price, an investor option on the issuer's credit spread, and an issuer's call option on interest rates. The zero-coupon convertible pays no periodic coupon (simply an accreted value payable at maturity or conversion) and redeems at par if not converted. Investors can benefit from both credit spread tightening and equity appreciation, and retain a rolling put feature; the put strikes generally rise as maturity approaches in order to preserve a constant yield-to-put. The issuer, through the callable feature, is protected from rising interest rates. All other benefits and risks found in conventional convertibles apply to zero-coupon convertibles.

In a reverse convertible bond the issuer, rather than the investor, holds the conversion option. This means that the investor is long a fixed income security and short a call option, and therefore receives premium via an enhanced coupon. The reverse convertible allows the issuer to make the decision regarding conversion; this adds a degree of certainty to the timing of equity funding, though it still does not guarantee that an equity infusion will occur (e.g., the equity option may remain out-of-the-money). The mandatory convertible, in turn, is a security that requires the issuer to convert the fixed-income instrument into a preset amount of shares at some future time and price; neither the investor nor the issuer have any flexibility in the matter.

Bonds with Warrants

Bonds with warrants represent another class of equity-based option-embedded securities. Warrants are long-dated options that can be bought, sold, and valued just as other options we have discussed. They are often attached to bonds in order to allow an issuer to lower financing costs (just as in a convertible bond) and give investors the potential benefits of both fixed-income and equity returns (again, as in a convertible). Both securities lead to dilution if conversion/exercise takes place.

While bonds with warrants appear to be similar to convertibles, they feature important differences. For instance, the conversion option in a convertible involves the exchange of an asset with fluctuating value (the bond) for shares of stock. The warrant option involves the exchange of cash for shares of stock. In addition, while the conversion option is embedded in the convertible and cannot be separated, warrants can generally be detached and traded separately in the secondary market. Finally, convertible bonds are often callable (forcing conversion), while warrant bonds tend to be noncallable.

Consider a warrant bond issued by ABC Inc, with details reflected in Table 4.5.

T A B L E 4.5

ABC XYZ Warrant Bond Terms

Bond	
Issuer	ABC Inc.
Amount Issued	$817.9m
Nominal (par) value	$475
Coupon	4.50%
Maturity	5 years
Warrant details	
Warrants per bond	1
Conversion	1 warrant for 1 common share
Strike price	$475
Exercise period	Up to 3 years after issue date
Market price of stock	$932

T A B L E 4.6

Dilution via Warrant Bond

Shares Issued on exercise of warrants	1,721,939
Shares acquired with proceeds from exercise*	(877,598)
Additional shares outstanding	844,341
Current shares outstanding	15,000,000
Shares outstanding after exercise	15,844,341

$$\text{*Detail: } \frac{(\text{warrants outstanding} \times \text{strike price})}{\text{current market price}} = \frac{(1,721,939 \times 475)}{932} = 877,598$$

Relevant calculations related to the warrant bond include the following:

$$\text{number of bonds issued} = \frac{\text{amount issued}}{\text{bond denomination}} \qquad (4.8)$$

$$= \frac{817,921,000}{475} = 1,721,939$$

total number of warrants
$$= (\text{warrants per bond}) * (\text{number of bonds issued})$$
$$= (1) * (1,721,939) = 1,721,939$$
total number of shares issuable
$$= (\text{shares per warrants}) * (\text{number of warrants})$$
$$= (1) * (1,721,939) = 1,721,939$$

If investors exercise the ABC warrants, the firm's earnings will be diluted, since the total number of shares outstanding will rise. Table 4.6 and the computations that follow illustrate the dilutive effect of the warrants, assuming that the company earns \$40m and has 15m shares outstanding.

To compute the change in earnings per share (EPS) based on this data we note the following:

EPS before exercise of warrants: $\text{EPS} = \dfrac{\text{earnings}}{\text{shares outstanding}}$

$$= \frac{40,000,000}{15,000,000} = 2.67$$

EPS after exercise of warrants: $\text{EPS} = \dfrac{\text{earnings}}{\text{shares outstanding}}$

$$= \dfrac{40,000,000}{15,844,341} = 2.52$$

$$\text{Change in EPS} = \left[\left(\dfrac{2.52}{2.67} \right) - 1 \right] = -5.6\%$$

Thus, EPS declines by 5.6%, from 2.67 to 2.52 as a result of the warrant exercise.

CALLABLE AND PUTTABLE BONDS

The second major class of option-embedded securities we consider centers on callable and puttable bonds, or packages comprised of fixed-income instruments and long or short options on interest rates.

Callable Bonds

A callable bond is a package of a bond and a long issuer call option on bond prices (or long issuer put option on interest rates) that allows the issuer to call the security at particular price and/or time intervals. We can distinguish between an American callable bond (which is callable at any time before maturity), a European callable bond (which is callable only once, generally one or two periods before final maturity), and a Bermudan callable bond (which is callable at regular, though not continuous, intervals, such as every 6 or 12 months during the life of the bond). U.S. issuers tend to issue callables primarily in American form, while European and Japanese issuers often opt for the European or Bermudan form.

In exchange for granting the issuer the call option, the investor collects a premium in the form of an enhanced coupon. If the issuer chooses to exercise the call at the call strike price implied by the security, the investor delivers the bond and receives a principal repayment amount equal to the price-based strike, times the quantity of bonds. For instance, a bond may be issued at par, in denominations of $10,000/bond, with a call price (strike) of 105. If the price of the bond rises to 107, as an example, and the issuer elects to call, investors will present their bonds for redemption at a price of $10,500 (and not $10,700, which represents the market value of the security). Figure 4.3 illustrates the basic callable bond structure.

F I G U R E 4.3

Callable Bond

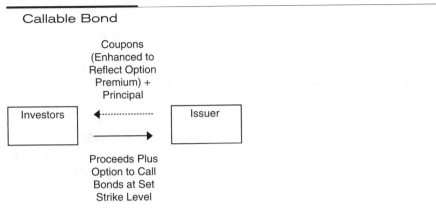

F I G U R E 4.4

Long Issuer Call Option in Callable Bond

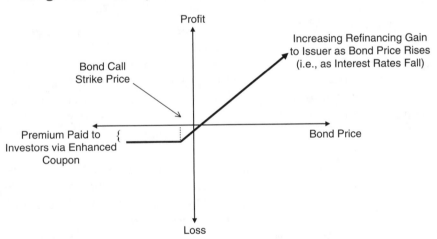

    The callability of a security is primarily a function of interest rates. Issuers floating callable bonds will choose to call their outstanding debt when rates are declining and opportunities to refinance in the new lower-rate environment expand. As rates fall, the outstanding bonds become more valuable (e.g., prices rise). Figure 4.4 examines the embedded call option from the issuer's perspective. Assume that at a current rate of 4% the bond is worth par; as rates fall to 3.5% the price rises to the call price (strike) of

105. At any point after this the issuer may find it advantageous to call the bonds and refinance in the market (i.e., at a level of 3.5% or less). While interest rates dominate the option exercise decision, it is important to note that credit spreads can also play a role in the process. Since an issuer's all-in funding cost (as reflected in the coupon) is a combination of the risk-free interest rate level and the relevant credit spread, it is conceivable that static rates coupled with a significant tightening of the issuer's credit spread may also lead to exercise of the call. If the issuer's credit has improved dramatically in market terms, the issuer will be able to call the security and reissue new debt at the tighter market spread, so reducing funding costs.

Because a callable bond is a combination of noncallable bond and a long issuer call option, it can be valued by examining the price of an identical noncallable bond and deducting the price of the call option. Once the theoretical value of the option is determined, the equation can be inverted to see if the noncallable bond price is accurate (e.g., noncallable bond price = callable bond price + call option price). This exercise is equal to deriving the implied noncallable bond price through observed callable bond prices and theoretical option values.

The value of a callable bond is based, in part, on the value of the option. However, determining the price requires calculating both the noncallable bond price and the call option price simultaneously, meaning it is difficult to shift from a quoted price on a bond to a yield for a given level of volatility—both variables change as yield changes. Furthermore, since the forward price must be computed, the price of the option depends not on a single yield, but on the entire yield curve. As a result, the market has turned towards the use of option-adjusted yields based on bond price and volatility. The noncallable bond is said to have a fair price when the option-adjusted yield for the callable bond is equal to the yield for a noncallable bond with the same features.

Bond value is simply the present value (PV) of all future cash flows (principal and interest) and, if the bond is riskless, it is the PV of the replicating portfolio of the risk-free benchmark. The replicating portfolio is valued at the risk-free zero-coupon value. If the bond is risky, a spread must be introduced to compensate for the risky nature of the cash flows. The resulting static spread is the spread that makes the PV of the cash flows from the bond, when discounted via the risk-free zero-coupon curve, equal to the bond's price.

Unfortunately, this static spread fails to take account of future interest rate volatility that could affect cash flows on a callable (or puttable) bond: the greater the interest rate volatility, the greater the likelihood that the call (or put) embedded in the security will be exercised (though the decision is still dependent on other factors, including remaining time to maturity, call (or put) strike, and so forth). The future path of interest rates thus determines option exercise and, by extension, potential value. Under the option-adjusted yield framework we can develop a zero-coupon curve and assumed spread for each possible interest rate path. The average of all PVs can then be computed; if the average PV is equal to the market price of the bond, then the spread added to the zero-coupon rates equals the option-adjusted spread (OAS); if it is not equal, a new path is computed. An OAS can therefore be interpreted as the average spread over the risk-free zero-coupon curve based on future interest rate paths. We discuss OAS in greater detail in Appendix I.

Convexity, or price sensitivity of the bond to large changes in rates, is an important dimension of the price performance of callable bonds—especially for price movements in a declining rate environment (before the call strike is reached). In practice the actual amount of upward price movement in the bond tends to be limited given the potential exercise of the call; this phenomenon, known as price compression (negative convexity), means that while the price of a noncall bond may continue to rise as rates fall, the price of the callable bond will tend to lag. In the extreme, a callable bond that is currently callable (e.g., one where the strike has been passed) but remains outstanding will feature significant compression as the probability of the security being called at any moment is very high; this compression is, of course, a manifestation of negative convexity. We can examine various yield scenarios to understand the impact of price compression on a noncallable bond, a callable bond that has been called, and a callable bond that remains outstanding. Figure 4.5 reflects the fact that as yields decline, the probability of call exercise increases and price compression begins to set in; however, when yields are positioned above the strike, the callable and noncallable bonds feature similar price/yield movements.

In practice, callable bonds may feature call prices (strikes) that change over time. For instance, in order not to dissuade investors from committing capital when rates are declining, an issuer may establish a relatively high call price for the first few years of a

F I G U R E   4.5

Callable and Noncallable Bonds and Price Compression

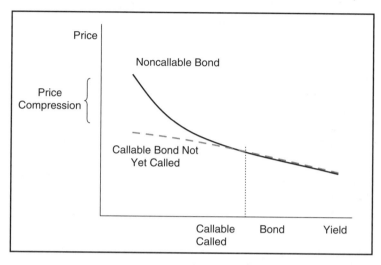

multiyear issue, helping ensure that the bonds can be successfully placed. Only after the passage of several years might the call price ratchet down to a lower level, increasing the likelihood of callability. The reverse may also occur: a step-up callable bond may feature increasingly higher strikes to induce the issuer to call sooner, rather than later, in the life of the bond. Naturally, an issuer is under no obligation to call securities, even if it appears optimal to do so (i.e., even if the option is in-the-money). In fact, there are instances where issuers may prefer to preserve a particular type of financing. This may occur when the issuer wants to keep an investor base intact, or when the issuer believes that a particular form of capital (e.g., maturity, market, coupon) may be difficult to refinance in a given environment). In general, however, an investor in callable securities must be prepared for a call event.

Puttable Bonds

A puttable bond is a package of a bond and a long investor put option on bond prices (long investor call option on interest rates) that allows the investor to put the security back to the issuer at particular price or time intervals. In exchange for granting investors the put option, the issuer collects a premium in the form of a reduced coupon. If investors decide to exercise the put at the strike

F I G U R E 4.6

Puttable Bond

Coupons
(Reduced to
Reflect Option
Premium) +
Principal, Plus
Option to Put
Bonds at Set
Strike Price

Investors		Issuer

Proceeds

price embedded in the security, they deliver the bonds and receive principal repayment equal to the price-based strike, times the quantity of bonds. For example, a bond may be issued at par, in denominations of $10,000/bond, with a put price (strike) of 103. If the price of the bond falls to 99, for instance, and investors decide to exercise their puts, they present their bonds for redemption at a price of $10,300 (and not $9,900, which represents the market value of the securities). Note that unlike the callable bond, which involves a single exercise decision on the part of the issuer, the puttable bond represents discrete decisions by each individual investor holding an eligible security. Figure 4.6 illustrates the basic puttable bond structure.

We can also view the structure in terms of the standard long put payoff profile, as in Figure 4.7. In this instance we note that as the price of the bond falls (e.g., rates rise), the option becomes more valuable to the investor base, which will be motivated to exercise once the strike has been breached. By exercising the option and delivering bonds back to the issuer, investors crystallize a gain and can then reinvest capital in the new, higher-rate, environment. As with the callable bond, the puttable bond may be exercisable by investors if rates are static but the issuer's credit spread widens beyond the strike; under this scenario it is advantageous for the investor base to put the securities back to the issuer.

The valuation techniques noted above are applicable to puttable bonds, since their construction is very similar. Ultimately the

F I G U R E   4.7

Long Investor Put Option in Puttable Bond

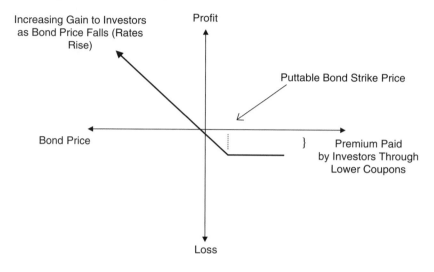

theoretical puttable bond price is simply the value of the nonputtable bond plus the value of the put option.

MORTGAGE-BACKED SECURITIES

The third fundamental class of option-embedded securities we consider is the mortgage backed security (MBS). An MBS is a fixed-income instrument backed by pools of mortgages (or other mortgage securities). The securities are issued from a bankruptcy-remote SPE or trust; the capital obtained from investors through the issuance of securities is used to fund the portfolio of mortgages acquired from the mortgage originator. MBS can be broadly divided into pass-through securities, CMOs, and stripped mortgage products; each can be further decomposed into a series of unique products, some of which we consider below. We include MBS in our discussion of option-embedded securities as most classes of MBS are sensitive to prepayments, or the speed at which mortgages are repaid. Because mortgage borrowers hold the option to prepay the mortgage loans they have taken out, investors in MBS are short options whose value depends critically on the level of prepayments; prepayments, in turn, are a function of interest-rate levels, home sales, and other factors we consider in greater detail in Appendix III.

Pass-through Securities

The pass-through security, as the name suggests, is a mechanism that collects and passes through cash flows from an underlying pool of mortgages to the investor holding the security; the SPE or trust deducts a small amount of the cash flow in the form of fees, and then passes through all interest and principal flows to investors. The frequency of the pass-through payment to the investor depends primarily on the payment frequency of the mortgages in the pool; in most cases borrowers are obliged to make payments on a monthly basis, meaning cash flows passed to investors also occur on a monthly basis; quarterly pay structures also exist. The basic pass-through framework is reflected in Figure 4.8.

The U.S. market features agency pass-through securities, which are arranged and issued by three major agencies (Federal National Mortgage Association (FNMA), Federal Home Loan Mortgage Corporate (FHLMC), Government National Mortgage Association (GNMA)) and private label residential and commercial pass-through securities, which are originated by private sector institutions. Agency pass-throughs include only those mortgages that meet specific size, loan-to-value (LTV), and credit criteria established by each agency; these are known as "conforming mortgages." In general mortgages included in agency pools are fixed-rate,

FIGURE 4.8

Fundamental Mortgage Pass-through Structure

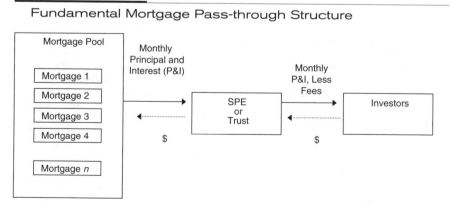

level-pay, single-family residential loans of less than $250,000 (and with LTVs below 80%), and may have explicit guarantees from other governmental agencies. Private label residential pass-throughs, in contrast, feature loans with parameters that diverge from agency criteria (i.e., "nonconforming loans"), including those that exceed the maximum loan threshold, those with higher LTVs, or those granted to subprime borrowers. Commercial MBSs are supported by mortgages extended to finance commercial development, including multifamily residential dwellings, hotels, offices, industrial parks, shopping/retail developments, and so forth; such loans are often extremely large. Non-U.S. pass-throughs represent an important component of the overall market; various countries have introduced government-related or private label pass-through structures over the past two decades, some of which have become very liquid (e.g., U.K., Denmark).

Agency Pass-through Securities

The U.S. agency pass-through market forms the core of the global MBS market. Agency pass-throughs are created when an authorized agency purchases a pool of conforming mortgage assets from a mortgage originator and issues securities backed by the pool to investors; each pool may be composed of thousands of mortgages with similar features (e.g., single or multifamily residential home loans with 15–30 year original maturities, fixed or adjustable rates, maximum loan size, and loan-to-value percentage). Pools may feature loans that are new or seasoned; seasoned pools are characterized by relatively stable prepayments.

GNMA, FNMA, and FHLMC[3] issue agency pass-throughs as fully modified or modified assets. Through the fully modified

---

3 GNMA, which is explicitly guaranteed by the U.S. government, issues only fully modified MBS under its GNMA I and GNMA II programs. FHLMC is a private institution that does not carry the explicit backing of the U.S. government. Given its role in the mortgage market, however, the agency and its modified and fully modified participation certificates (PCs) trade on the basis of an "implied guarantee." FNMA, like FHLMC, is private institution that lacks an explicit U.S. government guarantee, but enjoys some degree of implicit support. FNMA issues fully modified pass-throughs under various programs. All three agencies provide investors with the opportunity to swap outstanding pass-through securities for a pro-rata share in a large combined pool of securities. The amalgamation of smaller pieces of pass-throughs into single larger securities helps create more liquid benchmark issues based on a broadly diversified portfolio of mortgages. These swap/amalgamation securities are issued as FHLMC Giants, FNMA Mega-Pools, and GNMA Platinums.

pass-through structure the agency provides investors with a guarantee of timely payment of principal and interest, regardless of when the agency receives the underlying cash flows from the mortgage pool borrowers. Thus, if a default or delinquency occurs in the pool, the agency will absorb the loss or delay, meaning the investor will suffer no financial consequences. In the modified pass-through structure the agency guarantees payment of principal and interest, but only the interest is guaranteed to be timely. If a default or delay occurs, the investor receives the interest cash flow but may have to wait a period of weeks or months before receiving the principal component. Each agency pass-through security is defined by issue date, underlying collateral, coupon, original pool balance, current pool balance, pool factor (proportion of the original principal balance outstanding as of a particular date), weighted average maturity (WAM, which is the average time that a dollar of principal remains outstanding), and weighted average coupon (WAC, which is the average coupon of the pool, rather than the security; the difference between the WAC and the security coupon is known as the servicing spread). As a result of their special government-related status, agency pass-throughs are exempt from SEC registration requirements.

Private Label Pass-through Securities

Private label pass-throughs, sometimes referred to as conventional pass-throughs, nonagency pass-throughs, or A/Bs, are issued directly by financial intermediaries, including banks, savings & loans, and securities firms. As noted above, the collateral pool underpinning private label securities includes residential mortgage loans that fail to conform to agency requirements; not surprisingly, the pools are typically far less homogenous, and may include mortgages of varying size, LTV, and credit quality. Unlike agency MBS, private label securities carry no timely or ultimate guarantee of principal or interest, and must be registered with regulators. Most need to be rated via the public credit-rating agencies and actually achieving a rating similar to the AAAs of the agency market generally requires some form of credit enhancement.

The primary component of the private label market is based on jumbos, or loans that are at least three times larger than those granted by the agencies (and with LTVs that are often below 80%, i.e., more borrower equity is involved). Jumbos are extended to affluent borrowers, so credit default experience is generally much more favorable than on other loans. Jumbos tend to have faster prepayments than conventional mortgages, as borrowers are more attuned to interest rates and refinancing opportunities; the large loan size makes borrowers particularly sensitive to any possible savings that can be obtained through refinancing. Jumbo pools are often concentrated in regions that feature higher real estate prices (e.g., in the U.S. this can include California, the Northeast, and Florida).[4]

Because private labels carry a greater element of credit risk than agency securities and cannot offer the same guarantee of timely/ultimate repayment of principal and interest, many feature some form of credit enhancement in order to generate AAA or AA ratings and make the securities more appealing to a broader base of buyers. Common forms of credit enhancement include third-party guarantees or bond insurance (i.e., from monoline insurers or financial guarantee companies), bank letters of credit, or senior/subordinated structuring (e.g., issuance of senior and subordinated tranches backed by the same pool, with the senior investor holding priority over the collateral and the subordinated tranche absorbing the first loss component). The preferred form of credit

---

4 Private-label pass-throughs may also be created using so-called "alternative A" (Alt A) loans as the backing collateral. Alt A's are moderate/high credit quality loans, generally up to 30% larger than conforming loans (but smaller than jumbos), with LTVs that may exceed agency limits. Alt-A loans are often supported by limited borrower documentation, and borrowers may feature debt to income ratios that are below those required by the agencies. Alt-A loans are not lower credit quality loans, but loans with characteristics that are different from those in conforming pools; true low quality loans form part of the subprime sector, discussed below. The prepayment experience of Alt-A pools is generally mixed; borrowers may not initially have access to the same refinancing opportunities as conventional agency borrowers as a result of their unique characteristics, suggesting lower prepayments versus agency pools in a declining rate environment. This, however, appears to be true only in the short term; over the medium term, Alt-A pools seem to exhibit greater prepayments than agency pools as a larger number of "slow" refinancers begins to take action.

The subprime (B&C) loan sector forms the third part of the private label market. As the name suggests, subprime loans are credits extended to borrowers with a prior history of credit problems. In general, loan balances are smaller, and LTVs are lower, than in conforming pools so that lenders receive additional collateral protection. Pool diversification is considerable in order to spread the risk of borrower defaults across a broad portfolio. Because lower-quality borrowers tend not to have the same financing options as conforming borrowers, sensitivity to refinancing opportunities is much lower. Indeed, B&C prepayments from declining interest rates are much lower than on standard agency paper: in fact, refinancing is driven primarily by credit upgrades of borrowers, which tends to be a much slower process.

enhancement is generally a guarantee from the sponsoring institution, as this can help lower the cost of the transaction; however, this is only achievable when the sponsor is highly rated. In practice the most common form of credit enhancement is senior/subordinate tranching, with the subordinated, or junior, tranche occupying the first loss position.

STRUCTURED NOTES

The fourth major class of option-embedded securities we consider in the chapter centers on the structured note market. This sector includes fixed income securities that are paired with equity, fixed income, currency, commodity, or credit options to create unique risk, funding, and investment management opportunities. Structured notes are available in various generic forms, including:

- Principal protected: The investor is at risk only for loss of coupons in the event a defined risk event occurs.
- Coupon increased: The investor's principal is at risk in unleveraged or leveraged form, generally up to the entire amount of principal.
- Coupon reduced: The investor receives full repayment of principal, and an extra payment if a defined risk event occurs; if no event occurs, the coupon is reduced.
- Step-up: The investor receives a larger coupon for each occurrence of a defined risk event.

Structured notes are generally comprised of a host bond (three to seven years in maturity) and one or more options (they can also be created using embedded swaps and forwards, but these are outside the scope of our discussion). The design of a structured note must take account of various factors, including desired investor participation levels in future market movements, degree of principal protection, payment of interest or dividends, and optimal use of derivatives. For instance, if the investor is amenable to the use of an average price rather than a terminal price in the determination of principal redemption, then an Asian option can be embedded in the securities. Because the Asian option is typically cheaper than the European or American option, the investor can benefit through an increased participation rate. Alternatively, if the investor is willing to assume a greater amount of risk in exchange for a higher participation level, the investor can sell the note issuer a higher strike option.

Bonds can be coupon-bearing, zero-coupon, amortizing, bullet, or balloon. Host issuers, generally AAA or AA corporate or supranational organizations, allow intermediaries to issue structured liabilities on their behalf in exchange for a fee or reduced funding cost. Investors purchasing such securities thus face little default risk associated with the host issuer—coupon and principal-based returns are based solely on external references that are incorporated into the relevant payoff formula. Issuance also occurs via repackaging vehicles. Such vehicles, organized as bankruptcy-remote SPEs or trusts, were originally introduced in the late 1980s, but gained true popularity in the mid-1990s during the first cycle of structured note business. Most major financial institutions operate their own repackaging vehicles, which they use to acquire assets, repackage cash flows, and issue notes to investors. Most vehicles are created for multiple issuance in order to improve cost efficiencies; indeed, once a vehicle is established, the costs of new note issuance are generally very modest, making the process economically viable for both intermediaries and investors.

Though construction and valuation of structured notes can be an involved task, the individual components of any given security can be examined separately to determine proper design and pricing. For instance, a bond with an embedded option can be decomposed and each leg can be priced separately. In an arbitrage-free market environment, the decomposition process helps ensure some degree of price equilibrium.

Interest-Rate-Linked Notes

Structured notes with embedded interest rate options are common, appearing frequently when interest rates are low, the yield curve is steep, and interest rate volatility is on the rise; each one of these factors can benefit investors and issuers. Key option-based structures in this category include capped and collared floating-rate notes (FRNs), range FRNs, and step-up bonds.

Financial institutions and corporations seeking to lock in funding levels routinely issue capped and collared FRNs. The capped FRN is a package comprised of an FRN and a long issuer cap that establish a maximum borrowing cost. If forward rates are high (e.g., the curve is steep) or short-term rates are especially volatile, the cap is expensive, meaning a higher return for investors; high forward rates increase the "lock in" value for each reset date, and the high volatility increases the time value for each date. In some instances, the caps sold by investor via the note may be misvalued; this is particularly true when the curve is very steep. In such cases the issuer can sell an equivalent cap at a higher price in the market, using the differential to lower its funding costs. Another version of this structure, the collared FRN, incorporates a short issuer floor to give investors a minimum market return while defraying some (or all) of the issuer's cap premium cost. When the curve is steep, forward rates are significantly higher than current rates; this means that the floor the issuer has sold may be in-the-money in a current period but may move out-of-the-money in a future period; the reverse scenario occurs for the cap. If the issuer can sell the floor to investors at a relatively high level and repurchase an identical floor at a lower cost in the market, funding costs are lowered. Cost savings can run to more than 50 bps. In certain other situations the reverse transaction can also be arranged (e.g., the issuer sells a cap and buys a floor). Figure 4.9 illustrates the collared FRN.

Note that several other variations seek to capitalize on the same arbitrage opportunities. Collared FRNs with multiple

FIGURE 4.9

Collared FRN

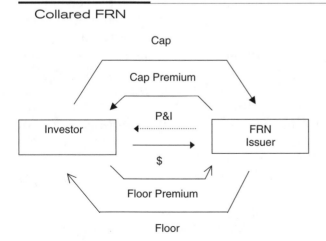

cap/floor strikes can be arranged, with each caplet/floorlet featuring a unique strike; this reverts to our discussion in Chapter 2. Ratchet collared FRNs are similar in concept, but contain caplet/floorlet strikes that increase at particular intervals; such structures are most valuable to issuers when the implied forward rates suggest greater moneyness will accrue to the caplets. Capped and collared FRNs with participating caps/floors are also available. These, for example, may allow for increased participation levels as the cap strikes rise for each sequential coupon period, with a payoff equal to (cap strike – participation rate ∗ (strike rate – LIBOR)).[5]

The range floater structure (also known as an accrual note) is similar to the collared FRN, except that the caps and floors are replaced by digital options that provide a payout/coverage of either a fixed amount or zero. The range floater pays interest to note investors only on days when LIBOR (or some other floating-rate index) falls within the boundaries established by the upper and lower strikes of the digital options; for every day within a period that LIBOR falls outside the range, interest ceases to accrue. If LIBOR falls outside the bands for an entire quarter, investors lose interest for the full quarter. In exchange for potential risk of loss on the coupon, investors receive an enhanced coupon while the benchmark rate remains within the band. This suggests, of course, that investors are selling the issuer a strip of digital options, with the enhanced coupon representing premium.

Let us examine an example of this structure. Assume that an investor buys a three-year range floater paying an enhanced coupon of three-month LIBOR + 40 bps in a market when LIBOR is equal to 5%. The note features a step-up range, where year one has a range of 5–6%, and years two and three have a range of 6 –7%. We can determine the number of days the range floater can trade outside the range and still be equal to a standard FRN (i.e., the breakeven LIBOR level at which the range floater is equivalent to a standard FRN trading at LIBOR flat). In this example the extra revenue earned over a full year amounts to 40.5 bps; the cost of trading outside of the range for one day is equal to approximately 1.4 bps, meaning that the breakeven position is 29 days. This suggests that if LIBOR trades inside the range for more than 29 days,

---

5 Obviously not all collared or capped structures reference LIBOR; other rates, including constant maturity Treasury (CMT), EURIBOR, bank bills, and so forth, can also be used.

the investor's position is profitable. A more extreme version of the range floater, the knock-out floater, is comprised of a series of knock-out options rather than digital options, suggesting that if the reference rate trades outside of the range for even a single day, the coupon for the entire (quarterly) period is sacrificed (e.g., it knocks-out as the barrier level is reached); these are particularly risky versions of the accrual structure.[6]

The step-up note is also common. Under this structure, which first appeared in the market in the late 1980s, the investor receives an above-market rate during the note's noncall period (generally one or two quarterly periods), and then receives increasingly higher rates (step-ups) for each period in which the note is not called by the issuer (in general, the step-up rates are likely to be below market rates for the first few periods). The investor in this instance has sold the issuer a strip of call options, with the initial above market rate constituting the premium.

Currency-Linked Notes

Bonds with embedded-currency options can be structured to give an issuer exposure to a particular currency. For instance, a company may issue a fixed-rate bond with a long embedded-currency option, paying the investor premium via an enhanced coupon. The value of the option impacts redemption: if the currency option remains out-of-the-money the investor receives par at maturity; if, however, the option moves in-the-money, the principal redemption payable to investors declines on a sliding scale related to the level of moneyness (the further in-the-money, the lower the redemption to a minimum floored level). Principal reduction may be defined by a formula such as:

$$P * \left(1 - \frac{strike - spot}{spot} \right) \tag{4.9}$$

---

6 It is worth noting that investors in capped/collared FRNs and range floaters face different risks. Investors in capped/collared notes are speculating that the rates implied by the yield curve are too high; if correct, they preserve the enhanced coupon representing the premium. Investors in range floaters, in contrast, are taking a view primarily on interest rate volatility (yield curve moves are only secondary); specifically, they must believe that the premium received via the enhanced coupon will be sufficient to make up for a potential loss in daily yield driven by volatility.

where P is principal, strike is the strike price of the currency option, and spot is the spot level at maturity.

Consider, for instance, a $100m structured currency note that pays investors an enhanced coupon and par redemption while the dollar trades weaker against the yen (versus a current spot and strike rate of Y105$). As the dollar begins to strengthen, the principal redemption begins to decline, meaning that the issuer of the note has purchased an embedded dollar call/yen put. Assume that at note maturity the dollar strengthens to Y110/$. Under this scenario investors will receive principal redemption of $95.5m (i.e., $100m * (1 − (105 − 110)/110))).

Notes can also constructed with embedded currency baskets (e.g., emerging market currencies) or exotic currency options, including barriers, digitals, lookbacks, and cliquets; these, not surprisingly, are somewhat less common, and appear in response to specific investor demand.

Equity-Linked Notes

Equity-linked securities are floated in a variety of forms, including FRNs and bonds with embedded options referencing individual stocks, baskets/sectors, or indexes. An investor in a typical equity-linked note purchases a security that pays no coupon (or pays a below market coupon), in exchange for appreciation (e.g., a call) or depreciation (e.g., a put) in the equity reference. The redemption of the note is typically set at par (i.e., a minimum guaranteed fixed payment) plus a percentage of the appreciation or depreciation in the reference equity index. The issuer of the note (e.g., bank, company, or SPE) benefits from a lower cost of funding through the receipt of the premium payment (e.g., the zero-coupon or below-market coupon rate on the note). As with the other notes mentioned above, the issuer may purchase a similar/ identical option in order to monetize value. Figure 4.10 summarizes this structure.

This type of equity-linked security is created through a multi-step process that begins with computation of the issuer's funding level. Once the target level is known, it is converted into a fixed rate covering the term of the note; this generates the value of the implied zero-coupon bond. For example, if the funding level suggests a 75% zero-coupon threshold is required, $75 of each $100 of note proceeds is used to purchase a zero-coupon security, which

F I G U R E   4.10

Equity-Linked Note

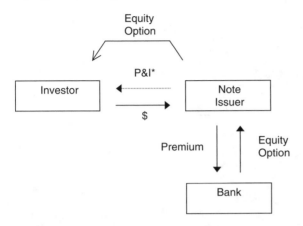

*Principal redemption increased if option moves in-the-money; interest
coupon decreased as a form of premium payment

grows to $100 by maturity. The balance of the note proceeds is used
to acquire an option (e.g., a call). If an option has a market value
of $20, the maximum amount of call coverage is $25/$20, or
$125 per $100 of note issuance. In practice, some amount of the
remaining $25 balance must be used to cover issuance fees and/or
to pay an interim coupon (on nonzero coupon deals). It is easy to
see that if principal protection is reduced (e.g., the $100 is not guar-
anteed at maturity) larger coupons and/or larger participation can
be introduced into the process. In fact, the coupon/principal value
of the note is a function of interest rates, maturity, option moneyness, option volatility, and desired level of equity participation. A
note with an out-of-the-money equity option commands less premium (and thus more coupon), but also provides less upside potential; one that is at- or in-the-money commands a greater premium
(and thus a lower coupon), but provides larger upside potential. In
general, as moneyness increases, the participation rate increases; the
same is true if volatility increases. For example, a note might feature
a five-year maturity and a 2% semiannual coupon plus 90% of the
appreciation in the S&P 500 above a strike price of 650, with a minimum redemption of par (i.e., no principal at risk). The investor
retains $0.90 of every dollar earned after the S&P exceeds the 650
strike. In the opposite form of this structure investors write the
issuer equity calls or puts in exchange for a higher coupon.

F I G U R E 4.11

Equity Note with Embedded Collared

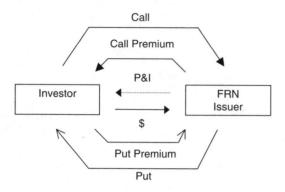

Put-based structures tend to be less popular than call-based structures, as investors often prefer to participate when markets are in an uptrend. This suggests that put-based structures may be cheaper, allowing a greater level of embedded investor participation. Other types of equity notes can be created, including those with synthetic collars, where an investor receives both a minimum and a maximum return; the investor is thus long a put and short a call via the note (meaning, of course, that the issuer is short a put and long a call). Figure 4.11 illustrates the collared equity note.

Coupons may also be embedded with call spreads that set minimum and maximum boundaries for a particular quarter or semiannual period (e.g., minimum appreciation of 1% and maximum appreciation of 5% in any quarter); the short call on the upside (e.g., sacrificing gains above 5%) increases the investors' participation rate. Other notes may feature embedded cliquet options that lock in unrealized value even if markets subsequently retrace; more extreme versions feature lookback options, supplying investors with the maximum gain achieved during the life of the transaction.

Commodity-Linked Notes

Commodity-based structures are created on common commodity references, such as oil, gold, silver, and aluminum, as well as broader commodity indexes. In some instances the notes/loans are issued by commodity producers, which use the instruments to hedge core commodity risks. In other cases intermediaries or other institutions seeking to monetize a market view issue them; monetization can help lower funding costs or increase investment returns.

As above, issuers selling embedded commodity options lower their funding costs by offering investors a lower yield (i.e., one that is equivalent to the theoretical premium on the options, amortized over the maturity of the note). Investors receive the upside or downside of the commodity if it moves in-the-money. An issuer selling a commodity option that is not required for the issuer's own operations typically repurchases an identical option from an intermediary in order to neutralize the risk; even after paying the premium, the issuer's all-in funding costs can be lower than that of a straight issue, though this depends on the relative strikes of the two options.

Consider an issuer that wants to float a three-year fixed-rate bond with a coupon of 9% and embedded gold call options; each option gives the investor the right to buy one oz of gold at $400. If the bond alone is a par valued security and the PV of the entire structure is 109.45, then the value of the call embedded in each bond is $9.45. In order for the funding arbitrage to work properly, the premium on the gold option the issuer repurchases must be less than $9.45. For example, if the issuer purchases an offsetting call at $8.75 the yield on the bond may decline to 8.45%, a 55 bp savings. If the issuer opts not to hedge the short call exposure, the issuer has a speculative position that negatively impacts the cost of funds as the price of gold rises.

Commodity producers can also use embedded options. For instance, a copper producer may borrow funds via a bond, with a cost that declines through the sale of embedded copper calls; since the producer owns the underlying copper, the producer is writing covered call options on a portion of production and using the premium to lower funding costs. If the price of copper rises, the calls move in-the-money and the bond investors receive an enhanced coupon or principal; the copper producer is indifferent to the increased payout, however, as the producer earns more on the core copper stock.

Credit-Linked Notes

The basic credit linked note (CLN) is a package consisting of a low-risk bond or FRN and a simple or structured credit option (or swap/forward), and provides investors with the returns of a credit-risky investment without the need to own the underlying credit asset. In certain instances the host fixed-income vehicle may be a loan, rather than a bond or FRN, though this structure is less common. The "vanilla" CLN is generally issued at par with a payout calibrated to a defined credit event. Because payout is dependent on the credit event, the investor typically serves as the credit protection seller. As with other structured notes, the issuer often acts as a "pass-through," selling the credit derivative purchased from investors to the bank arranging the transaction in order to reduce funding costs. The vanilla structure can settle in cash or physical: if a credit event occurs, the note terminates and the investor receives as principal repayment the cash difference between the asset's value pre- and postdefault, or it delivers the reference asset and receives the postdefault market price.

CLNs can be created using bonds and default options or credit spread options that provide the buyer with a payment if the spread on a reference credit defaults or widens/tightens. For instance, the credit spread note, which embeds a credit spread call or put option in a host security, creates an exposure to the spread movement of a reference asset. An investor purchasing the note monetizes a view on expected versus implied forward credit spreads. Thus, if the note is created using a call option, the investor anticipates a tightening of spreads; if a put option is used, then a widening of spreads is expected. In exchange for purchasing the put or call, the investor pays a premium by accepting a lower coupon yield.

The credit default CLN, which packages a host bond with a credit default option, is similar to the credit spread note, but generates a payoff that relates only to default of the reference asset. The default note allows an end user to invest in default risk (through the embedded sale of the default option) and an issuer, such as a financial intermediary, to hedge default risk (through the purchase of the option). Notes issued by corporates rather than financial institutions generally include back-to-back options between the corporate issuer and the bank in order to transfer the economics of the default option. Under the standard structure the note provides the investor with an enhanced yield based on the value of the default option being sold, along with par redemption at maturity if no default occurs or par redemption less a default payment if an event occurs. The default payment can be set as a percentage of recovery or the change in the reference asset price between issue

F I G U R E   4.12

Default-based CLN

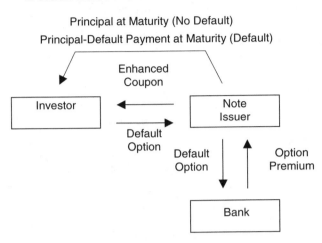

date and the default date. The default event can be defined specifically or generally, though the industry's move towards standardized definitions typically means that bankruptcy, restructuring, cross default, failure to pay, repudiation, and moratorium are included. Figure 4.12 summarizes the default-based CLN structure.

The callable credit default note is an extension on the standard default CLN. This structure, which is a package of an FRN, default option, and issuer call option, functions just like a default note, but gives the issuer the right to call the note back at regular intervals (generally every quarter or semiannual interest payment date). If the bond is not called the coupon steps up to a higher predefined margin over LIBOR. Through this structure the issuer determines on each call date whether or not to preserve the default protection; if the note is not called, it may indicate that the reference credit is deteriorating, meaning that the cost of protection via the higher coupon is justifiable. A further variation is the principal-guaranteed credit default note, which allows the investor to participate in the credit risk exposure without placing principal at risk; this can be structured as a risk-free bond and a call option on the credit reference. Another extension is a default CLN linked to the credit performance of the asset and continued convertibility in a local marketplace. This structure, which is often applied to local currency emerging market bond investments where capital controls present an additional dimension of risk, features a coupon/principal payout that is a function of default and restricted convertibility. If either event occurs, principal redemption is adjusted.

CHAPTER EXERCISES

1. Consider the following convertible bond issued by Company JKL:

Nominal value	$1,000
Conversion price	$78
Stock price at issuance	$61
Current share price	$63
Bond market price	$95

   a. Calculate the conversion ratio.
   b. Calculate the conversion premium.
   c. Calculate the conversion value.
   d. Calculate the parity.
   e. Calculate the premium.

2. A convertible bond is a package of:
   a. Short bond and short investor call option
   b. Long bond and long investor call option
   c. Long bond and short investor call option
   d. Short bond and long investor call option
   e. None of the above

3. The convertible bond conveys which of the following benefits?
   a. Increase in an issuer's cost of funds and decrease in an investor's returns
   b. Minimum value in an investor's returns and decrease in the issuer's cost of funds
   c. Increase in dividends and capital appreciation
   d. Increase in shareholder dilution
   e. None of the above

4. Which of the following is/are true of a convertible bond?
   a. Dilution always occurs
   b. Dilution never occurs

    c. Dilution may occur

    d. Dilution will vary

    e. None of the above

5. A callable bond is a package of:

    a. A long bond and a long issuer call

    b. A long bond and a long investor call

    c. A short bond and a short issuer call

    d. A short bond and a short investor call

    e. None of the above

6. The theoretical value of a callable bond is equal to:

    a. Noncallable bond + call option

    b. Callable bond – call option

    c. Noncallable bond – call option

    d. Callable bond + call option

    e. None of the above

7. A puttable bond is a package of:

    a. A long bond and a short issuer call

    b. A long bond and a short investor call

    c. A long bond and a long investor call

    d. A long bond and a short investor put

    e. A long bond and a long investor put

8. A collared FRN features:

    a. A long issuer floor and a short issuer cap

    b. A long investor floor and a short investor cap

    c. A long issuer floor and a long investor cap

    d. A short issuer floor and a long investor cap

    e. None of the above

9. In a credit-spread-linked credit-linked note with an embedded call option on credit spreads, the principal/coupon is:

    a. Increased as spreads widen

    b. Increased as spreads tighten

    c. Decreased as spreads widen

    d. Decreased as spreads tighten

    e. None of the above

Option-Embedded Derivatives

INTRODUCTION

We continue our discussion and analysis of structured option instruments by considering the general class of option-embedded derivatives. Packages comprised of swaps or forwards and one or more options have become extremely popular over the past two decades, and are often used in conjunction with option-embedded securities in order to more precisely match or hedge cash flows of structured instruments.

In this chapter we consider several of the most common types of option-embedded derivatives, including swaptions, callable, puttable, and extendible swaps, callable asset swaps, puttable asset swaps, and asset swaps variations.

SWAPTIONS

A swaption, as the namely indicates, is a combination of a swap and an option. We know from Chapter 1 that an interest rate swap involves the periodic exchange of interest/currency coupons on a fixed- or floating-rate basis, while the option grants the purchaser the right to buy or sell a particular asset at a set strike price. A swaption, then, is a synthetic derivative contract that grants the buyer the right to enter into a swap with a fixed rate defined by the strike. It can be further described as:

- The payer (or put) swaption, which grants the buyer the right to enter into a swap where it pays a fixed rate (i.e., the strike level) and receives floating (e.g., LIBOR)
- The receiver (or call) swaption, which grants the buyer the right to receive the fixed rate and pay the floating rate[1]

If the buyer chooses to exercise the option, all terms related to the swap come into force, including rates, payment frequency, notional amount, and final maturity.

The market quotes swaptions in terms of a strike rate, option maturity, and swap maturity. For instance, a 1×3 5% $ payer swaption grants the buyer a one-year option to enter into a three-year swap where it pays $ fixed at 5% and receives $ LIBOR flat. If rates rise above 5% during the 12-month period, it becomes economically rational for the buyer to exercise the swaption to pay 5% and receive LIBOR for a period lasting three years; conversely, if rates remain below 5% the contract remains unexercised. Like other options, swaption exercise can be defined in American, European, or Bermudan terms, and settlement may be arranged in cash or swap terms. Swaption quotes are available on a range of global rates and a series of common structures related to the tenor of the option, the tenor of the underlying swap and the fixed-rate strike (note that the fixed-rate strike is quoted as an absolute rate rather than as a spread to a benchmark). Dealers provide bid-offer pre-

T A B L E 5.1

Sample Swaption Quotes

Swaption Structure	Fixed-Rate Strike (%)	Receiver Spread (bps)	Payer Spread (bps)
1×3	5.00	5–10	70–75

Premium dealer pays for buying the fixed payer swaption

Premium dealer demands for selling the fixed payer swaption

---

1 The put and call swaption terminology can be compared with that of a standard bond option: a call option on a bond gives the purchaser the right to receive the bond's cash flows once a certain strike level has been reached; similarly, a call swaption grants the right to receive fixed cash flows under a swap. The reverse is true for bond put options and put swaptions.

mium spreads for both payer and receiver flows for each of these structures, as noted in Table 5.1; these premiums are applied to the notional value of the transaction to generate a dollar value premium.

The strike level influences the value of a swaption, like any other option, time to maturity, volatility, and risk-free rate. For instance, a receiver swaption with a high strike is more valuable than one with a low strike, as it provides the buyer with a larger cash flow upon exercise; a payer swaption with a higher strike is less valuable than one with a lower strike, as it requires the buyer to pay a larger cash flow on exercise. Swaptions with a longer time to maturity are more valuable than those with shorter maturity as they provide more time for the contract to move in the money. Similarly, a more volatile market increases swaption value as greater volatility can force a contract in-the-money (or further in-the-money).

Exercise of the swaption depends on the market level of interest rates. If rates fall through the strike of the swaption, the buyer of a payer swaption will not exercise as it is economically favorable to pay the lower market rate, while the buyer of a receiver swaption will exercise as it will receive an above market rate. If rates rise above the swaption strike the reverse occurs: the buyer of the payer swaption will exercise in order to lock in a maximum payment level, while the buyer of the receiver swaption will choose not to exercise. These four states are summarized in Table 5.2.

Swaptions are highly flexible and can be used to meet a range of goals. An institution may purchase a swaption in order to lock in a known or anticipated funding, hedge, or investment level for a future date, and it might sell a swaption to take advantage of a view on the movement and/or volatility of interest rates, or to monetize value in a callable or puttable bond structure.

An institution believing rates will rise can purchase a payer swaption or sell a receiver swaption; one believing that rates will fall can sell the payer swaption or buy the receiver swaption. For

T A B L E 5.2

Swaption Exercise States

	Rates Rise through Strike	Rates Fall through Strike
Payer swaption	Exercise	No exercise
Receiver swaption	No exercise	Exercise

instance, if a bank expects rates will rise, it can buy a payer swaption; if rates rise, it can exercise the right to pay fixed at below market levels and receive higher market floating rates. Alternatively it can exercise and then sell the swap in the market for its intrinsic value, or enter into a reverse market transaction where it receives the higher market fixed rate against floating (thus locking in the spread on the fixed legs). Or, it may simply sell the in-the-money swaption in the marketplace to another party. If rates decline, the institution will let the swaption expire unexercised and simply lose the premium it paid to acquire the contract. It may also sell the receiver swaption to capitalize on its expectation of rising rates. The institution believing that rates will decline can sell the payer swaption and collect premium; if rates remain below the strike the contract will expire unexercised and it will have earned premium income (naturally, if rates rise above the strike, the institution's liability increases). Alternatively, it can buy the receiver swaption, exercising to lock in a higher fixed rate if market rates fall below the strike. We will consider other swaption-based monetization strategies in Chapter 7.

Standard swaptions are usually structured as European options with a single exercise date. Market practitioners are generally not eager to price American swaptions due to the broken date nature of the resulting underlying swap if the swaption is exercised. Bermudan swaptions serve as a middle ground, allowing exercise of the swaption on specific dates during the life of the transaction; this makes the entire package easier to price and risk manage. In fact, the Bermudan swaption creates a product that bridges the gap between the multiexercisable cap and floor suite of interest rate option products discussed in Chapter 2, and the single exercise opportunity of the standard swaption. They are particularly useful for bond issuers and investors who have either issued, or are trading, bonds with embedded options that can be exercised at various points during the life of the bond.

Consider a six-month LIBOR, two-year cap with a forward start date of two years. The cap buyer has the option to exercise caplets at 24, 30, 36, and 42 months. Next, consider a standard 2-×-2 swaption; the contract allows the buyer to exercise into a two-year swap once, in two years. The product will not cover any adverse rate changes after the two-year period. Finally, consider a four-year no-call two-year Bermudan swaption with annual exercise. This structure allows the buyer to exercise two times: at the end of year two, entering into a two-year swap, or at the end of year three,

FIGURE 5.1

Cap and Swaption Exercise Opportunities

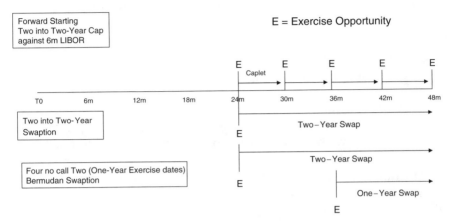

entering into a one-year swap. The spectrum of exercise opportunities of the three products is summarized in Figure 5.1.

We can imagine that introducing shorter exercise periods generates a more complete continuum of alternatives. Consider, for instance, a four-year, no-call six-month Bermudan swaption. This structure provides the buyer with one of seven opportunities to exercise into a swap, as noted in Table 5.3.

Though not as flexible as a standard cap, the Bermudan swaption features considerable advantages over a standard American or European swaption. It is worth noting that Bermudan swaptions

TABLE 5.3

No Call Six-Month into Four-Year Swaption

Time	Exercised Swap
Today	No call
6 months	3.5-year swap
12 months	3-year swap
18 months	2.5-year swap
24 months	2-year swap
30 months	1.5-year swap
36 months	1-year swap
42 months	0.5-year swap

are useful when attempting to hedge or monetize value in a callable or puttable bond. Most such bonds do not have a single call/put date, meaning that a swaption with multiple exercise opportunities is necessary.

CALLABLE, PUTTABLE, AND EXTENDIBLE SWAPS

Callable and puttable swaps, like swaptions, are structured derivatives that are created by combining swaps and options. A callable swap is a swap with an embedded option that allows the fixed-rate payer the right to terminate the transaction at some future point. The puttable swap allows the fixed-rate receiver to terminate a swap. We can view these synthetic structures in terms of their constituent components. For instance, a five-year swap that is callable in three years is equal to a standard five-year swap and a three-year receiver swaption on a two-year swap. Similarly, a five-year swap that is puttable in three years is equal to a five-year swap and a three-year payer swaption on a two-year swap. Since callable and puttable swaps are constructed from swaps and options, put-call parity relationships hold, primarily for European structures. For example, knowing that a callable swap is simply a package of a swap and a receiver swaption, we note that a callable swap and a short receiver swaption are precisely equal to a swap, as are a puttable swap and a short payer swaption.

Let us consider the puttable swap in more detail. A puttable swap gives the fixed-rate receiver the right to terminate the underlying swap transaction at some future date, meaning that the fixed-rate payer is selling a receiver swaption on an underlying swap that starts during the life of the swap and terminates at maturity. In exchange for selling the right to cancel, the fixed-rate payer receives a premium in the form of an up-front cash flow or a higher fixed rate on the underlying swap. The purchaser of the puttable swap can choose to enter into this type of transaction if the purchaser is unsure of the need to preserve the swap at some point in the future or expects that interest rates will decline. One common puttable swap structure is the index amortizing rate (IAR) swap, where the notional principal of the swap amortizes as interest rates decline through particular thresholds (i.e., strike levels).[2] This can

---

2 IARs can also be viewed as swaps with embedded digital options.

be viewed as a strip of partial cancellations of the swap tied to the downward movement of rates. In this instance the fixed-rate payer pays the fixed-rate receiver the higher rate (premium) for the right to cancel portions of the swap as rates fall. IARs have proven to be quite popular as hedges for securities/transactions with uncertain cash flows that depend on the movement of rates (e.g., MBS, leases).[3]

Callable and puttable swaps can also be used to synthesize callable/puttable bonds. For instance, an issuer may find it economic to convert a callable bond into a synthetic FRN using a callable swap. Indeed, the all-in funding cost can be lower on the synthetic FRN because the issuer can purchase the call embedded in the callable bond at cheap levels and sell it in the swap market at higher levels. We can consider a scenario where a firm issues a fixed-rate callable bond and enters into a callable swap where it receives fixed and pays LIBOR. If rates rise, no change in the structure occurs, meaning the issuer continues to fund on a floating-rate basis. If rates fall, however, the callable swap counterparty will terminate the swap transaction, the issuer will call the fixed rate bond, and will then reissue in the FRN market directly, again achieving a desired floating-rate funding. Puttable bonds can also be converted into synthetic FRNs using the puttable swap. Consider, for example, a company that issues a 10-year fixed rate bond that is puttable after five years and enters into an associated puttable swap where it pays LIBOR against fixed rates. If rates rise after year five, investors in the puttable bond will put the security back to the issuer, who will terminate the swap. It will then issue new floating-rate funding in the market directly, maintaining the same LIBOR-based funding profile. If rates fall, the bond and the swap remain outstanding for the full 10 years, meaning that the issuer achieves the goal of maintaining floating-rate financing.

The reverse scenario is also possible: noncallable debt, for instance, can be created synthetically by pairing a callable bond with a callable swap. This opportunity again arises when investors demand less for the call embedded in the callable bond than its true worth; the issuer, long the call, can issue the bond, and sell a callable swap granting the counterparty (which pays fixed) the right to terminate the underlying interest rate swap associated with the funding. If rates decline, the issuer calls the bond and funds at

---

3 In fact, IARs feature positive convexity, which makes them ideal for hedging negative convexity securities such as MBS.

a new lower floating rate; the callable swap counterparty, in turn, calls and terminates the swap. Throughout this transaction the issuer continues to pay floating rate (e.g., via the callable swap until call date, and via the FRN market when refunding occurs), as if the underlying callable bond was actually noncallable.

The extendible swap, like the callable or puttable swap, is a structured derivative package comprised of an interest rate swap and an option that grants one party the right to require its counterparty to continue a previously contracted swap under existing terms for an additional period of time. The payer extendible swap, for instance, is a combination of a fixed payer interest rate swap and a payer swaption. Assume that the purchaser enters into an underlying swap paying 5% and receiving LIBOR for two years and a swaption that gives the purchaser the right to preserve the 5% rate for a further three years. If rates rise above 5%, the purchaser can exercise the payer swaption so that the purchaser continues paying 5% for an additional three years, effectively extending the original two-year swap into a synthetic five-year contract. If rates decline, the option expires unexercised. This example is highlighted in Figure 5.2. The receiver extendible swap, in contrast, is comprised of a fixed receiver swap and a receiver swaption. In this case the buyer can extend the underlying swap and receive fixed rates for an additional period of time; the buyer will do so if rates fall below the strike level of the swaption. As in all other option-based structures, the party purchasing the option to extend pays a premium, either up-front or as an adjustment to the rates payable/receivable under the swap.

CALLABLE AND PUTTABLE ASSET SWAPS

We now extend our discussion by considering callable and puttable asset swap packages, and asset swap switches. A callable asset swap (also known as a remarketable asset swap) is similar to a standard asset swap package comprised of a bond and fixed/floating swap, or an FRN and a floating/fixed swap. However, in the callable asset swap the bank selling the package to the investor retains a call option on the underlying fixed- or floating-rate asset, allowing it to repurchase the asset at a given spread at some future time. The total package can thus be seen as a combination of a callable swap (itself a package of a swap and an option) and an underlying fixed- or floating-rate bond. The option

F I G U R E 5.2

Payer Extendible Swap

(a) Original Two-Year Interest Rate Swap

LIBOR

5% Fixed

+ (b) Three-Year Payer Swaption

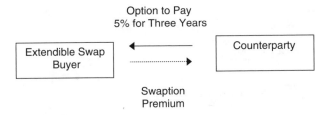

Option to Pay
5% for Three Years

Swaption
Premium

= (c) Synthetic Five-Year Swap

LIBOR

5% Fixed +
Premium

generally has a European or Bermudan exercise that is synchronized with the coupon dates of the asset, and the call spread (i.e.,
the strike level) is generally equal to the investor's initial purchase
level. If the spread on the asset tightens during the life of the transaction (e.g., the price of the asset rises as a result of specific or general market/credit conditions), the swap bank calls the package
away from the investor; the investor receives proceeds equal to the
strike spread plus invested principal from the swap bank. The
swap bank can then sell the underlying asset in the marketplace at
a profit, or enter into a new callable asset swap with a new investor
at the tighter market spread; this process helps realize mark-to-
market value on the deal. Naturally, if the spread widens, the swap

bank will not exercise the option and the investor will preserve the package until the contracted maturity date. The investor, in exchange for giving the swap bank the right to call the package away, receives an incremental yield representing the premium from selling the option. This synthetic structure gives both parties specific benefits: the swap bank preserves the ability to efficiently crystallize value by liquidating or reselling the structure if asset spreads tighten, while the investor earns an incremental yield for granting the option. The callable asset swap structure (based on a fixed-rate bond) is summarized in Figure 5.3 (a) and (b).

F I G U R E 5.3

Callable Asset Swap

(a) Initial and Ongoing Flows Assuming No Exercise

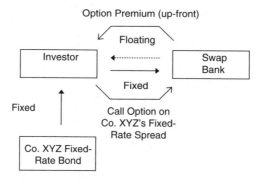

(b) Terminal Flows Assuming Swap Bank Exercises

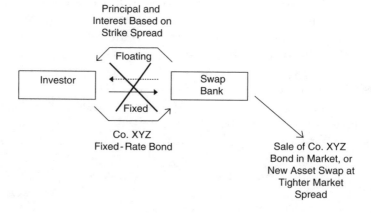

A puttable asset swap functions in a similar way, except that the investor, rather than the bank, enjoys the benefit of the option feature. Specifically, the investor acquires a package comprised of an asset (e.g., fixed-rate bond or FRN) and a puttable swap, where the put feature allows the investor to sell the entire asset/swap package back to the bank at a predetermined strike spread. As with the callable structure above, the put option generally has a European or Bermudan exercise that is synchronized with the coupon dates of the asset and the strike spread is typically set equal to the investor's purchase spread. If the spread widens during the life of the transaction (e.g., the price of the asset falls as a result of specific or general market/credit conditions), the investor puts the package to the bank, receiving principal and interest defined by the strike spread. The swap bank may then retain the asset in its portfolio, sell it in the marketplace, or attempt to arrange a new asset swap structure with another investor at the new (albeit wider) spread level. Depending on carrying value, the bank may or may not post a mark-to-market loss. If the spread tightens, the investor will not exercise the option and will thus continue to preserve its package until the contracted maturity date. The investor, in securing the right to put the package back to the bank, pays an option premium; this may be in the form of an up-front option payment or a lower yield on the asset swap coupon. As above, both parties obtain benefits through this synthetic structure: the swap bank receives incremental income from selling the put option (and either temporarily or permanently removes the underlying asset from its balance sheet), while the investor obtains de facto downside protection against spread widening on the underlying asset. Note that the puttable asset swap structure is also an essential element of callable bond investing, because investors must have comfort that they can terminate the swap component of a callable/puttable asset swap strategy if the underlying bond is called back by the issuer. Absent this feature, investors would be left with naked swap positions upon exercise of the bond call. The puttable asset swap structure (based on a fixed-rate bond) is summarized in Figure 5.4 (a) and (b).

Asset swap switches are another form of structured asset swap packaging. Asset swap switches, as the name implies, involve the exchange of two different asset swap packages. Under the most basic version an investor acquires an asset swap package from a bank or financial intermediary, and simultaneously agrees to deliver the package and accept another one in return if the

F I G U R E 5.4

Puttable Asset Swap

(a) Initial and Ongoing Flows Assuming No Exercise

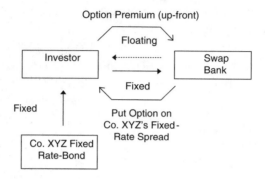

(b) Terminal Flows Assuming Investor Exercises

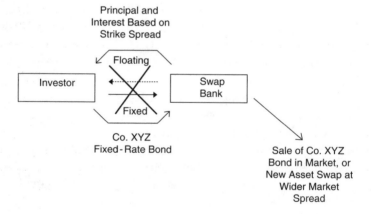

spread on the second package widens to a particular level; the two asset swap packages are generally uncorrelated. By agreeing to "swap" the two packages, the investor receives an enhanced yield on its investment; this is equivalent to receiving a premium for having sold the option to be exercised against. Assume, for example, that an investor owns an asset swap package on credit reference ABC at LIBOR + 30 bps and agrees with Bank D to exchange it for an asset swap package on XYZ, currently trading at

LIBOR + 50 bps—but only if XYZ's trading spread widens to +70 bps. Bank D essentially bought a put option that gives it the right to sell the XYZ package to the investor, while simultaneously calling back the ABC package. In order for this transaction to function from an economic perspective, the investor and the bank must have different views on the current and future creditworthiness of ABC and XYZ. For instance, the investor must believe that XYZ represents good value at +70 bps, but is too rich at +50 bps. The bank is clearly exposed to 20 bps of spread widening before it can trigger the swap, but is able to acquire default protection through the structure.

CHAPTER EXERCISES

1. Which of the following trades would represent the cheapest hedge for a borrower who thought interest rates were going to fall but needed protection if rates rose over the next two to five years?
   a. Pay fixed on a forward starting swap
   b. Buy a standard payer swaption
   c. Buy a five-year, no-call three-year Bermudan swaption with semiannual exercises
   d. Buy a three-year cap forward starting in two years
   e. All would be approximately equivalent
2. A borrower who has issued a callable bond with an exercise date in three years wants to monetize the value of that bond. Which of the following would be suitable?
   a. Sell a standard payer's swaption
   b. Sell a standard receiver's swaption
   c. Sell a Bermudan payer's swaption
   d. Sell a Bermudan receiver's swaption
   e. None of the above
3. A long payer swaption:
   a. Grants the buyer the right to receive fixed rates
   b. Obligates the buyer to receive fixed rates
   c. Grants the buyer the right to pay fixed rates
   d. Obligates the buyer to pay fixed rates
   e. None of the above

4. Which of the following is/are true?
   a. A payer swaption is equal to a put swaption
   b. A payer swaption is equal to a call swaption
   c. A receiver swaption is equal to a payer swaption
   d. a and b
   e. b and c

5. Which of the following is/are true?
   a. A receiver swaption with a high strike is more valuable than one with a low strike
   b. A payer swaption with a low strike is more valuable than one with a high strike
   c. A swaption with a longer time to maturity is more valuable than one with a shorter time to maturity
   d. All of the above
   e. None of the above

6. Assume the following market/product scenarios:

   Current LIBOR = 5.00%
   Payer swaption strike = 4.00%
   Receiver swaption strike = 3.00%

   Which of the following is/are true?
   a. The payer swaption will be exercised
   b. The payer swaption will not be exercised
   c. The receiver swaption will not be exercised
   d. a and c
   e. b and c

7. A six-year, no-call-year Bermudan swaption with annual exercise allows for how many exercise opportunities?
   a. 6
   b. 5
   c. 4
   d. 3
   e. 2

8. A seven-year callable swap that is callable in three years is equal to:
   a. A seven-year swap and a three-year receiver swaption on a four-year swap

    b. A seven-year swap and a three-year payer swaption on a four-year swap

    c. A seven-year swap and a four-year receiver swaption on a three-year swap

    d. A seven-year swap and a four-year payer swaption on a four-year swap

    e. None of the above

9. A payer extendible swap is equal to a package of:

    a. Floating payer swap and payer swaption

    b. Floating payer swap and receiver swaption

    c. Fixed payer swap and callable swap

    d. Fixed payer swap and receiver swaption

    e. Fixed payer swap and payer swaption

10. If a bank has sold an investor a callable asset swap package it will exercise against the investor when:

    a. Credit spreads have widened beyond the strike

    b. Interest rates have exceeded a fixed level

    c. Credit spreads have tightened inside the strike

    d. Interest rates have fallen below a fixed level

    e. None of the above

CHAPTER 6

Option Strategies

INTRODUCTION

In the last four chapters we have introduced basic and exotic options, and options that are embedded in other financial assets. Nearly all of the products that we have considered up to this point have either been single options, or created with single options. In this chapter we extend our discussion by considering how options can be combined in groups of two or more to create specific risk and investment management profiles. Such multiple option strategies have become very popular over the past few decades, and are a significant driver of activity in both the listed and OTC markets.

In this chapter we consider directional and volatility strategies. Directional strategies, which include bullish and bearish price strategies, provide exposure to, or protection against, the direction of a particular reference asset, such as stock or bond prices, or currency rates. Volatility strategies, which include combinations such as straddles, strangles, butterflies, condors, and calendar spreads, are based on the volatility of the asset's price, rather than its direction. In fact, we will see that most volatility strategies feature a directionally neutral position so that an institution can express a pure view on volatility.

DIRECTIONAL OPTION STRATEGIES

Directional option strategies are designed to take advantage of the direction of a reference asset, without direct regard for the volatility of the market (though an increase or decrease in volatility will ultimately influence the magnitude of a directional move; the buyer of an option is thus taking a long position in volatility, while the seller is taking a short position). We consider several directional strategies in this section, including outright single bullish/bearish option positions and bullish/bearish price spreads.

Single-Option Bullish/Bearish Positions

Though most of our discussion in this chapter is based on multiple options, we begin with a review of single-option positions. The most elemental directional option strategy an investor or speculator can create involves a single option. As noted in Chapter 2, the purchase or sale of a call or a put is a way of expressing a bullish or bearish position on a reference asset.

The purchase of a call is a popular bullish strategy used by institutions that believe the price of the reference asset will rise above some strike level. If the price rises above the strike, the option purchaser generates a profit. Naturally, if the price does not rise as expected, the purchaser loses premium. This means that the purchaser will take the position only if the market is expected to rise. This position exposes the purchaser to less downside risk (loss) than an outright position in the asset, as losses are limited to premium paid, rather than the full downside move of the reference price; this is, of course, characteristic of the unilateral payoff profile of options. The success of this type of bullish strategy depends on the purchaser's ability to select an asset that will rise in price, an expiration month that ensures the expected underlying price increase will occur before the option expires, and a strike price in which the potential benefits of the advance are balanced with the possibility of losing the entire premium paid.

A bullish strategy can also be created through the sale of a put. In this case the intent of the institution is not to capitalize on an upward or downward move above or below the strike, but to hope that the reference asset trades in a narrow range. If the option remains out-of-the-money (or does not move further in-the-money), the institution, as an option seller, preserves the premium received. The bullish expression of this strategy comes through selling puts in a market that is expected to rise: if the view proves correct and the asset price is in a bullish phase, it will rise and keep (or move) the option out-of-the-money.

T A B L E 6.1

Single-Option Bullish/Bearish Positions

Position	Directional View	Upside/Downside
Long call	Bullish	Price above strike/premium paid
Short put	Bullish	Premium received/price below strike
Long put	Bearish	Price below strike/premium paid
Short call	Bearish	Premium received/price above strike

Bearish strategies can be created by selecting the opposite positions. The classic single-option bear strategy is, of course, the purchase of a put. The institution in this instance expects the reference asset price to decline, and will generate a profit (over and above premium paid) as the bearish move plays out and the option moves in-the-money. Of course, if the market rallies and forces the asset price up, the institution will lose the premium it paid for the contract. The sale of a call option in a market that is expected to decline represents another bearish strategy. The logic of this position follows along the lines we have discussed for the short put/bullish position above: if the market remains relatively range bound, the call will remain out-of-the-money and the seller will preserve premium received.

Table 6.1 summarizes these single-option bullish/bearish positions.

Single options are often paired with underlying asset positions to generate additional income or to obtain a degree of price protection. These positions include covered calls and protective puts.

An institution writes a covered call by simultaneously selling a call option and buying the underlying asset, or by selling a call option against an underlying asset position that it already owns. By selling the call option, the institution receives premium income, and is contractually obliged to sell the reference asset to the call buyer if the option is exercised. Institutions that believe the price of the underlying asset will remain neutral to very moderately bullish (but below the strike offered) and who seek additional income write covered calls.

An institution obtains a protective put by simultaneously purchasing a put option and buying the underlying asset, or by purchasing a put against a position that it already owns. The intent is to obtain some degree of downside price protection against an asset that it wants to hold. The cost of doing so is, of course, the premium that it pays the put seller. Institutions that believe the price of the underlying asset will decline (perhaps significantly) but that do not want to sell the underlying asset purchase protective puts.

Multiple-Option Bullish/Bearish Positions

We now broaden our discussion to consider multiple-option positions that are created to express a directional view. The most popular of these positions is the price spread, sometimes known as a vertical spread or money spread. The strategy can be created in four different forms: bullish call spread, bearish call spread, bullish put spread, and bearish put spread. We consider each in turn.

In the bullish call spread an investor buys a call option with a lower (i.e., closer-to-the-money) strike and sells a higher strike call option; the purchase of the closer-to-the-money option results in a net outflow of premium, but locks in a profit equal to the difference between the two strikes. The bullish put spread is created when an investor sells the high strike put and buys the low strike put; in this case the sale of the closer-to-the-money put creates a premium inflow, and locks in a liability equal to the difference between the strikes as the market sells off.

Bearish spreads are created in the opposite manner. In a bearish call spread the investor sells the low strike call and buys the higher strike call, generating a premium inflow and locking in a known liability as the market rallies. In a bearish put spread the investor purchases the high strike put and sells the low strike put, paying a net premium but locking in a gain equal to the strike differential as the market trades down. Table 6.2 summarizes these positions.

T A B L E 6.2

Bullish and Bearish Call/Put Spreads

	Bullish	Bearish
Call spread	Buy low strike	Sell low strike
	Sell high strike	Buy high strike
Put spread	Sell high strike	Buy high strike
	Buy low strike	Sell low strike

F I G U R E 6.1

Bullish Call Spread Payoff

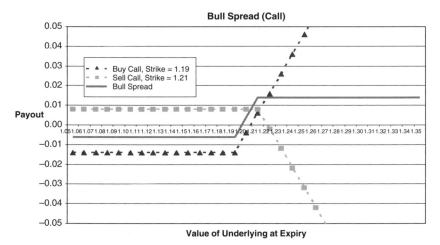

Let us consider examples of bullish and bearish price spreads using the foreign exchange market as the reference asset class. Assume a bank is bullish on spot €/$ and believes that it will rise from a current level of 1.19 over the next 30 days (though not above the 1.22 level). To monetize this view the bank structures a bullish call spread by purchasing an at-the-money call struck at 1.1900, paying a premium of 140 FX points (e.g., 0.014 €/$), and simultaneously selling an out-of-the-money call at 1.2100, receiving a premium of 60 FX points. The net cost of expressing this view through the bullish call spread is 80 FX points. Figure 6.1 illustrates the payoff profile of the bullish call spread position.

We can examine various market scenarios to understand the potential upside/downside the bank faces. The call spread has a maximum profit of 120 FX points. This is calculated using 1.2100 as the best rate at which the buyer will sell €, less the current spot rate of 1.1900, less the 80 points of premium. The trader will make money provided the €/$ rate goes above 1.1980, which is the current rate plus the net premium paid. The maximum payout of 120 points is achieved at a rate of 1.2100.

We can also consider the bearish put spread illustrated in Figure 6.2. The position is created when the bank buys an at-the-money put at 1.1900, paying a premium of 140 FX points, and sells

F I G U R E 6.2

Bearish Put Spread Payoff

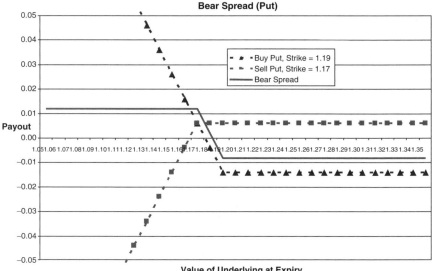

an out-of the-money put at 1.1700, earning a premium of 60 FX points. The bank in this case makes a profit if the rate goes below 1.1820; the profit is capped at 1.1700 when the short put moves in-the-money. In this instance the bank can only lose a maximum of 80 FX points, which is the net premium paid.

We note the opposing views at work in both examples. In the case of the bullish call spread (i.e., the bank buying the closer-to-the-money strike call and selling the farther out-of-the-money call) the institution on the opposite side of the transaction expects a bearish €/$ scenario. That is, it expects €/$ to weaken (or remain stable) so that it can preserve the 80 points of net premium it earned. Likewise, the institution on the opposite of the bearish put spread expects a bullish €/$ market: it believes €/$ will strengthen (or remain stable) so it can, again, preserve as much of the net premium received as possible.

Table 6.3 summarizes these key directional multiple-option strategies.

T A B L E 6.3

Multiple-Option Bullish/Bearish Positions

Position	Directional View	Upside/Downside
Long call spread	Bullish	Price above strike/premium paid
Short put spread	Bullish	Premium received/price below strike
Long put spread	Bearish	Price below strike/premium paid
Short call spread	Bearish	Premium received/price above strike

VOLATILITY OPTION STRATEGIES

Volatility options strategies are created to take advantage of the volatility (or price variability) of a market or asset, without specific regard to the direction of the market. As noted earlier, most volatility strategies are created with neutral market direction exposure. Though many volatility strategies can be created by combining two or more options, we focus our discussion on several of the most popular, including straddles, strangles, butterflies, condors, and calendar spreads.

Straddle

The straddle is a common multioption position, taken in order to profit from, or protect against, volatility. The basic long straddle is created through the purchase of a call and a put on an underlying reference at the same strike price and with the same maturity. In exchange, the buyer pays the seller a premium. By creating a straddle the buyer seeks to take advantage of market volatility; the buyer is relatively indifferent (or uncertain) as to the direction of the market, but simply attempts to capitalize on a large market movement expressed through rising volatility. Thus, if the market moves up sharply (i.e., volatile on the upside), the call leg of the straddle increases in value. The reverse is true in the case of a sharp downward movement in the market (i.e., volatile on the downside).

The seller, in contrast, sells a straddle in expectation of a relatively quiet market. If the reference trades in a narrow range, neither leg of the straddle will appreciate in value, meaning that premium received from selling the package of options will be preserved. In fact, premium decay will accelerate as time to maturity draws closer,

F I G U R E 6.3

Payoff Profile of Long Straddle Position

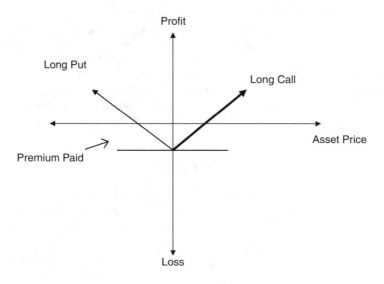

particularly if the market remains range bound. Figures 6.3 and 6.4 highlight the payoff profiles of long and short straddles by illustrating the individual options comprising the strategy.

Let us return to our foreign exchange example to consider the mechanics of the long straddle. Assume a bank believes market movements in €/$ will be significant (i.e., the market will be volatile), but it is uncertain as to direction. It therefore purchases a straddle, giving it a long position in volatility. Specifically, it buys a call and a put on €/$ struck at 1.1900 (at-the-money), each with a premium of 200 FX points (400 FX points total). The solid line in Figure 6.5 depicts the payoff profile, while the broken lines reveal the payoff profiles of the call and put legs. If €/$ stays at 1.1900, suggesting a low-volatility market, the bank loses the entire premium of 400 points. However, if the rate moves up or down by a significant degree, the initial loss declines and becomes a profit once €/$ goes below 1.1500 or above 1.2300. Naturally, the premium the bank pays for the straddle depends on the level of volatility and the time to expiry: the lower the volatility and the shorter the time to maturity, the smaller the premium paid. However, this also means that the straddle stands less of a chance of moving in-the-money.

FIGURE 6.4

Payoff Profile of Short Straddle Position

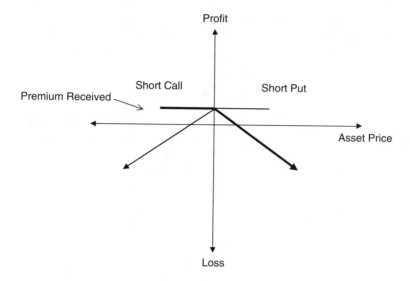

FIGURE 6.5

Long FX Straddle Position

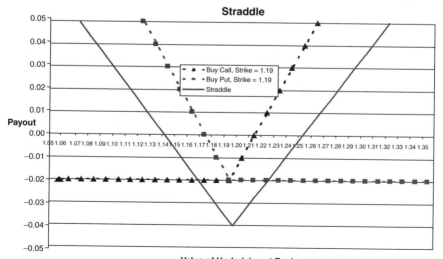

The seller of the straddle is, of course, taking the opposite view. The seller expects that €/$ volatility will be stable or decline, allowing spot to trade in a relatively narrow range (e.g., 1.1500 – 1.2300). The seller earns maximum returns if the rate stays at the current level of 1.1900. Of course, the seller faces a potentially large liability if volatility spikes and forces one leg of the position in-the-money.

Strangle

The strangle is a variant of the straddle. The buyer of the strangle, like the buyer of the straddle, seeks to take advantage of increased volatility by using a put and a call with the same expiry date. Unlike the straddle, however, the strangle's put and call strikes are different, suggesting that a greater amount of volatility is required before a position moves in-the-money (or further in-the-money). This means that the strangle buyer pays less premium for the position than it would for a straddle, and that the seller can withstand a greater amount of market movement before a potential liability begins to accrue. The basic long strangle thus consists of the purchase of a call and a put on an underlying reference at different strike prices but with the same maturity, as illustrated in Figure 6.6; the seller's position is reflected in Figure 6.7.

F I G U R E 6.6

Payoff Profile of Long Strangle Position

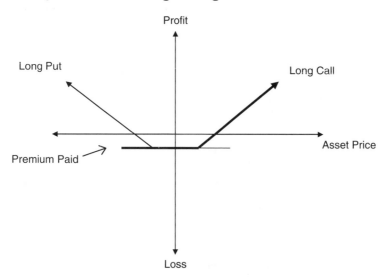

F I G U R E 6.7

Payoff Profile of Short Strangle Position

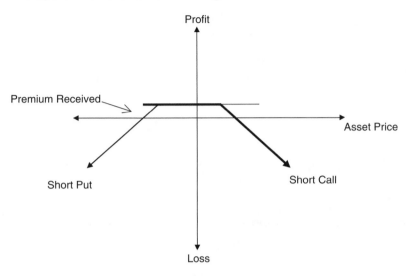

Let us consider a strangle in the context of our continuing €/$ transaction. In the straddle the bank selected put and call strikes of 1.1900, while in the strangle sets them at 1.1700 and 1.2100. The premium for the two options amounts to 280 FX points (versus 400 points on the straddle), resulting in breakeven rates of 1.1420 and 1.2380. Figure 6.8, which illustrates the strangle from the buyer's perspective, suggests that a greater amount of market movement will be required for spot €/$ to move above or below the strikes; the bank is clearly hoping for a great deal of volatility. The seller, in contrast, expects a tranquil market that causes the spot rate to remain within the 1.1700–1.2100 range; the closer the rate stays to 1.1900, the more premium the seller preserves. Again, the seller faces a potentially large liability if volatility spikes and forces one leg of the strangle in-the-money.

Butterflies and Condors

The butterfly is the third major volatility-based multi-option strategy, and is created with unique combinations of long and short call/put options. A long butterfly is a package consisting of long low-strike option, a long high-strike option, and two short

F I G U R E   6.8

Long FX Strangle Position

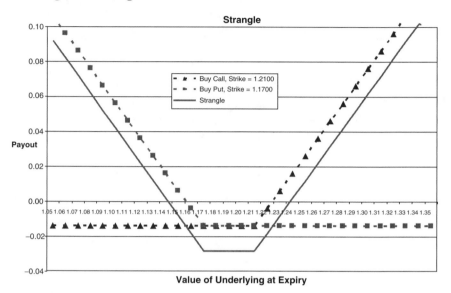

Value of Underlying at Expiry

midstrike options. This package can also be viewed as a short straddle combined with a long strangle (e.g., a short straddle without the extreme downside risk).

The short butterfly, in contrast, is a package consisting of a short low-strike option, a short high-strike option, and two long midstrike options; this again is equivalent to a long straddle and a short strangle. Figure 6.9 illustrates the payoff profile of the long butterfly; the payoff profile of a short butterfly, shown in Figure 6.10, is simply the "mirror image."

Let us consider the "protective" nature of the long buttery versus the short straddle by decomposing the constituent parts. The buyer of the butterfly

- Sells at-the-money call and put options with the same strikes and expiries; this is precisely equal to a short straddle (as in Figure 6.4)
- Buys out-of-the-money put and call options with the same expiry but different strikes; this is equivalent to a long strangle (as in Figure 6.6)

FIGURE 6.9

Payoff Profile of Long Butterfly Position

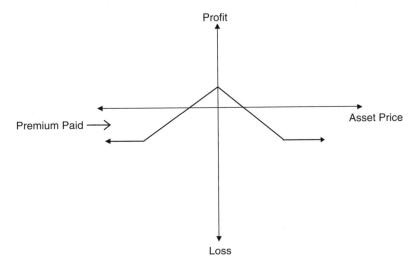

FIGURE 6.10

Payoff Profile of Short Butterfly Position

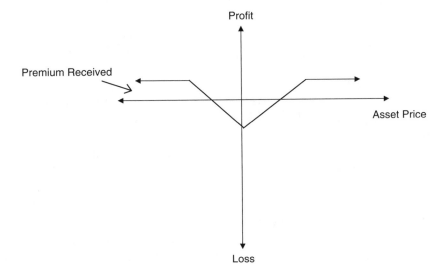

The purchase of the strangle creates the wings of the butterfly, meaning downside potential is limited. In fact, the purchaser of a butterfly expects a relatively tranquil market that trades near the money; this provides maximum gain. The butterfly seller, in contrast, hopes for greater volatility that forces one of the two out-of-the-money options in-the-money; that said, once one of the wing options moves in-the-money, the gain is capped by offsetting options in the package.

Let us consider an example of a short butterfly strategy from the interest rate market. Assume that a hedge fund expects interest rate volatility will increase and wants to monetize this view. It can buy a swaption straddle by purchasing a receiver swaption and a payer swaption (both with at-the-money strikes of 4.00%). In order to reduce the premium payable, however, it can also sell a swaption strangle, i.e., selling out-of-the-money receiver and payer swaptions. The resulting strategy creates the short butterfly payoff profile noted in Figure 6.11. The options and premiums comprising this butterfly include:

- Long receiver swaption with an at-the-money strike of 4.00% and premium payment of 20 bps
- Long payer swaption with an at-the-money strike of 4.00% and premium payment of 20 bps
- Short out-of-the-money receiver swaption with strike of 3.20% and premium receipt of 8 bps
- Short out-of-the-money payer swaption with strike of 4.80% and premium receipts of 8 basis points

The net premium outlay for the buyer of the butterfly strategy is 24 bps (i.e., (2 * 20 bps) − (2 * 8 bps)). This creates the peak of the "V" on the payoff profile. The combination of the four trades creates a worst-case scenario loss for the buyer of 24 bps (versus 40 bps for a long straddle). However, the buyer no longer has unlimited profit potential following a rise in volatility and a commensurate change in rates up or down. The maximum the buyer can make is 56 bps (i.e., the difference between 4.00% and 3.20% or 4.00% and 4.80%, less 24 bps).

The butterfly is attractive to the buyer because it reduces the overall premium outlay and possible maximum loss. In fact, the strategy may be attractive to the option buyer who believes volatility will rise within a limited range. If this view is correct, profits can

F I G U R E 6.11

Short Swaption Butterfly

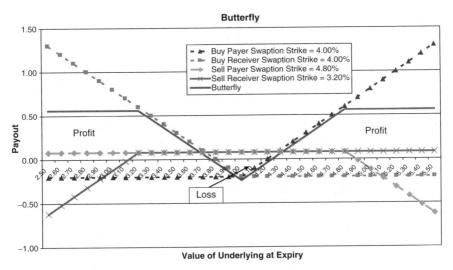

Butterfly

Legend:
- Buy Payer Swaption Strike = 4.00%
- Buy Receiver Swaption Strike = 4.00%
- Sell Payer Swaption Strike = 4.80%
- Sell Receiver Swaption Strike = 3.20%
- Butterfly

Payout axis (vertical): 1.50, 1.00, 0.50, 0.00, −0.50, −1.00

Profit   Profit

Loss

Value of Underlying at Expiry

be generated and premium payment can be minimized. The seller of the butterfly faces an inverted risk profile that also reflects a lower degree of risk: the seller is no longer exposed to unlimited losses, as in a short straddle.

The condor is an extension of the butterfly, with the middle strikes set further apart—meaning greater volatility is required to move the position in-the-money (or further in-the-money). The long condor is a package of long low- and high-strike options, a short midstrike low option, and a short midstrike high option. The short condor, by extension, is a package of short-low and high-strike options, a long midstrike low option, and a long midstrike high option. The payoff profile of a long condor is illustrated in Figure 6.12; the payoff profile of a short condor shown in Figure 6.13.

Calendar Spread

The calendar (or time) spread is a multioption strategy that seeks to take advantage of market volatility as related to time. Since options on the same underlying reference with identical strikes but different maturities trade at different levels, the use of long/short calendar

F I G U R E 6.12

Payoff Profile of Long Condor Position

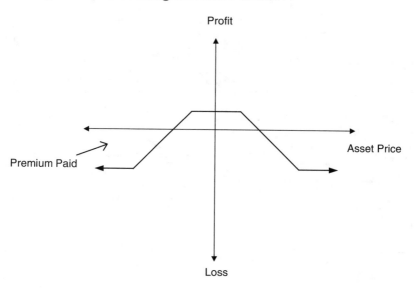

F I G U R E 6.13

Payoff Profile of Short Condor Position

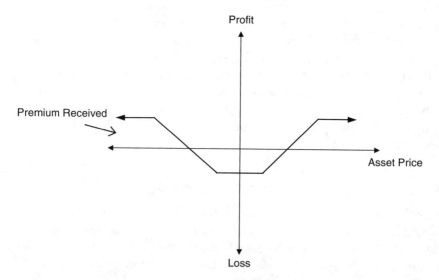

spreads allows an institution to capitalize on the differences. A short calendar spread, for instance, is created by buying a short maturity option and selling a longer maturity option, both with the same strike. The time value of the shorter maturity option decays more quickly than that of the longer maturity option; the seller thus hopes for a calm market in order to capture and preserve the net premium inflow. A long calendar spread is created in the opposite manner, and requires a volatile market in order to generate value for the buyer.

A calendar spread can be created as follows:

- Long calendar spread: buy long-dated option, sell short-dated option
- Short calendar spread: sell long-dated option, buy short-dated option

In both cases, the longer-term options have more time value since they have a greater time to expiry. This difference can be reduced, however, by the term structure of volatility. As we have noted, short-term options often feature higher volatility than longer-term options. The value of the trades can be adjusted so that the premium paid on the bought option equals the premium received on the sold option.

A time spread is different from other directional spreads because the value of the spread depends on movement in the underlying asset price as well as expectation of future asset prices reflected in the implied volatility of the individual components of the spread. Value is ultimately crystallized via time decay. Figure 6.14 shows the theta decay profile of two swaptions: a 6-month × 1-year swaption originally priced at 65 bps and a 1-×-1-year swaption originally priced at 40 bps. Both swaptions show the time decay characteristic of options. The top curved line shows the value of the longer-dated swaption at the expiration of the shorter-dated swaption. All other things being equal, and assuming that there is no change in the volatilities of the two swaptions, we would expect the 1-×-1-year swaption to have the same price in six months as the 6-month-×-1-year swap has now (e.g., 40 bps).

To capitalize on a specific volatility/time view, an institution can buy the long-dated payer swaption and sell the short-dated payer swaption, as noted in Table 6.4.

Establishing this trade costs 25 bps. In six months, the short-term swaption originally bought expires and the long-term option will then be reduced to the same tenor. Provided interest rates have

F I G U R E 6.14

Theta Comparisons

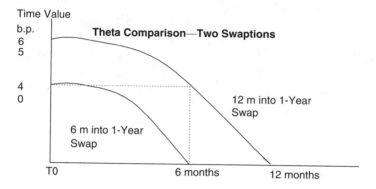

not changed, there has been no change in the shape of the yield curve or rate volatility, the premium for the 6-month-×-1-year swaption, at-the-money, will be 40 bps. However, the new 6-month-×-1-year swaption does not have an at-the-money strike of 4.11%; it has an out-of-the-money, original 1-×-1-year at-the-money strike of 4.34%. This means that the premium received if the option is sold today is approximately 30 bps, rather than the 40 bps for the at-the-money swaption. This results in a small profit, but may not be an acceptable return given the rate and volatility risks embedded in the trade. In fact, this type of calendar spread is more likely to be established around expected changes in the term structure of relative volatility. If the institution believes that longer-term volatility will increase relative to shorter-term volatility, it can buy the spread. Assume that in three months short-term swaption volatility has remained at 17.80%, but longer-term swaption volatility has increased to 25%. Under this

T A B L E 6.4

Swaption Time Spread

Period	Type	ATM Strike	Direction	Volatility	Premium	Nominal Principal
6 m into 1 Year	Payer	4.11%	Sell	17.80%	40	1,000,000
12 m into 1 Year	Payer	4.34%	Buy	20.10%	−65	1,000,000
Net Carry					−25	

TABLE 6.5

Summary of Multiple-Option Volatility Strategies

Position	Volatility View
Long straddle	Increasing
Short straddle	Decreasing
Long strangle	Increasing
Short strangle	Decreasing
Long butterfly	Decreasing
Short butterfly	Increasing
Long condor	Decreasing
Short condor	Increasing
Long calendar spread	Decreasing
Short calendar spread	Increasing

scenario theta for the shorter-term option is developing as expected and the premium value, at the same volatility figure of 17.80%, has declined to 25 bps. The longer-term option, with the new higher-volatility value of 25%, generates a premium of 60 bps, a decline of only five basis points. If the institution squares this position it earns 35 bps (60 bps – 25 bps); subtracting the original 25 bps points of cost for the strategy produces a net profit of 10 bps.

Table 6.5 summarizes the key multiple-option/volatility strategies noted above.

CHAPTER EXERCISES

1. Which of the following is/are true?
    a. Selling a put is a bullish strategy
    b. Buying a call is a bullish strategy
    c. Selling a call is a bearish strategy
    d. Buying a put is bearish strategy
    e. All of the above are true
2. What is the maximum net profit for an €/$ FX bull spread with a long at-the-money call of 1.20, a short call of 1.25 and a net premium of .005?
    a. .045
    b. .05

    c. .055

    d. .035

    e. None of the above

3. Which of the following is not a volatility strategy?

    a. Straddle

    b. Strangle

    c. Calendar spread

    d. Call spread

    e. Condor

4. Which of the following can be used to create a long Nikkei straddle?

    a. Buy 16,000 call, sell 18,000 put

    b. Sell 16,000 call, buy 18,000 put

    c. Buy 16,000 call, sell 16,000 put

    d. Sell 18,000 call, buy 16,000 put

    e. Buy 18,000 call, sell 16,000 put

5. A long butterfly is comprised of:

    a. A short call spread and a long strangle

    b. A long call spread and a short strangle

    c. A long straddle and a long strangle

    d. A long straddle and a short strangle

    e. A short straddle and a long strangle

6. The short butterfly is:

    a. Cheaper than a long straddle

    b. Provides less upside than a long straddle

    c. Is more expansive than a long straddle

    d. a and b

    e. b and c

7. Which strategy would be taken to capitalize on increasing volatility?

    a. Long call spread

    b. Short straddle

    c. Long strangle

    d. Short put spread

    e. Short strangle

Corporate and Investor Applications

INTRODUCTION

In the last chapter we discussed common directional and volatility strategies. We extend our analysis in this chapter by examining in greater detail key corporate and investor applications. For purposes of our discussion we categorize these into three classes: speculating, hedging, and arbitraging/monetizing. While we have already discussed some of these motivations in general terms (e.g., using options to take a speculative view or create additional premium income), our intent in this chapter is to examine the process in more detail through worked examples.

Before commencing let us define the nature and scope of key applications:

- Speculating: the process of creating an option strategy in order to take advantage of an expected movement in the direction or volatility of an asset.
- Hedging: the process of creating an option strategy to protect against a possible movement in the direction or volatility of an asset.
- Arbitraging/monetizing: the process of creating an option strategy to increase or realize profits with a limited downside range; the monetization of profits can be used as a liability management tool to lower funding costs.

SPECULATIVE APPLICATIONS

Intermediaries and end users regularly use options to express a specific speculative view on a market's direction and/or volatility. We have noted in the last chapter some of the basic outright positions that an institution can arrange to crystallize a speculative view. We review them in brief in this section.

Buying Naked Call Options

An institution purchasing a call option is expecting the price of the underlying reference asset to rise. By extension, it is expecting volatility to increase, because greater volatility can help move the call in-the-money. If the price of the underlying reference asset rises above the strike, the call option increases in value and can be sold in the secondary market or exercised. In theory there is no limit to the buyer's potential profit since there is no limit as to how high the price of the reference asset can rise. In practice, of course, there is a limit: one related to both time and asset volatility. We illustrate this basic speculative application in the context of a £ call/$ put option in Figure 7.1, where the speculator purchases a $1.50 strike £ call/$ put for a premium of $0.02.

The distance below the line from point E to A represents the premium cost of buying the option. The dotted line through points D and B represents the strike price of the option. Line DC shows the market price movement needed for the buyer to recover the premium

FIGURE 7.1

Long Naked £ Call/$ Put Option

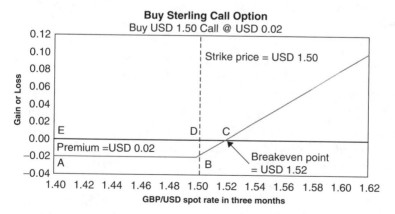

cost of the option—this is known as the breakeven point. Therefore, no profit will be realized on the option until the market price of the underlying moves to the right of point C (e.g., above 1.52). If the £/$ market price rises above the strike price, but less than distance DC, the buyer of the option will still exercise the contract; the result, however, will be a net loss since the cost of the premium is still greater than the gain on the option. Line BC measures the recovery of the option premium as the market price of the underlying increases.

Selling Naked Call Options

An institution selling a naked call option expects that the price of the underlying reference asset will remain unchanged or decline. This also implies that volatility is expected to remain relatively stable. If this view holds true, the time value of the call option will decrease (at an accelerating rate); this allows the option seller to retain some, or all, of the premium received at the time of sale. The maximum possible gain for the naked option seller is equal to the option premium. The maximum possible loss for a naked call seller is theoretically unlimited. As above, there is no limit on the upward price of an asset. In practice, of course, the same time and volatility constraints exist, so that the maximum possible loss may be significant but not unlimited.

We can return to the same £ call/$ put option example and illustrate the payoff profile, as in Figure 7.2, from the perspective of the naked option seller.

F I G U R E   7.2

Short Naked £ Call/$ Put Option

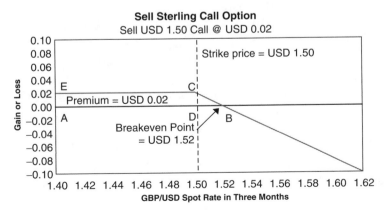

Sell Sterling Call Option
Sell USD 1.50 Call @ USD 0.02

Distance EA measures the seller's premium income. Line DC measures the erosion of that income as the market price of the underlying rises above the strike price of the option. A £/$ price movement from B to C will eliminate the premium income, and any movement to the right of point C will cause the option seller to sustain a loss. As we have noted, this loss is theoretically unlimited. Conversely, any £/$ price below $1.50 will result in the buyer's abandoning the contract, allowing the seller to preserve the premium as profit. As distance EA shows, the maximum profit for the writer of a naked call option will always be equal to the premium received.

Buying Naked Put Options

An institution purchasing a put option for speculative reasons expects that the price of the reference asset will decline below the strike price; this implies, once again, a long volatility position, because a rise in volatility will help push the option in-the-money. If the price of the asset falls, the put option will increase in value, resulting in a profit when the option is sold or exercised. Under this speculative scenario the maximum possible loss for the buyer is equal to the premium paid. The maximum possible profit is limited to the point where the asset price reaches zero, since the price of an asset cannot be negative. Again, for practical purposes the maximum profit will be closely related to both the volatility of the reference asset and the maturity of the put contract.

Let us again return to our £/$ example, this time examining the position from the perspective of the put buyer (e.g., long £ put/$ call). Assume, once again, the put strike is $1.50 and the premium paid for a three-month contract is $0.02. Figure 7.3 illustrates the payoff profile of the naked put position.

The buyer expects that the market price of £/$ will fall below the strike price of $1.50. Line AF measures the cost of the option premium, while the dotted line through points B and C represents the strike price. Exercise or sale will occur if the market price of the underlying falls below the strike price (any point to the left of C). Line CD measures the amount of downward price movement necessary for the buyer to recover the cost of the premium; line DE measures the gain the buyer would receive if £/$ fell to $1.40. If the market price of the currency moves higher than the strike price of the option (all points to the right of C), the put option will be abandoned.

F I G U R E 7.3

Long Naked £ Put/$ Call Option

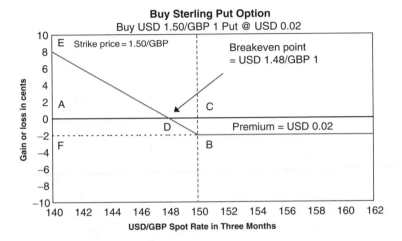

Selling Naked Put Options

An institution selling a naked put option expects that the price of the underlying asset will remain unchanged or increase modestly. This suggests that volatility is expected to be relatively stable. As with other sold option positions, the maximum gain possible for the writer is equal to the premium received. The potential loss is limited to the point where the price of the asset reaches zero; in practice the real loss is likely to be less than this amount, because the contract will be defined by specific time and volatility parameters that bound the price range. Figure 7.4 features the £ put/$ call example from the seller's perspective.

Line AF represents the premium income the seller receives. This income will be preserved if the market price of £/$ remains at, or above, the $1.50 strike price (i.e., all points to the right of C). Line BD represents the decline of premium as the market price of £/$ falls below the strike price. Line CD represents the amount by which the market price of the underlying must fall to offset exactly the premium income. Line DE measures the loss beyond the premium.

The examples above remind us of the basic directional strategies that a speculator can employ. We recall from the last chapter that speculative positions can be developed to express a view on volatility. Thus, the speculator expecting volatility to rise can buy a straddle or strangle, or sell a butterfly or condor. The speculator that

F I G U R E   7.4

Short Naked £ Put/$ Call Option

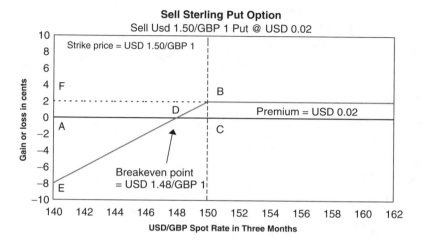

expects volatility to remain stable or decline can sell a straddle or strangle, or buy a butterfly or condor. Again, each one of these strategies allows the buyer or seller to express a specific speculative view.

Buying and Selling Exotic Options

Speculative positions can be created with many of the exotic options we described in Chapter 3. Some contracts, such as power options, are designed expressly to give the buyer a leveraged view on a particular asset or its volatility. For instance, if an institution believes LIBOR is set to rise over the coming months, it can buy a vanilla option that generates a profit as LIBOR rises. Alternatively, it can leverage that view by buying a power option that provides a leveraged payout of two times or three times the movement in LIBOR; it can even create an exponential payout of LIBOR squared or cubed, as noted in Figure 7.5. While the premium paid for any leveraged option is clearly much higher than it is on a conventional option, the potential payoff to the buyer is much higher—if the speculative market view proves correct.

Barrier options, the most common of the exotic class, are routinely used to create speculative positions. Down-and-in calls for instance, allow the speculator to construct an inexpensive option position in order to purchase an asset at a price thought to be undervalued. The smaller premium paid for securing the position can help boost overall returns if the strategy proves correct. Similarly, a

F I G U R E 7.5

Leveraged LIBOR Option Payouts

Profit/Loss

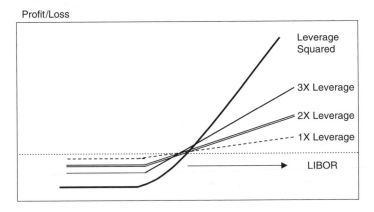

Leverage
Squared

3X Leverage

2X Leverage

1X Leverage

LIBOR

down-and-out call allows the purchaser to reduce option premium by extinguishing the contract at a time when it is perceived to have no value. The major drawback of barrier options is that a precise market view is required in order to specify the terms of the option. Forecasting the direction of market prices is difficult; adding in elements related to timing and magnitude of market moves complicates the picture significantly. A speculative user of barrier options must therefore have a clearly defined view.

Consider an example of a speculator who seeks to buy copper on weakness, hoping to profit from market fears that a holder of copper inventory may soon begin to liquidate its own positions. Assume further that volatility has risen to an all-time high, making outright naked options positions extremely expensive. The speculator is willing to take a long position, but only if the price of copper falls from the current level of $1,800/ton to $1,600/ton. To create this speculative view the speculator can consider two barrier positions:

- Purchase a down-and-in call: Under this strategy the option does not come into existence unless the price of copper falls to a certain level. Hence, it is ideal for the speculator wishing to buy a commodity if it is selling at a low price. In this case, the barrier can be set at the speculator's trigger price of $1,600/ton and the strike can be fixed at some level above $1,600 (e.g., $1,700). If the barrier is hit on the downside (perhaps as the large copper player liquidates copper stocks), the speculator holds an out-of-the-money call and will begin to profit when (if) copper prices begin to rally.

■ Purchase a reverse down-and-in call. As above, the copper call option does not come into existence unless the price of the underlying falls through the barrier. In this case, however, the speculator can buy at a strike price below the prevailing market price, creating immediate intrinsic value. For instance, the barrier can be set at $1,600/ton and the strike can be set at some level below that point (e.g., $1,500). Naturally, this speculative application will be more expensive than the first one as a result of the intrinsic value embedded in the contract. Nevertheless, it is still cheaper than the purchase of an outright call.

HEDGING APPLICATIONS

Intermediaries and end-users routinely use derivatives to hedge particular risk exposures. Though hedging can take different forms and be arranged to different degrees, the overall process includes any transaction that mitigates exposure to financial or market variables.

A company can protect itself against adverse price or rate changes by buying or selling a contract that establishes a price or rate today for some asset to be bought or sold in the future. When the contract totally or partly offsets some underlying exposure that is driven by the same price or rate, the company creates a hedge. It is important to stress that hedge instruments do not replace the underlying exposure generating the risk; they are layered on top of the exposure to neutralize some (or all) of its potentially damaging effects. In other words, hedge products are additional sets of cash flows that offset the adverse cash flows of the underlying position, generating gains as the underlying position incurs losses, and vice versa.

Let us assume that a company has a foreign currency (FC) exposure in the form of a payable. If the value of the foreign currency rises, the company's liability rises, and if the value of FC declines, the value of the liability falls. This relationship, which will serve us as we create a continuing example, is illustrated in Figure 7.6.

Symmetrical Hedging Products

In order to properly introduce the use of options as a hedging tool we first describe hedging that can be obtained through symmetrical, or bilateral, hedging products. This provides a useful point of comparison and contrast. We know from Figure 7.6 that rising

FIGURE 7.6

Foreign Currency Exposure

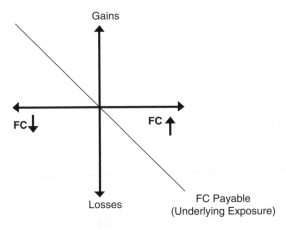

FC values lead to declining net income for the company (e.g., the lower right quadrant of the graph). To hedge this exposure, the company will seek a product that produces gains to offset the losses. Achieving this objective requires superimposing a product that will create gains as the FC rises; this combined position is illustrated in Figure 7.7.

By layering the hedge product onto the original exposure, the profits from the hedge offset the losses on the underlying exposure,

FIGURE 7.7

Foreign Currency Exposure with Symmetrical Hedge

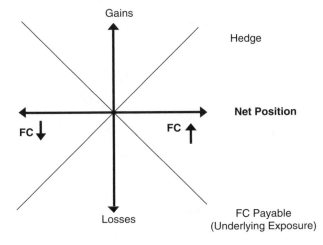

causing the two positions to net at the x axis. By adding the hedge to the original underlying exposure, the company effectively "locks in" the cost of its future FC payable. In this example, losses on the underlying exposure are offset by gains on the hedge just as gains on the underlying are offset by losses on the hedge. A hedge product that produces such a result is considered symmetrical. Examples of symmetrical products for currencies include forward foreign exchange contracts and currency swaps; similar symmetrical products can be obtained in other asset classes (e.g., interest rates, commodities, equities). Importantly, these products do not require an initial cash outflow, as in the case of options. They do, however, eliminate any possibility of profits from an opposing market scenario; in addition, they always give rise to potential credit risk exposure.

Asymmetrical Hedging Products

Based on our discussion of options and examination of option payoff profiles, we know that options comprise the general class of asymmetrical, or unilateral, hedging products. For example, a long call option, when combined with the FC payable, generates a payoff profile such as the one illustrated in Figure 7.8.

In this instance the hedge produces gains that offset the losses on the FC exposure. The resulting exposure protects the firm from adverse movements in currency rates, but allows for gains in the

F I G U R E 7.8

Foreign Currency Exposure with Asymmetrical Hedge

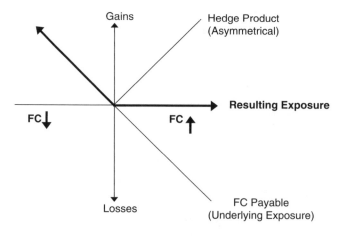

T A B L E 7.1

Forward and Option Hedging Strategies

Underlying	Risk	Forward Contract	Basic Option Hedge
FC payable	FC up	Buy FC forward	Buy option to buy FC
	DC down	Sell DC forward	(Buy FC call or DC put)
FC receivable	FC down	Sell FC forward	Buy option to sell FC
	DC up	Buy DC forward	(Buy FC put or DC call)

underlying should rates move in a favorable direction. This additional flexibility comes at a price, of course: payment of up-front premium, a cash expense that is not incurred with symmetrical hedging products.

We now consider a consolidated example of hedging foreign currency payables and receivables using both the symmetrical (e.g., forward) and asymmetrical (e.g., option) products. To hedge a foreign currency payable, a company purchases a foreign currency forward, as in Figure 7.5 above. To hedge a receivable, it sells the foreign currency forward. No matter which way foreign exchange rates move, the net of the hedge position and the underlying position is constant for either the payable or receivable positions. Foreign currency options can mitigate the opportunity cost associated with forward transactions, providing downside hedge protection but not affecting the upside—though only for an up-front premium payment. The advantage of the option is the favorable asymmetry in the option return. Like forwards, foreign currency options generate gains when the underlying position has losses, but they do not generate losses when the underlying position generates gains.

Table 7.1 illustrates basic hedging solutions for foreign currency (FC) payables and receivables relative to a company's domestic currency (DC).

Let us explore various scenarios to expand on the hedging concept.

Hedging Foreign Currency Payables with Calls

Assume that a U.S.-based company needs to hedge a £100m payable that is due in three months. It can select from various strategies, such as buying a currency forward or an at-the-money

T A B L E 7.2

Hedge Results for Various Market Prices—P&L ($) of £100m Payable:

Spot £/$ Rate (in Three Months)	1.45	1.50	1.55
1. At original spot rate ($)	(150)	(150)	(150)
2. At current rate ($)	(145)	(150)	(155)
3. Net gain/loss due to spot movement ($)	5	0	(5)
4. Cost of call ($)	(2)	(2)	(2)
Exercise call	No	No	Yes
5. Payment received under call	0	0	5
Total cost ($) under current market conditions [2 + 4 + 5]	(147)	(152)	(152)
Total cost expressed as spot rate (£/$)	1.47	1.52	1.52
Cost of forward contract (£/$)	1.50	1.50	1.50

call option with a strike price equal to the market price of the forward. Table 7.2 compares the results of the two strategies for a range of market price scenarios.

We know from the preceding that the call option allows the company to take advantage of a weaker £ rate should it be available in three months. If £ is weaker than $1.50 at expiration of the option, the right to buy £ at $1.50 will be worthless. The company will buy the required £ in the spot market at a better rate, and the only cost will have been the option premium of $0.02. Conversely, if £ is stronger than $1.50, the company will exercise the option to buy £ at the strike of $1.50, suggesting an all-in cost of $1.52. We note that the breakeven point on the forward contract (defined as the forward rate less the option premium) is $1.48. If £ weakens below $1.48, the call is the preferred alternative; if it strengthens above $1.48, the forward contract is cheaper. The breakeven point in this example is defined as the forward FX rate less the option premium.

Hedging Foreign Currency Receivables with Puts

A company can employ a similar process to hedge a receivable denominated in a foreign currency (i.e., the reverse of the position above). Under this scenario it can either sell a currency forward or buy an at-the-money put. Let us again assume the firm has a £100m

T A B L E   7.3

Hedge Results for Various Market Prices—P&L ($) of £100m Receivable:

Spot £/$ Rate (in Three Months)	1.45	1.50	1.55
1. At original spot rate ($)	150	150	150
2. At current rate ($)	145	150	155
3. Net gain/loss due to spot movement ($)	(5)	0	5
4. Cost of put ($)	(2)	(2)	(2)
Exercise put	Yes	No	No
5. Payment received under put ($)	5	0	0
Total profit ($) under current market conditions [2 + 4 + 5]	148	148	153
Total profit expressed as spot rate (£/$)	1.48	1.48	1.53
Profit from forward contract (£/$)	1.50	1.50	1.50

receivable that it wants to hedge; its alternatives, and the results under various scenarios, are depicted in Table 7.3.

As above, the currency put option allows the company to take advantage of a stronger £/$ exchange rate if it is available in three months. If £ is stronger than $1.50 at expiration, the right to sell pounds at $1.50 will be worthless, and the company will abandon the option. Instead, it will sell the currency in the spot market at a better rate. The only additional cost will be the $0.02 premium it paid for the option. The breakeven rate against the forward contract is $1.52, because the put option costs $0.02 per pound. In other words, the breakeven point for a put option versus a forward contract is the forward currency rate plus the cost of the option. If the pound strengthens above $1.52, then the put option is preferred. Otherwise, the forward contract is preferred.

Hedging with Participating Forwards

A participating forward is a forward/option hybrid that can also be used to create an effective hedge. The basic participating forward requires the simultaneous purchase of a forward contract and call option to hedge a foreign currency payable, or the sale of a forward contract and the purchase of a put option to hedge a foreign currency receivable. Changing the ratio of forward contracts to foreign currency options changes the "participation level."

Consider the hedge of a payable created with a 50% forward and a 50% long call. This package provides full downside protection along with partial (50%) participation in favorable moves in the exchange rate. Figure 7.9 and Table 7.4 illustrate the use of a 50% participating forward in the hedge of £100m of payables.

Because the participation rate of this strategy is 50%, the participating forward costs only half as much as the basic foreign currency call option strategy. Of course, in return for the lower cost the buyer forfeits 50% of the benefits that accrue from a favorable move in exchange rates.

The table illustrates the cash flows from the buyer's perspective. In this case, the purchased call option has a strike of $1.50 and covers one-half of the notional (£50m); the forward contract at $1.50 covers the balance. The spot sterling rate in the first line is the spot rate at the time the payable is due.

If the dollar strengthens relative to the pound, the participating forward strategy is cheaper than a pure call option strategy. However, when the dollar weakens below $1.50, the call strategy becomes less expensive than the participating forward, because it allows full participation as the dollar weakens.

Hedging with Collars (Range Forwards)

Institutions can also use options to create collar (or range forward) hedges. The basic collar strategy, illustrated in Figure 7.9, involves the purchase of an out-of-the-money call and sale of an

F I G U R E   7.9

Hedging Payables with a 50% Participating Forward

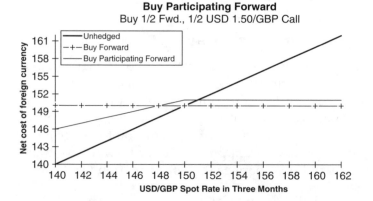

Buy Participating Forward
Buy 1/2 Fwd., 1/2 USD 1.50/GBP Call

T A B L E 7.4

Hedge Results for 50% Participating Forward—P&L ($) of £100m Payable:

Spot £/$ Rate (in Three Months)	1.45	1.50	1.55
Cost ($) of £100m payable:			
1. At original spot rate ($)	(150)	(150)	(150)
2. At current rate ($)	(145)	(150)	(155)
3. Net gain/loss due to spot movement ($)	5	0	(5)
Call structure:			
4. Cost of call ($)	(1)	(1)	(1)
Exercise call	No	No	Yes
5. Payment received under call (for ½ notional)	0	0	2.5
Forward structure:			
6. Payments/receipts for ½ notional ($)	(2.5)	0	2.5
Total cost ($ under current market conditions [2 + 4 + 5 + 6]	(148.5)	(151)	(151)
Total cost expressed as spot rate ($/£)	1.485	1.51	1.51
Cost of straight call strategy ($/£)	1.47	1.52	1.52

out-of-the-money put (or vice versa). The relative strikes of the put and call dictate whether a "zero-cost" structure can be created. A zero-cost collar, as the names suggests, means that an institution need not pay a premium to secure some level of hedge protection.

In this example, the cost of buying the calls is equal to the revenue from selling the puts, resulting in zero premium. Selecting different strike prices will lead to a net premium debit or credit, though the overall payoff profile will still approximate the one reflected in Figure 7.10. The collar guarantees that the net cost of the currency will fall within a predefined band. The buyer "caps" the cost of the currency at the call strike but relinquishes the right to participate in gains below the put strike. Table 7.5 illustrates the hedge cash flows from the buyer's perspective. The long call option has a $1.55 strike and the short put option has a $1.45 strike. The premium received on the put offsets the premium paid on the call.

Hedging Interest Rate Risk with Caps and Floors: The Borrower's Perspective

Options can be used to hedge other risks as well. Interest rate hedging via the options market, for example, is extremely popular.

F I G U R E   7.10

Hedging Payables with a Collar

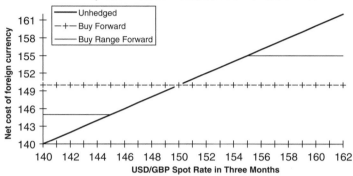

Buy Range Forward
Buy USD 1.55/GBP Call, Sell USD 1.45/GBP Put

USD/GBP Spot Rate in Three Months

T A B L E   7.5

Hedge Results for Collar—P&L ($) of £100m Payable:

Spot £/$ Rate (in Three Months)	1.43	1.50	1.58
Cost ($) of £100m payable:			
1. At original spot rate ($)	(150)	(150)	(150)
2. At current rate ($)	(143)	(150)	(158)
3. Net gain/loss due to spot movement ($)	7	0	(8)
4. Cost of range forward ($)	0	0	0
Exercise call	No	No	Yes
Exercise put	Yes	No	No
5. Call receipt/put payment ($)	(2)	0	3
Total cost (USD) under current market conditions [2 + 4 + 5]	(145)	(150)	(155)
Total cost expressed as spot rate ($/£)	1.45	1.50	1.55

While institutions can, and in practice do, manage rate risk using symmetrical interest rate products such as swaps and forward rate agreements (FRAs), asymmetrical products can offer interesting alternatives. To demonstrate this process we consider hedging examples using caps, floors, and FRAs.

To review, a cap ensures that the buyer will be protected if interest rates rise above a specified strike level; conversely, a floor ensures the buyer that a certain minimum rate will be achieved.

T A B L E   7.6

Cap/Floor Premiums

Strike Rate	Cap Premium (bps)	Floor Premium (bps)
6.00%	63	2
6.25%	42	6
6.50%	25	14
6.61%	19	19
6.75%	12	26
7.00%	5	44
7.25%	2	66

Caps and floors can thus be considered call and put options on FRAs for several periods. As we know, a single cap or floor is comprised of a strip of options, one for each evaluation period until maturity. Thus, a two-year cap with six-month evaluation periods is comprised of seven caplets.

Let us consider the case of Company XYZ, which can fund itself through a bank facility at three-month LIBOR + 100 bps. Assume XYZ is borrowing $10m when the current three-month LIBOR FRA rate is 6.61% and the quoted three-month cap/floor premiums for a variety of strikes are as shown in Table 7.6.

FRA Alternative

In order to hedge its borrowing cost under the $10m facility, XYZ can create a long position in a three-month FRA at 6.61% (for which it would make no up-front premium payment). This locks in the cost for the three-month period starting in three months, at 7.61% (6.61% plus the credit spread of 1%). This position is reflected in Figure 7.11.

The FRA strategy provides a known all-in borrowing cost over all possible LIBOR outcomes during the three-month horizon. The unhedged line illustrates how the interest cost of the underlying position rises in the absence of protection. Similarly, the opportunity cost of the FRA hedge is evidenced by the fact that XYZ does not benefit from lower LIBOR rates.

Cap Alternative

Instead of entering into an FRA, XYZ can purchase a cap; this eliminates the potential opportunity cost of an FRA—at a price. Since the

F I G U R E 7.11

Hedging with FRAs

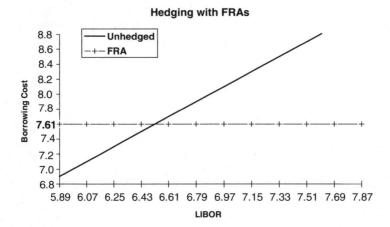

cap is an option to buy an FRA, XYZ will not exercise when rates are unfavorable (i.e., when LIBOR is below the 6.61% strike). This means that it is not locked into a particular funding cost as LIBOR falls, as it would be through a symmetrical instrument.

Assume that the company selects an at-the-money strike rate of 6.61%, paying a premium of 19 bps, or $4,750 (e.g., $10m * 0.0019 * 90/360). Table 7.7 illustrates cash flows using a 6.61% cap under various rate scenarios.

Regardless of how much LIBOR rises in three months, XYZ's effective borrowing cost will be no higher than 7.80% (6.61% plus the credit spread of 1% plus the annualized cap premium of 0.19%). Thus, if LIBOR in three months is higher than 6.61%, the company

T A B L E 7.7

LIBOR Hedge Scenarios

LIBOR in 3 Months:	6.00%	6.61%	7.00%
Interest expense at LIBOR + 1% $	(175,000)	(190,250)	(200,000)
Cap cost $	(4,750)	(4,750)	(4,750)
Exercise cap	No	No	Yes
Payment received under cap $	0	0	9,750
Total cash outflow $	(179,750)	(195,000)	(195,000)
Expressed as a %	7.19%	7.80%	7.80%

F I G U R E   7.12

FRA versus Cap Alternatives

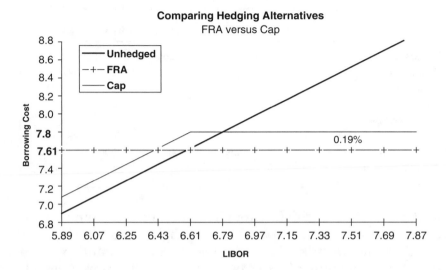

will exercise the option and receive the difference between the three-month LIBOR and the cap rate of 6.61%. For example, when LIBOR is 7.00%, XYZ receives $9,750 [(7.00% − 6.61%) × 90/360 × $10,000,000]. However, if LIBOR falls to 6.00% in three months, XYZ will allow the cap to expire worthless, thus facing an effective borrowing cost of 7.19% (LIBOR of 6.00% plus the 1% credit spread plus the 0.19% cost of the cap). In this case, the company's effective cost is 42 bp less than the symmetrical FRA hedge. The payoff profiles of these hedge alternatives are illustrated in Figure 7.12.

The figure clearly demonstrates that the cap alternative carries a higher borrowing cost than the FRA as rates rise. But if rates fall, the cap is abandoned and the borrowing cost falls along with LIBOR (plus the additional cost of the premium). This indicates that the cap is the best alternative when rates fall. In fact, the point at which the cap becomes cheaper than the FRA occurs when interest rates fall below the FRA rate less the cap premium; in this example, the breakeven point appears when LIBOR falls below 6.42% (6.61% − 0.19%).

Collar Alternative

Of course, XYZ may not want to bear the cost of purchasing a cap, and may thus choose to arrange a collar, where premium from the

TABLE 7.8

LIBOR Hedge Scenarios

LIBOR in 3 Months:	6.00%	6.25%	6.61%	7.00%
Interest expense at LIBOR + 1% $	(175,000)	(181,250)	(190,250)	(200,000)
Cap cost $	(4,750)	(4,750)	(4,750)	(4,750)
Floor premium $	1,500	1,500	1,500	1,500
Exercise cap	No	No	No	Yes
Floor exercised	Yes	No	No	No
Cap receipt/floor payment $	(6,250)	0	0	9,750
Total cash outflow $	(184,500)	(184,500)	(193,500)	(193,500)
Expressed as a %	7.38%	7.38%	7.74%	7.74%

sale of a floor can help defray (or eliminate) the premium paid on the cap. The collar provides XYZ with a maximum borrowing cost defined by the cap strike. However, the short floor simultaneously establishes a minimum effective borrowing rate. If interest rates fall below that minimum (defined by the floor strike), XYZ cannot benefit economically.

Assume XYZ wants to protect against LIBOR exceeding 6.61%. It can obtain that protection by buying an at-the-money cap with a strike price of 6.61% for an annualized premium of 19 bp. It can then sell a floor, such as a 6.25% strike for 6 bps. This premium income offsets the premium paid on the cap, bringing XYZ's all-in hedging costs to 13 bps. Table 7.8 illustrates the company's cash flows using the collar for its next rate resetting under various assumed LIBOR levels.

XYZ is thus certain that in three months its borrowing cost will not be higher than 7.74% (6.61% LIBOR + 1% credit spread + 0.13% net cost of collar), or lower than 7.38% (6.25% LIBOR + 1% credit spread + 0.13% net cost of collar). The net cost of this hedging strategy is $3,250 ($10m * 0.0013 * 90/360, or $4,750 – $1,500). Figure 7.13 illustrates the FRA and collar hedging alternatives, where the collar has a 6.61% strike cap and a 6.25% strike floor.

Comparing All Three Alternatives

The three hedging alternatives can be combined in a single diagram (see Figure 7.14) to illustrate the relative advantages and disadvantages of each one. Indeed, it is useful to see how each performs under

F I G U R E   7.13

FRA versus Collar Alternatives

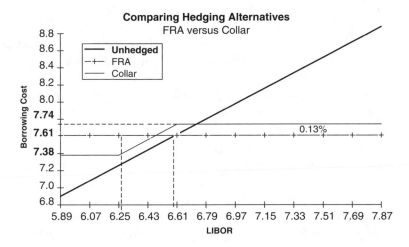

F I G U R E   7.14

FRA, Cap, and Collar Alternatives

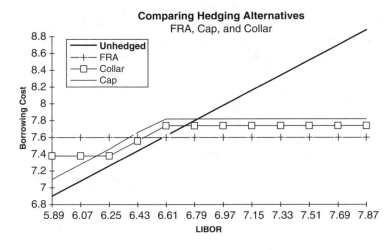

different interest rate scenarios (assuming any "no hedge" alternative is excluded). Examining the results we note the following:

- The FRA is the best strategy when rates rise.
- The cap is the best hedging strategy when rates fall.
- The collar is the best strategy when rates fall modestly (but not below the floor strike).

Hedging Interest Rate Risk with Caps and Floors: The Investor's Perspective

Hedges can also be constructed to protect an investor's risk to interest rates. Let us assume that an investor has a portfolio of LIBOR-based floating-rate investments and is concerned that short-term rates may fall in the next three months. Following the logic developed above, we know that the investor can hedge with symmetrical products (i.e., selling an FRA); this locks in a rate three months hence. But if rates rise substantially over the period, the investor suffers an opportunity loss. Instead of selling an FRA, the investor can buy a floor (i.e., the right to sell an FRA).

Assume the investor buys an at-the-money floor with a strike of 6.61%, paying 19 bps in premium. It now has the right to receive 6.61% against payment of three-month LIBOR in three months. If LIBOR in three months is greater than 6.61%, the investor will allow the floor to expire worthless. If LIBOR is less than 6.61%, the investor will exercise the option and receive the difference between LIBOR and 6.61%, in effect ensuring it has achieved a minimum investment rate. The minimum return after accounting for the cost of the floor amounts to 6.42% (LIBOR of 6.61% − 0.19% cost of the floor). Figure 7.15 illustrates the FRA and purchased floor alternatives.

It is worth noting that the cap/floor/collar examples we have described above have been simplified by considering only

F I G U R E   7.15

FRA and Floor Alternatives

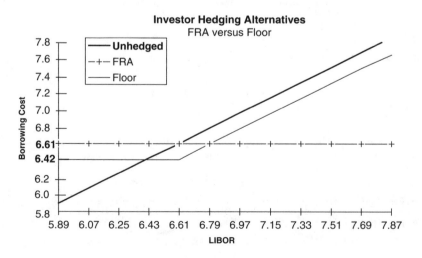

single-period payouts. The same hedging concepts apply for multiple-period characteristics of the typical cap/floor. Assume a company has a French subsidiary that borrows at EURIBOR + 50 bps. The subsidiary wants to lock in a maximum EURIBOR base rate of 9.00% for the next two years (which is equal to the current swap market rate), but wants to take advantage of any reduction in rates over that period; current three-month EURIBOR is 8.60%.

The subsidiary can purchase a two-year, 9.00% cap on three-month EURIBOR for an up-front premium of 75 bps; a €10m cap therefore costs €75,000. The subsidiary will have the right to exercise its option under the cap on seven different dates over the next two years, and will do so when EURIBOR is greater than 9.00% on the rate reset dates. It is useful to consider how much the up-front premium adds to the company's borrowing cost. To do so we must amortize the cost over the life of the financing, and convert the cost to a per annum basis. To put the 75 bps on a quarterly effective per annum basis, we assume the proper two-year quarterly effective discounting rate is 9.00% (at-the-money two-year strike rate, which is the two-year swap rate). Using the time value of money functions of a financial calculator or spreadsheet we note the results in Table 7.9

T A B L E 7.9

Amortization of Cap Costs

	TVM key	Value
1) Input cash outflow	[PV]	−0.75
2) Input future value	[FV]	0
3) Input number of three-month periods	[n]	8
4) Input the quarterly discount rate:		
input the annual discount rate		9
divide by 4		÷ 4
input result as discount rate	[i]	2.25
5) Solve for quarterly payment	[PMT]	0.035
6) Convert result to annual nominal rate:		
multiply by 360		× 360
		37.2558
		÷ 91.25
divide by 91.25 days		**0.4083**

The subsidiary's total borrowing cost at each rate reset over the next two years will not be more than 9.91% (9.00% cap rate + 0.50% credit spread + 0.41% effective per annum cost of cap).

Hedging with Barrier Options

Barrier options are often employed to hedge cash flows and input/output risks given their relative cost-efficiencies. The most commonly used barrier options for hedging are those which knock out as the price of the reference asset moves through the barrier. In particular, hedging strategies are often developed using the down-and-out call and the up-and-out put. Each structure knocks out when the contract is out-of-the-money and hedge protection is no longer required. Let us consider examples of both forms.

We know that the down-and-out call is very similar to a standard call except that it extinguishes if the market value of the asset falls below the barrier price. This suggests that it is appropriate for hedging input risks (e.g., oil prices, power prices, raw material commodity prices). Let us assume a company is interested in hedging the input risk associated with a commodity and faces the trade parameters for European and down-and-out calls noted in Table 7.10.

Let us also project some price path (as in Figure 7.16) that illustrates the asset rising above the strike (providing gains on the option as the hedger suffers losses on the input) and then dipping below the strike (providing no gains on the option but allowing the hedger to generate savings on the input). The extreme condition

T A B L E 7.10

European and Down-and-Out Call Parameters

Specifications	European Option	Barrier Option
Type	Call	Call
Maturity	180 days	180 days
Spot price	300	300
Strike	310	310
Volatility	20%	20%
Knockout barrier	N/a	290
Premium cost	11	5.7

F I G U R E 7.16

Price Path on Down-and-Out Call

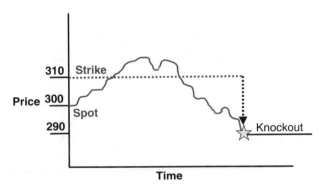

occurs as the asset price falls to low levels and knocks out; at this point the hedger's core exposure is well in-the-money, so it may be relatively indifferent to the fact that it has a naked exposure—particularly since the initial cost of the protection is relatively inexpensive compared to the European option.

Hedgers often target a price range for the underlying exposure that they are trying to manage. In this example the hedger needs to purchase assets (e.g., production inputs) between 290 and 310. The hedger may also believe that if prices fall to 290 they will continue to decline further. If the barrier is touched, the option ceases to exist and the hedger has three choices: do nothing; purchase the underlying input at the lower price and lock in a "gain"; wait for the price to fall even further before locking in with a new, cheaper, call option.

Let us consider the example of an airline that must purchase 10m barrels of oil in six months to cover its jet fuel requirements (note that jet fuel is one of the light products that is derived from crude oil). The airline is concerned that jet fuel prices will increase if oil cartel policy changes. However, if the policy does not change, supply will be readily available, meaning oil (and jet fuel) prices will decrease. The optimal solution in this case is for the airline company to buy a knockout call option on crude oil. If the price of oil rallies immediately, the knockout acts just as a regular call (though it is much cheaper than the regular call). If the price of oil hits the barrier prior to expiry, the airline can lock in the lower prices by buying a standard call at a much cheaper level than it could have initially. Trade details are summarized in Table 7.11 for

T A B L E   7.11

European and Down-and-Out Crude Oil Call Parameters

Specifications	European Option	Barrier Option
Type	Call	Call
Maturity	180 days	180 days
Spot price	50	50
Strike	55	55
Volatility	30%	30%
Knockout barrier	n/a	45
Premium cost	1.23	0.65

T A B L E   7.12

European and Up-and-Out Put Parameters

Specifications	European Option	Barrier Option
Type	Put	Put
Maturity	180 days	180 days
Spot price	300	300
Strike	290	290
Volatility	20%	20%
Knockout barrier	N/a	310
Premium cost	12.75	6.6

each option contract; a hedge of 10m barrels would require the purchase of 10,000 contracts (e.g., 1,000/barrels per contract).

The up-and-out put is another common barrier hedge. In this structure the put extinguishes if the market value of the asset rises above the barrier price. This suggests that it is appropriate for hedging outputs (e.g., the goods the company produces or extracts). We can again illustrate the general principles by examining a sample trade, as in Table 7.12 and Figure 7.17. In this case the hedge remains in place as long as the asset price remains below the barrier. When the price falls below the strike, the hedger gains on the put but loses on the underlying exposure; when the price rises above the strike the hedger no longer gains on the put, but gains on the underlying exposure. Once the barrier is reached, the hedge disappears.

FIGURE 7.17

Price Path of Up-and-Out Put Option

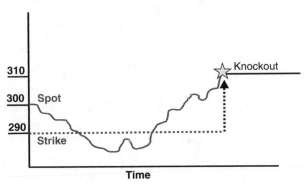

Let us again examine a transaction in light of actual details. Assume a U.S. computer manufacturer wants to purchase specialized graphics chips from Korea. Each computer that uses this chip can be sold for $55 more than a computer without the chip. The current Korean won (KRW)/$ exchange rate is KRW1200/$; each chip costs KRW 60,000, or $50 at the current exchange rate.

The company contracts to buy 100,000 chips to be delivered in six months, at which point the full purchase price will be due. Let us assume the following three scenarios:

- Scenario 1: The computer company decides not to hedge. After six months pass, the KRW exchange rate has strengthened to KRW 1000/$. The company must buy KRW 6b in the spot market, which is equal to $6m. As a result, each chip costs the company $60, suggesting that an anticipated profit of $5 per chip has become a loss of $5 per chip.
- Scenario 2: The computer company hedges with a standard European option. The company purchases a $ put/KRW call struck at KRW1200/$. If the KRW strengthens to KRW 1000, the profit margin of $5 per chip is protected. However, the actual cost of the European option may be high as a result of volatility.
- Scenario 3: The computer company hedges with an up-and-out barrier option. The company purchases a $ put/KRW call struck at 1200 KRW/$ with a barrier at KRW 1300/$. If KRW strengthens (e.g., to KRW 1000), the $5 profit margin is protected. If KRW weakens above the barrier level of

KRW 1300, the company loses the hedge protection, but only at a point where the profit margin is greater than $5/chip. It will also have arranged the hedge at a cheaper cost than the European alternative.

ARBITRAGE AND MONETIZATION APPLICATIONS

Options are often used to arbitrage or monetize value. Pure arbitrage, in the classic sense of creating a riskless profit through the simultaneous purchase and sale of two positions, is relatively difficult to achieve in an era of technology and information; price discrepancies which drive such opportunities are exploited very rapidly, meaning that a true riskless position can be hard to establish. However, relatively low-risk arbitrage strategies that can enhance yield/return or allow monetization of value are quite common. When constructed properly, these applications can generate reasonable profits without generating the same level of risk as pure speculative strategies. We consider various examples of this type of application in the section that follows.

Swaption-driven strategies are popular. For instance, a floating-rate borrower who does not believe that interest rates will decline can sell a receiver swaption to generate premium that reduces funding costs; a borrower who believes rates will fall can sell a payer swaption to achieve the same result. Or, an institution that owns an interest-rate sensitive asset can buy a payer swaption as protection, while one that is managing an interest gap created by short-duration assets and long-duration liabilities can buy a receiver swaption. Swaptions can also be used to protect or leverage a volatility position: the issuer of a callable bond can sell a receiver swaption to monetize value, while the issuer of a puttable bond can buy a payer swaption to protect against rising rates. Regardless of the specific strategy, the premium inflow or outflow must be considered as part of the all-in funding cost or investment return computation.

Let us consider an FRN issuer who sells an out-of-the-money payer swaption (where fixed rates are below the forward rates associated with the option's final maturity): If rates fall and the buyer of the payer swaption exercises, the issuer/seller effectively converts a portion of its FRN funding into fixed rates. If rates do not fall, the debt remains floating, but the issuer earns premium from the swaption sale that can be used to offset all-in funding costs. We can imagine the opposite scenario: an investor holding an FRN can sell a receiver swaption, earning premium on the sale. If the swaption remains unexercised, then the investor enjoys the benefit of enhanced portfolio yield via the earned premium; if the swaption is exercised, the investor locks in a fixed rate on a portion of the FRN position.

We can consider another example where the issuer of a fixed-rate puttable bond receives a lower funding cost from the initial sale of the put option and can supplement this by entering into a fixed/floating interest rate swap to exchange the issuer's funding into LIBOR, and buying a receiver swaption from the put date to the final bond maturity. If rates fall and investors do not exercise their puts, the issuer can exercise the receiver swaption to keep the borrowing at lower floating rates (which offsets the sum paid for the swaption).

Swaptions can be used to monetize value in the callable and puttable bonds described in Chapter 4. Monetization generally arises from an arbitrage opportunity that makes it possible to buy "cheap" options and sell "rich" ones. The arbitrage works because of pricing discrepancies that periodically appear between issuers, investors, and intermediaries. Empirical evidence suggests that the implied volatility of options in the capital markets is often lower than in the derivatives market, as investors tend to focus on yield rather than total return when determining value. This means that investment decisions are made on a yield-to-worst basis, ascribing zero value to the optionality in the securities. Investors also tend to lack information on corporate posture regarding callablility and the probability of a call action, generally believing that no such calls will occur. Further pricing discrepancies can arise from relative value differentials among synthetic or structured securities, and between the swap curve and the corporate credit curve. For example, if the swap curve is flat to inverted versus the corporate curve, implied forward rates are lower in the swap market—this means that receiver swaptions in the swap market are worth more than call options in the corporate market, leading to potential arbitrage opportunities. An issuer of a callable bond de facto purchases a cheap call option from investors via the bond and can then sell a receiver swaption to an intermediary, which gives the intermediary the right to exercise into a swap where the intermediary will receive fixed and pay the issuer floating. If rates fall, the intermediary will exercise the swaption, paying LIBOR and receiving fixed; the issuer, in turn, will call the bond and refinance via an FRN at a new lower rate. Rather than paying fixed rates to the original bond investors, the issuer then pays fixed rates to the swaption intermediary; the floating cash flows the issuer receives from the intermediary are redirected to the new FRN investors. Naturally, if rates rise, the entire bond/swaption package remains outstanding until maturity. Figure 7.18 summarizes this example. Note that this structure works if the swaption can be sold for more on a present value basis than the market yield on straight debt (e.g., excall option); if it cannot, then the arbitrage does not work and the issuer is better off issuing noncall debt directly.

When forward swap rates are high, payer swaptions are worth more than put options in the corporate market, leading again to profit opportunities with puttable bonds. For instance, an issuer might float a 15-year fixed-rate bond that is puttable at par after five years. The issuer, which is short the put to investors, can buy a five-year payer swaption on a 10-year fixed rate—and achieve an arbitrage if the swaption is cheaper than the option sold via the puttable bond. If this occurs, then the issuer's all-in cost will be lower than a straight bond and value will have been monetized. If rates fall below the issuance yield in year five, the bond will remain outstanding

FIGURE 7.18

Callable Bond/Receiver Swaption Arbitrage

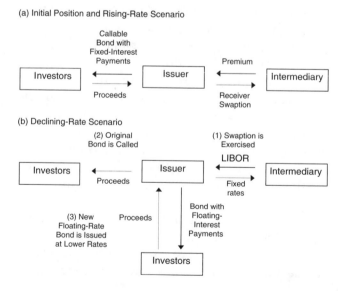

and the swaption will remain unexercised. If rates rise, investors will put the bond back to the issuer and the issuer will exercise the payer swaption to continue paying a known fixed rate versus LIBOR.

In general, swaption arbitrage tends to appear when interest rates are volatile (which increases the value of the options), the yield curve is relatively flat, and credit spreads are either tight (callable bonds) or wide (puttable bonds). The swaption arbitrage does not always exist; in fact, it appears to be a cyclical phenomenon driven by issuance activity in specific credit sectors, the needs of investors, and the creation of new structured liability opportunities.[1] It is also important to stress that the actual net swaption arbitrage that is achieved is a function of an issuer's future creditworthiness; if credit deterioration occurs, so that the spread over LIBOR or a government benchmark widens, the actual funding arbitrage will compress.[2]

---

1 While investor undervaluation of embedded options has historically been a market driver, greater sophistication within the investment community, as well as access to better modeling tools and corporate information, mean that the arbitrage may begin to compress or appear less frequently.

2 An investor can purchase a payer swaption or purchase a receiver swaption and a forward starting swap; the two results are identical. Synthetic construction can also be used to create different forms of funding. Noncallable/nonputtable bonds, for example, can be converted into callable/puttable equivalents, and callable/puttable bonds can be converted into fixed or floating noncallable and nonputtable equivalents—all through the use of the appropriate underlying asset and a swaption.

Consider that an issuer can create synthetic noncall debt by issuing a callable bond and selling a receiver swaption, which creates fixed-rate funding to the call date and synthetic fixed-rate funding from the call date to the maturity date. Thus, if a company issues a fixed-rate callable bond with a five-year final maturity and sells a payer swaption, it will have a fixed-funding profile regardless of what happens to rates: if rates rise, the bond will remain outstanding and the swaption will go unexercised; if rates decline, the bond will be called and the swaption buyer will exercise the swaption to receive fixed in a swap with the issuer. These scenarios make it appear as though the callable bond is, in fact, noncallable for its entire life. Synthetic callable bonds can also be created using noncallable debt and swaptions.

An issuer can also synthesize a puttable bond from a package that includes a callable bond and the sale of back-end receiver and payer swaptions. The buyer of the swaptions thus has the option to exercise either swaption and force the issuer to pay fixed or received fixed. One of the two swaptions purchased is used to offset the option embedded in the callable bond, while the other serves to create the puttable structure. Thus, if the issuer floats a seven-year bond that is callable after year five and rates rise, the buyer of the swaptions will exercise the contract to receive floating for the final two years of the issue. The issuer thus has fixed funding for the first five years and floating rate funding for the last two. If rates fall, the buyer will exercise the contract to receive fixed for the last two years; the issuer then calls the outstanding bond and funds via a new FRN in the lower-priced market. Puttable bonds can also be converted into nonputtable securities using similar techniques.

T A B L E 7.13

Swaption Financing Computation

	TVM key	Value
Input total amount received		
(100% principal + 0.80% swaption premium)	[PV]	100.80
Input principal repayment	[FV]	−100
Input annual coupon payment	[PMT]	−9.35
Input number of year	[n]	5
Solve for yield	[I]	9.14

Let us review a simple example of monetization using swaptions. Assume that a borrower can issue five-year noncallable debt at 9.25% or five-year debt, callable after one year, at 9.35%. A one-year receiver swaption can be sold for 80 bps. Under the terms of the receiver swaption the swaption buyer has the right, in one year, to exercise and cause the seller (i.e., the debt issuer) to enter into a four-year interest rate swap where the seller receives 9.35% and pays LIBOR.

If four-year swap rates are less than 9.35% in one year, the swaption buyer exercises and the four-year swap commences. Once this occurs, the borrower will call the debt and refinance in the cheaper floating-rate market. The net result is that the borrower continues to pay 9.35% for four years. If rates are greater than 9.35% in one year, the swaption buyer will allow the swaption to expire worthless. The borrower does not call the outstanding debt and continues to pay 9.35%.

In either case, the borrower ends up paying a 9.35% coupon for five years. But with the callable bond plus swaption combination the borrower reduces the cost of five-year funds from 9.25% (available with a five-year noncall issue) to 9.14%, which is demonstrated via the computation in Table 7.13.

This represents a savings of 11 bps (9.25% − 9.14%). We can also view this transaction as an arbitrage between two markets: the borrower buys an option in the callable debt market for 10 bps (e.g., 9.35% vs. 9.25%) and sells the same option in the swaption market for 21 bps (9.35% − 9.14%).

CHAPTER EXERCISES

1. Speculative positions can be created by:
   a. Selling a strangle
   b. Buying a straddle
   c. Buying a power call
   d. Selling a put spread
   e. All of the above

2. An up-and-out call can be a benefit to speculators because:
   a. It is cheaper than a vanilla option
   b. It allows crystallization of a very defined market view
   c. It can be applied across asset classes
   d. All of the above
   e. None of the above

3. The maximum payoff to a speculator on a down-and-in put struck at 1,000, with a barrier of 900 and a terminal price of 750 is:
   a. 250
   b. 100
   c. 150
   d. 350
   e. None of the above

4. If a company has a foreign currency payable that is unhedged its liability will:
   a. Increase if the foreign currency increases
   b. Decrease if the foreign currency increases
   c. Increase if the foreign currency remains unchanged
   d. Depend on market volatility
   e. None of the above

5. To hedge a foreign currency receivable exposure a company can:
   a. Sell a foreign currency forward
   b. Buy a foreign currency put option
   c. Buy a domestic currency call option
   d. All of the above
   e. None of the above

6. A 75% participating forward is created through a package of:
   a. 25% forward, 75% option
   b. 75% forward, 25% option
   c. 50% forward, 50% option
   d. 10% forward, 90% option
   e. 100% forward

7. Consider the following collar transaction:
   Long call struck at 100, premium of 3
   Short put struck at 95, premium of 2
   If the price of the underlying moves to 105, the net P&L on the collar is:
   a. 3
   b. 4
   c. 5
   d. 2
   e. 1

8. Given the transaction details in 7, what is the net P&L if the price of the underlying moves to 91?
   a. −2
   b. −1
   c. 0
   d. −3
   e. 3

9. If a company is hedging a $10m 12-month interest-rate risk at 5% through the purchase of a cap that costs $62,000, what is the maximum all-in funding cost?
   a. 5%
   b. 5.26%
   c. 5.62%
   d. 5.72%
   e. None of the above

10. A company might choose to hedge with a collar to:
   a. Reduce its hedge cost
   b. Create more upside
   c. Create more downside
   d. All of the above
   e. None of the above

PART 2

Valuation Tools

An Overview of Option Pricing

INTRODUCTION

Proper valuation of options is an essential ingredient in any successful hedging or speculating program. The options market has undergone significant, and continuous, advances in valuation methodologies since the earliest work put forth in the early 1970s. Refinements and expansions continue to the present time, helped by advances in financial mathematics and computing power. Our intent in this chapter (and the one that follows) is to present some of the key elements involved in the valuation of options. In keeping with the practical focus of this book our approach is qualitative and intuitive, rather than mathematical. That said, a list of relevant mathematical works is included in the reference section for readers wishing to examine the financial mathematics of the pricing process.

In this chapter we set the stage by considering intrinsic value and time value and analyzing the inputs that are commonly used to price options. We then introduce an intuitive approach to option pricing by developing a simple binomial tree. We shall supplement this discussion in the next chapter by considering the key option pricing models used by intermediaries and end users.

INTRINSIC VALUE AND TIME VALUE OF OPTIONS

We have noted in Part I of the text that the premium that a buyer pays the seller is comprised of two components: intrinsic value and time value.

The intrinsic value of an option, often referred to as "money-ness," is the profit (if any) that can be earned by immediately exercising the option. Since an option is an asymmetric contract, intrinsic value can never be less than zero; in other words, the option buyer can never be forced to pay out on an option.

Suppose that the current forward FX price is $1.50/£. The intrinsic value of a call with a strike price of $1.40 is $0.10:

Current price to purchase sterling	$1.50
Right to purchase sterling with exercise of option	$1.40
Intrinsic value	$0.10

In other words, since one pound can be purchased $0.10 below the market price of pounds, the call has intrinsic value of $0.10. We can contrast this with the intrinsic value of a put with a strike price of $1.40:

Current price to sell sterling	$1.50
Right to sell sterling with exercise of option	$1.40
Intrinsic value	$0.00

In this case, one pound can be sold only at an exchange rate higher than the rate prevailing in the market. Because this option has no intrinsic value, the buyer would simply abandon the contract rather than exercise it.

An in-the-money option therefore has an intrinsic value that is greater than zero. For calls, this occurs when the option buyer can purchase the underlying asset below the market price. For puts, this occurs when the owner can sell the underlying at a price that is above the market. The following relationships are true for in-the-money options:

- Calls: Market price > Strike price
- Puts: Market price < Strike price

With an exchange rate at $1.50, the $1.45 call and $1.55 put are both in-the-money, i.e., both have intrinsic value.

An out-of-the-money option has no intrinsic value. The call at the $1.55 strike and the put option at $1.45 strike are both out of the money, i.e., they cannot be exercised for immediate gain. The following are true for out-of-the-money options:

- Calls: Market price < Strike price
- Puts: Market price > Strike price

The greater the difference between the market price and the strike price, the farther out-of-the-money the contract. Premium decreases as the option moves further out-of-the-money, since there is no intrinsic value (and time value, discussed below, is low).

Time value is the time remaining until the expiry of the option, and can be computed as the difference between the option premium and the option's intrinsic value. For instance, assume that the premium of the $1.40 £ call option is $0.17. The time value of the call is simply:

$$\text{Time value} = \$0.17 - \$0.10 = \$0.07$$

The time value of the $1.40 put option, also assuming a premium of $0.07, is:

$$\text{Time value} = \$0.07 - \$0.00 = \$0.07$$

This simple example demonstrates that time value for options (whether puts or calls) is identical as long as they have the same strike and expiration.

We can also interpret time value as an element of the option's price that accounts for the fact that the price of the underlying asset might change between now and option expiration. The longer the option maturity, the better the chance that the option will end in-the-money, i.e., a profit to the buyer, a loss to the seller. Accordingly, and all other things equal, an option with a longer maturity will carry a larger premium. However, since time is a wasting asset, the time value of the option declines to zero as expiration approaches. The value of an option at expiration is therefore

F I G U R E   8.1

Time Value and Intrinsic Value

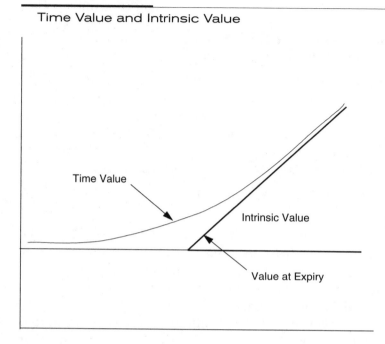

comprised solely of intrinsic value (if it is in-the-money). The actual rate of time value decay accelerates as expiration approaches. Thus, a longer-term option has a slower rate of time premium decay than a shorter-term option.

An at-the-money option has a strike price equal to the market price of the underlying. For instance, if the forward exchange rate for £ is $1.50, then the $1.50 call and put options are at the money. At-the-money options have intrinsic values of zero since they cannot be exercised for current gain. However, time value is larger for at-the-money options than for in-the-money or out-of-the-money options; we can observe this from Figure 8.1.

OPTION PRICING INPUTS

We have indicated that option prices are derived from mathematical models based on various inputs. Arbitrage forces help ensure that market prices and theoretical prices track one another closely over time. In this section we note the variables that determine the value of an option. These valuation variables, or input factors, vary slightly by type of reference asset, but are ultimately centered on same core "suite," which includes the underlying asset, volatility of the asset, strike price of the option, maturity (time to expiry), and risk-free rate; for options on equities and other dividend paying securities we must also consider the level of dividends. We describe the impact each of these variables has on both calls and puts using stock options as an example (and note that we can easily substitute other asset underlyings to obtain similar results).

Underlying Asset Price

We already know that the price of a call option increases, and the price of a put option decreases, as the price of the underlying stock increases—all other variables remaining constant. In fact, the price of the underlying asset is the single most important variable in determining value, as it indicates the level of intrinsic value the option carries at any point in time. Not surprisingly, when the stock price rises, the price of the call option rises as the chances of contract exercise increase. The price of the put, by extension, falls. The reverse scenario appears when stock prices fall, as noted in Figure 8.2.

Strike Price

Changing the strike price of an option has a decided impact on the value of the contract. For instance, call prices decrease and put prices increase as the strike price increases—again, all other variables being held constant. Conversely as the strike price decreases,

F I G U R E 8.2

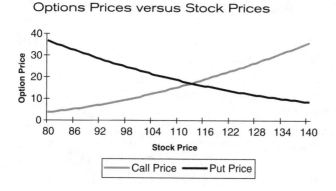

Options Prices versus Stock Prices

F I G U R E   8.3

Options Prices versus Strike Prices

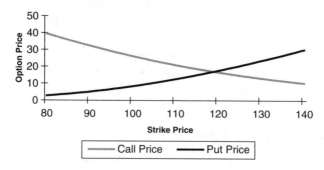

call prices increase and put prices decrease. This relationship is, of course, directly related to the intrinsic value of an option, as noted above. Figure 8.3 highlights this relationship.

Volatility of the Asset

Volatility, a driver of many of the strategies we have considered in Part I, is a key pricing parameter. Volatility reflects the level of uncertainty regarding the future value of the underlying reference asset. The greater the degree of future uncertainty, the greater the value of the option. This makes intuitive (as well as mathematical) sense, because a reference asset, such as a stock, that is very volatile stands a greater chance of moving in-the-money (or deeper in-the-money) than one that is very stable. Thus, as volatility rises, option buyers (puts or calls) are willing to pay more, since they expect to profit from greater price movement; option sellers, facing the same scenario, will demand a greater premium as the likelihood of a large (or larger) liability is much higher. Accordingly, as the volatility of the underlying stock increases, call prices increase and put prices increase (all other variables remaining constant). Similarly, as volatility decreases, call prices decrease and put prices decrease. Mathematically, the measurement of uncertainty corresponds to the calculation of the statistical standard deviation of price movements. As we'll note in the next chapter, volatility can be measured retrospectively (through examination of historical data) or prospectively (through the use of market-implied data). The option price/volatility relationships are depicted in Figure 8.4.

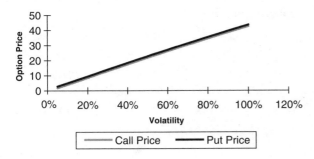

FIGURE 8.4

Options Prices versus Volatility Levels

Time to Expiration

Time to Expiration

We have noted that time value is an integral component of option premium. Accordingly, time to expiration has a direct impact on the prices of puts and calls. Holding all other inputs constant, an increase in the amount of time until expiration increases call and put prices; by extension, a decrease in the amount of time decreases call and put prices. This makes intuitive sense, as an option with a long time to expiration provides more time for the market to move the option in-the-money (or further in-the-money).

Time is, of course, a decaying asset. As time passes and an option approaches its expiration date, its time value decays. The decay accelerates as the expiration date approaches, because the likelihood of the option ending in-the-money (or further in-the-money) declines. This relationship is illustrated, for various call options, in Figure 8.5.

Dividend Payout

The dividend payout variable (which is, again, applicable to options on stocks, stock indexes, and other dividend-paying assets) is the dividend amount paid out on the underlying stock during the life of the option. As a company's dividend payout increases, call prices decrease and put prices increase—all other variables remaining constant. Conversely, as the dividend decreases, call prices increase and put prices decrease. Cash dividends have the effect of reducing the stock price on the "ex-dividend date;" in

F I G U R E 8.5

Options Prices versus Time to Expiration

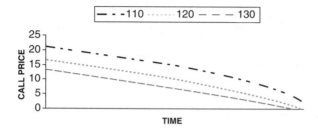

F I G U R E 8.6

Options Prices versus Dividend Rate

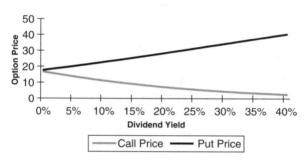

other words, the stock price is adjusted downward by the amount of the dividend. Accordingly, the larger the dividend payout, the larger the impact on the stock's price. This anticipated decrease in the price of a stock has a predictable impact on the related options, as illustrated in Figure 8.6.

Risk-Free Rate

Interest rates have an impact on the value of all options. While they clearly have a major influence on the value of interest rate options (e.g., bond options, caps, floors), they also have an effect on other classes of options, including stock options. As short-term (risk-free) interest rates increase, call prices rise and put prices fall, all other variables held constant; as short-term interest rates decrease, call prices fall and put prices rise. This relationship, illustrated in

FIGURE 8.7

Options Prices versus Risk-Free Rate

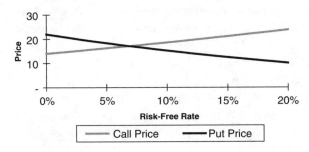

Figure 8.7, exists because the risk-free rate is translated into the time value of money and the forward price of the stock: when interest rates rise, forward prices also rise, meaning a call moves toward (in) the money, while a put moves (farther) out-of-the-money.

The variables impacting the value of a stock option are summarized in Table 8.1. We can create similar tables for other classes of underlying reference assets based on an understanding of how the variables noted above interact with call and put payoffs.

TABLE 8.1

The Effect Key Inputs on Option Prices

Key Input	Movement	Call Price	Put Price
Asset price	Up	Up	Down
	Down	Down	Up
Strike price	Up	Down	Up
	Down	Up	Down
Volatility	Up	Up	Up
	Down	Down	Down
Dividends*	Up	Down	Up
	Down	Up	Down
Time to expiry	Up	Up	Up
	Down	Down	Down
Risk free rate	Up	Up	Down
	Down	Down	Up

* where relevant

INTUITIVE APPROACH TO OPTION PRICING

To introduce a basic intuitive pricing framework we present a simple analogy based on a game of chance. Let us assume that an institution (or individual) pays an entry fee to drop a ball down a board that is filled with pegs. The pegs direct the ball in different directions. If the ball lands to the left of position X, the player receives nothing and forfeits the entry fee; if the ball lands to the right of position X, the player will receive a payoff. If the ball consistently falls to the right side every time it hits a peg, the payoff continues to grow, until it becomes very large. This simple game is illustrated in Figure 8.8.

An interesting issue centers on how much a participant might pay to play the game. If we can successfully answer the question, the result we obtain can actually guide us toward developing a simple option-pricing framework. Before developing an approach

FIGURE 8.8

A Game of Chance

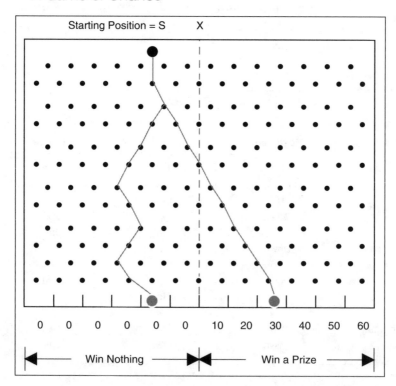

let us first compare the key elements of the game with those of a financial option by noting that:

- The dividing line (X) on the board between a prize/no prize is equal to the strike price of an option.
- The starting position (S) of the game is equal to the current market price of an option's reference asset.
- The vertical distance the ball drops is equal to an option's expiry.
- The "bounce" of the ball hitting the pegs is equal to the level of an option's volatility.
- The entry fee required to play the game is equal to an option's premium.

In fact, the peg-board diagram above is a pictorial representation of a binomial tree, which is a popular technique for estimating option prices. As noted above, these "variables" are crucial in determining the value of an option.

Pricing and Hedging with a Binomial Tree

Let us introduce a £/$ currency option to help us illustrate the binomial process. Assume that the one-year forward price for £/$ is $1.5000, meaning that the value of £1.00 in 12-months' time is $1.50. For the moment we make a simplifying assumption that the spot £/$ rate in one-year's time will take one of two possible values, as in Figure 8.9 (note that this is simply a representation of one "node" of the peg board shown above).

F I G U R E   8.9

Two States of £/$ in 12 Months

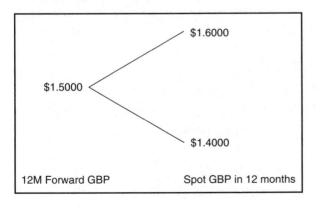

Note that we are starting with today's 12-month forward £/$ rate, rather than today's spot £/$ rate, and we simplify the world so that the actual spot rate in 12 months can yield only one of two possible values. We assume further that the probability that the rate will be higher or lower in 12-months' time is completely unknown. In fact, one of the most powerful advances of the binomial model (and others) is that neither the buyer nor seller of the option needs to have a specific view about the probability of the price rising or falling.

The key to establishing the price of a £/$ with a $1.5000 strike relates to the process of hedging the call after it is sold. If the option is hedged correctly, the all-in profit and loss (P&L) will be the same whether the rate goes up or down. If this occurs, then the option seller is indifferent to the probability of the currency rate rising or falling, meaning there is no need to know the relevant probabilities. P&L is comprised of three components:

- Option payout: the potential payout the seller must make to the buyer if the option moves in-the-money.
- Hedge profit: any potential profit from the hedge.
- Premium: the premium the seller receives from the buyer.

We can measure each one of these in both the up and down scenarios to understand its impact. We know from earlier that the value of a call at expiry is equal to the maximum of intrinsic value or zero, or call = max (0, (underlying price – strike price)). In order to hedge the call, the option seller must either buy or sell £/$ 12 months forward. Before doing so, the option seller must know whether to buy or sell the £/$ forward, and in what quantity.

If the option buyer chooses to exercise, which will be certain if the final spot rate is above the strike of $1.5000, the seller must deliver £ to the buyer in exchange for the buyer's $. To hedge this position, the option seller must therefore buy £/$ forward. The seller must then determine the proper size of the £/$ hedge. Buying a forward position at the forward rate of $1.5000 will have a positive or negative P&L impact, depending on whether the rate goes up or down. The hedge P&L can be described as:

$$\text{Hedge P\&L} = \text{Hedge (spot} - \text{forward)} \qquad (8.1)$$

In order to calculate the correct amount of the forward hedge, the P&L when the rate rises must be set equal to the P&L when the rate falls. When the rate rises, the P&L is comprised of two

T A B L E 8.2

Hedge P&L 1

Case		Call	Hedge
Up	P&L =	− max(0, up − strike)	+ hedge * (up − forward)

T A B L E 8.3

Hedge P&L 2

Case		Call	Hedge
Up	P&L =	(strike − up)	+ hedge * (up − forward)

T A B L E 8.4

Hedge P&L 3

Case		Call	Hedge
Down	P&L =	− max(0, down − strike)	+ hedge * (down − forward)
Down	P&L =	0	+ hedge * (down − forward)

components, one related to the call and the other to the hedge. These are given in Table 8.2.

The payout on the call is stated in favor of the option buyer. The payout for the option seller, by extension, is negative. This can be simplified when the rate moves up, as in Table 8.3.

When the rate falls, the call will not be exercised as it will be out-of-the-money, so the down P&L is comprised of only one part, the hedge. Down scenarios are reflected in Table 8.4.

The correct hedge makes the P&L equivalent for both the up and down scenarios. This means we can solve for the hedge amount by setting the two scenarios equal to each other, as in Equation (8.2):

$$\text{(strike − up)} + \text{(hedge * (up − forward))}$$
$$= \text{(hedge * (down − forward))} \tag{8.2}$$

This condenses algebraically to:

$$\text{Strike} - \text{Up} + \text{Hedge} \times \text{Up} - \text{Hedge} \times \text{Forward}$$
$$= \text{Hedge} \times \text{Down} - \text{Hedge} \times \text{Forward}$$
$$\text{Hedge} \times \text{Up} - \text{Hedge} \times \text{Down} = \text{Up} - \text{Strike}$$
$$\text{Hedge}_{\text{Call}} = \frac{\text{Up} - \text{Strike}}{\text{Up} - \text{Down}} \tag{8.3}$$

Since all three values are known, the solution for the forward hedge is given as:

$$\text{Hedge}_{\text{Call}} = \frac{\text{Up} - \text{Strike}}{\text{Up} - \text{Down}} = \frac{1.6000 - 1.5000}{1.6000 - 1.4000} = \frac{0.10}{0.20} = 50\%$$

This means that by buying a 50% forward £/$ position the option seller can properly hedge the call, and will face the same financial result whether the market moves up or down, as noted in Table 8.5.

The option seller thus loses $0.05 in either case. To bring the P&L back to a flat state under both scenarios, the option seller will need to earn $0.05 of premium at the end of the year. The price of the option is $0.05 per £1.00, i.e., what the option must be worth in one year. To calculate the up-front premium payable by the buyer, we must discount this future value back to the present. If we assume that 12-month $ interest rates are 10%, the fair value of the option premium today is:

$$\frac{\$5}{1 + 10\%} = \$4.55$$

TABLE 8.5

Hedge P&L 4

Case		Call	Hedge	All-in
Up	1.6000	(1.50 − 1.60) = 0.10	+ 50% * (1.60 − 1.50) = + 0.05	− 0.05
Even	1.5000			
Down	1.4000	0	+ 50% * (1.40 − 1.50) = − 0.05	− 0.05

T A B L E 8.6

Hedge P&L 5

Case		Put	Hedge
Up	P&L =	0	+ hedge ∗ (up − forward)

T A B L E 8.7

Hedge P&L 6

Case		Put	Hedge
Down	P&L =	(down − strike)	+ hedge ∗ (down − forward)

We can follow the same general approach for a put option. Knowing that a put is the opposite of a call leads us to believe that when the price of the market reference moves up, the only factor of relevance is the hedge, as in Table 8.6.

When the price moves down, however, there is an impact on both the put and the hedge, as noted in Table 8.7.

Setting these equal to each other and solving for the hedge yields:

$$\text{Hedge} \times (\text{Up} - \text{Forward})$$
$$= (\text{Down} - \text{Strike}) + \text{Hedge} \times (\text{Down} - \text{Forward})$$
$$\text{Hedge} \times \text{Up} - \text{Hedge} \times \text{Forward}$$
$$= \text{Down} - \text{Strike} + \text{Hedge} \times \text{Down} - \text{Hedge} \times \text{Forward}$$
$$\text{Hedge} \times \text{Up} - \text{Hedge} \times \text{Down} = \text{Down} - \text{Strike} \tag{8.4}$$
$$\text{Hedge}_{\text{Put}} = \frac{\text{Down} - \text{Strike}}{\text{Up} - \text{Down}}$$

Because the down value is always less than the strike, in this simplified approach the hedge of the put is a negative number, meaning that the hedge of a put involves the sale of a specific amount of the underlying asset. This is true of all puts: the buyer of the put has the right to sell the asset to the seller, so the writer's hedge must involve selling some amount of the asset.

Binomial Tree Valuation

In order to illustrate the binomial framework above we made a simplifying assumption, i.e., the £/$ exchange rate movements in one year are assumed to occupy one of two states ($1.60 or $1.40). To make the process more realistic we can replace this assumption with calculations that depend on market conditions:

- The number of steps in the binomial process is increased to provide a larger number of possible spot values at option expiry.
- The percentage of up or down movement is determined by the amount of uncertainty in the underlying instrument, i.e., the volatility of the instrument. The upward or downward moves at each time step are based on the volatility adjusted by the amount of time.
- The weight given to an upward or downward movement is determined by:
  - □ the size of the up/down moves at each time step
  - □ the level of interest rates in both £ and $

The weights are selected so that the weighted average of the possible future spot rates at each time step equals the market forward rate. By adding more time intervals and allowing the rate to move up or down at each step, the possible movement of the currency rate assumes the shape of a lattice, as illustrated in Figure 8.10. This is, of course, a representation of the simple pegboard game introduced above.

F I G U R E 8.10

General Binomial Lattice

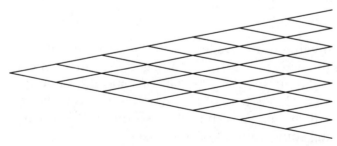

As more steps are included in the lattice, the number of possible final spot rates grows to reflect the continuous range of final spot values assumed by the normal distribution. This means that more steps or nodes in the lattice lead to improved pricing—though the degree of improvement becomes very small once the number of steps becomes very large.[1]

This discussion serves as an introduction to basic option pricing. We shall expand on pricing in the next chapter, with a particular focus on more detailed construction of the binomial tree.

CHAPTER EXERCISES

1. The one-year forward price of an asset is 100. The forward price in one year will be either 85 or 115, as shown below:

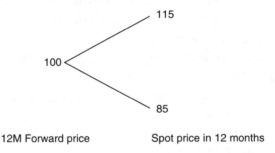

12M Forward price   Spot price in 12 months

   a. What is the correct hedge of a short put struck at 95 in terms of amount and position (e.g., purchase or sale)?
   b. What is the price of the put struck at 95 if the one-year interest rate is 5%?
2. What is the relationship between option premium, intrinsic value, and time value?
   a. Option premium + Intrinsic value = Time value
   b. Option premium = Intrinsic value + Time value
   c. Option premium + Time value = Intrinsic value
   d. Option premium < Intrinsic value + Time value
   e. None of the above

---

1 Binomial models return the same prices for European options as the closed-form Black-Scholes model we consider in the next chapter. The benefit of the binomial model is, of course, that it can be used to value American-style options and other options that cannot be accommodated via a standard Black-Scholes framework.

3. What is the intrinsic value of a put option on a one-year forward £/$ exchange rate with a strike of $1.5000, premium of $0.0765, and a market forward rate of $1.5200?

    a. 0

    b. 0.02

    c. –0.02

    d. 0.0765

    e. None of the above

4. What happens to time value as an option approaches expiration (other factors remaining constant)?

    a. Time value increases, but only for out-of-the-money options

    b. Time value is constant for in-the-money options

    c. Time value increases for in-the-money options

    d. Time value declines for all options

    e. None of the above

5. Which of the following is/are true for in-the-money options?

    a. Calls: market price > strike price, puts: market price < strike price

    b. Calls: market price < strike price, puts: market price > strike price

    c. Calls: market price > strike price, puts: market price > strike price

    d. Calls: market price < strike price, puts: market price < strike price

    e. None of the above

6. Which of the following is/are true for out-of-the-money options?

    a. Calls: market price > strike price, puts: market price < strike price

    b. Calls: market price < strike price, puts: market price > strike price

    c. Calls: market price > strike price, puts: market price > strike price

   d. Calls: market price < strike price, puts: market price
      < strike price
   e. None of the above
7. Consider the following positions:
   Long call, strike 100, current asset price 101
   Long put, strike 99, current asset price 101
   Time value of call: 1
   Time value of put: 1
   Which of the following is/are true?
      a. Call intrinsic value = 1, time value = 1 option price = 2
      b. Put intrinsic value = –1, time value = 1, option
         price = 0
      c. Call intrinsic value = –1, time value =1, option
         price = 0
      d. b and c are true
      e. None are true
8. Which of the following is not an input into the pricing of
   a currency option?
      a. Domestic interest rate
      b. Spot rate
      c. Volatility
      d. Dividends
      e. Time to expiry
9. If the strike price of a call option on gold is increased,
   the value of the option will:
      a. Increase
      b. Decrease
      c. Remain the same
      d. Depends on the volatility of gold
      e. None of the above
10. Rising volatility increases the value of:
      a. Call options
      b. Put options
      c. Call and put options

    d. Depends on the strike price

    e. None of the above

11. As dividends are increased on a stock:

    a. Call prices decrease and put prices increase

    b. Call prices increase and put prices decrease

    c. Call prices and put prices decrease

    d. Call prices and put prices increase

    e. None of the above

Option Pricing Models

INTRODUCTION

As we have noted in the last chapter, proper option valuation is essential in order for market participants to be able to arrange efficient and accurate hedge and speculative positions. Academics and financial intermediaries have made considerable advances in developing option pricing models over the past few decades, and new variations and enhancements appear on a relatively frequent basis to accommodate new types of option products (i.e., new exotic option variants). In this chapter we focus on the underpinnings of the key market models that are used in the equity, commodity, currency, and interest rate markets, with specific coverage of the seminal Black-Scholes model, the binomial model, and various one-factor and two-factor interest rate models. Our approach in this chapter is practical rather than academic. For those readers interested in the mathematical treatment, however, we provide a list of additional mathematical references in the notes.

THE BLACK-SCHOLES MODEL

Fischer Black and Myron Scholes published their groundbreaking paper on option pricing in 1973.[1] Prior to their work there was no established option pricing methodology that allowed buyers and

---

1 Robert Merton was also working on similar approaches at the same time.

sellers to agree on prices; indeed, pricing approaches were not particularly rigorous and often inaccurate. The Black-Scholes model was first used to price stock options. A key component of the model, risk-neutral valuation, suggested that in order to value a stock option, it was not necessary to determine a specific investor return; all that was needed was the risk-free rate. This discovery allowed stock options to be valued in a tractable manner.

The Black-Scholes model, designed as a closed-form solution for European options on nondividend paying stocks, has become a cornerstone of option valuation. Subsequent refinements and approaches have expanded the industry's valuation choices. To be sure, the Black-Scholes model has limitations (i.e., it is valid only for European-style options) and depends on various assumptions (i.e., volatility and interest rate inputs are constant). Nevertheless, market participants have adopted and enhanced the model over the years and many types of options are regularly traded to the Black-Scholes value.

The Formula

The Black-Scholes model builds on the general minimum value of an option (market price (S) – strike price (X) for a call, $X - S$ for a put) by considering both the present value of a potential payoff and the probability of option exercise. The underlying asset price is assumed to move up and down in very small increments, without price gaps or jumps. Since the option is characterized by a future exercise/expiry date, the present value of the potential payoff is discounted on a continuous basis; this yields a key component of the model. The next component relates to the probability that the price of the asset will rise to a level where the option becomes exercisable (within the allocated time frame)—this is simply the probability that the option will pay off, and is described by a value from the cumulative normal distribution function. The remaining component is simply the probability that the option will be exercised, and is again generated as a value from the cumulative normal distribution function.

From a descriptive perspective, we can describe qualitatively the value of a call and a put under the Black-Scholes framework as:

$$\text{Call price} = [\text{benefits of option} * \text{weight of benefits}] - [\text{costs} * \text{weight of costs}] \tag{9.1}$$

Put price = [costs * weight of costs]
               − [benefits of option * weight of benefits]   (9.2)

The "weights" shown above are dependent on the variables we have described in Chapter 8, including current price of the underlying reference asset, strike price, volatility, time to expiration, and interest rates. Note that dividends do not factor into the core Black-Scholes framework, which is based on nondividend paying stocks.

The mathematical formulas that correspond to this intuitive explanation are given as:

$$C = SN(d_1) - Xe^{-rt}N(d_2) \qquad (9.3)$$

and

$$P = Xe^{-rt}N(-d_2) - SN(-d_1) \qquad (9.4)$$

where

$$d_1 = \frac{ln\left(\dfrac{S}{X}\right) + rt}{\sigma\sqrt{t}} + \frac{\sigma\sqrt{t}}{2}$$

$$d_2 = d_1 - \sigma\sqrt{t}$$

and

S	is the current stock price
X	is the strike price
r	is the interest rate
t	is the time to expiration
σ	is the volatility
$N(\ )$	is the cumulative normal standard distribution function

The benefits and costs described above correspond, respectively, to the variables denoted by $N(\ )$, S, and $Xe^{(-rT)}$. Knowing this, we can gain some insight into the direction of call and put prices as variables change. For example, the call equation shows that a rise in stock price S will increase the call's value, while a rise in the strike price X will decrease its value. It is somewhat less obvious to see how an increase in interest rates or time to expiration affects call prices; however, if the "cost" of $Xe^{(-rT)}$ is known to decrease with an increase in r or T, then call prices will rise.

Valuation models and arbitrage forces indicate that the value of a call option less the value of a put option is equal to the present value of the asset price less the strike price. A call can thus be viewed as a leveraged position in an asset, protected by a put, while a put can be regarded as a short position in an asset, protected by a long call. This concept, known as put-call parity, means that the purchase of a European call option and the sale of a European put option with the same strike and expiry generates a leveraged investment in the underlying asset (less the value of cash payments on the underlying asset over the life of the option). This relationship is commonly shown as:

$$C - P = Se^{-rt} - X \qquad\qquad (9.5)$$

Volatility under Black-Scholes

Volatility relates to the variability in the daily prices of the asset underlying an option. For a stock option, this relates to daily stock prices, for a currency option it relates to daily spot rates, and so forth. Volatility, denoted in the Black-Scholes formula as standard deviation (σ), can be measured by analyzing historical price data. Specifically, volatility is defined as one standard deviation in the expected distribution of "log price changes." This can be illustrated through the process outlined below.

Given two consecutive closing prices (S_1 = closing price on day 1, S_2 = closing price on day 2), the daily return is the ratio of the two:

$$\text{Daily Return} = \frac{S_2}{S_1} \qquad\qquad (9.6)$$

This return is based on one day's change and represents daily compounding. A convenient way to calculate the amount of daily price change is based on continuous compounding, which involves calculating the natural logarithm of the daily price change:

$$\text{Daily Return} = ln\left(\frac{S_2}{S_1}\right) \qquad\qquad (9.7)$$

Thus, if a stock price closes at 50 yesterday and at 52 today, then the continuously compounded annual return of the daily price change is:

$$\text{Daily Return} = ln\left(\frac{52}{50}\right) = 3.9221\%$$

Using the natural log is convenient because an upward move in the asset price has the same relative price change as a downward move. For instance, if the price drops from 52 to 50 the next day, the change is again:

$$\text{Daily Return} = ln\left(\frac{50}{52}\right) = -3.9221\%$$

By way of comparison, if we calculate the price change in the usual discrete manner, the upward and downward changes do not yield the same answer. For instance, an upward move from 50 to 52 represents a gain of 4%:

$$\text{Daily Return} = \frac{52 - 50}{50} = 4.00\%$$

The downward move on the following day is, however, smaller:

$$\text{Daily Return} = \frac{50 - 52}{52} = -3.8462\%$$

Under the volatility framework we assume that the daily relative price changes are normally distributed. When the natural logarithm of a variable is normally distributed, the variable itself is said to be lognormally distributed. It is technically correct, therefore, to say that stock prices are lognormally distributed and daily relative stock price changes (or returns) are normally distributed.

The historical volatility of a price series is therefore computed as the standard deviation of the natural logarithm of relative price changes. Assume that the observed behavior of variables whose daily price changes are normally distributed is as shown previously. Common sense says that upward and downward price movements will be greater over longer periods of time. This belief is captured by assuming that the price returns are a random process subject to the normal distribution. The amount of relative change every day is not predictable, but an examination of daily relative changes over time shows that most of them are near zero, while only a few of them are very large. An important corollary of this is that each daily return is totally independent of the return achieved on any prior day. A consequence of this behavior is that the annual volatility and daily volatility of a normal distribution are related to one another as follows:

$$\sigma_a = \sigma\sqrt{T} \tag{9.8}$$

where

σ is the daily standard deviation
σ_a is the annual standard deviation
T is the option's maturity

For instance, if we assume that a year has 260 trading days, then:

$$\sigma_a = \sigma \,(16.1245)$$

Using the historical price data in Table 9.1, we illustrate the computation of daily and annual volatility.

If the 10 most recent days of data are used to compute volatility, the results are likely to differ from those based on the past 30, 50,

TABLE 9.1

Historical Price Data and Volatilities

Daily Price	Price Change	LN of Price Change
50		
51	1.0200	0.0198
53	1.0392	0.0385
52	0.9811	−0.0190
51	0.9808	−0.0194
48	0.9412	−0.0606
50	1.0417	0.0408
54	1.0800	0.0770
56	1.0370	0.0364
53	0.9464	−0.0551
51	0.9623	−0.0385
Daily Mean =		0.0020
Daily Volatility =		0.0468
Annual Volatility =		0.7546

or 100 days. Because the volatility experienced most recently is likely to produce option prices that best reflect the current market, a smaller number of days is preferable for the computation. However, if this is too little price data, the results may be suspect. The market generally balances these opposing forces by using approximately one month of daily market prices (i.e., 22 business days of rolling data).

As we have noted, the volatility needed to compute the price of an option that expires in the future is based on the daily price changes we expect between today and expiry. Clearly, this cannot be measured because it is based on events that have not yet occurred. To price an option, we must therefore express a view based on all available market information and any expectations regarding future events. We already know that volatility computed on what has occurred in the past is known as historical volatility. Traders and market-makers tend to supplement this computation with volatility contained in market prices, which is commonly known as implied volatility. To determine implied volatility, we observe traded option prices in the market and use them in the Black-Scholes formula to solve for (or imply) the volatility that generates the traded price. This implied volatility will vary from day to day, but by averaging the results over time (e.g., 30 days) variations can be smoothed. This value can then be used as a proxy for the volatility input into the Black-Scholes equation.

Extensions of the Black-Scholes Model

The success of the original Black-Scholes model, coupled with its somewhat restrictive assumptions, led ultimately to the development of various extensions, including:

- The Black-Scholes model with dividends: used for valuing options on dividend paying stocks
- The Black model: used for valuing commodity options and certain classes of interest rate options
- The Garman-Kohlhagen model: used for valuing foreign exchange options

The binomial model, which we discuss in detail later in this chapter, can also be viewed as a generalized version of the

Black-Scholes framework, where the Black-Scholes result is a special case of the binomial.[2]

The Black Model

Black developed a model to value options on futures contracts or commodities. When a futures call (put) option is exercised, the buyer acquires a long (short) position in a futures contract. This feature demands a refinement to the original model based on the following assumptions: execution costs are zero and tax consequences are negligible, interest rates are constant, and futures prices are governed by a random walk process. The Black model has been successfully applied to the valuation of futures options on individual commodities, interest rates, and foreign exchange rates.

That said, when the Black model is used to value bond options, it is implicitly assumed that the bond price volatility remains constant through the life of the option. This assumption contradicts an important aspect of bond prices: since a bond is always repaid at par at maturity, its price becomes less volatile as maturity approaches. As a result, when the Black model is used to price interest rate options, it is more appropriate to model the interest rate as the variable that changes through time. Note that there is also a subtle inconsistency in applying the Black model to interest rate options: the option's value is the probability-weighted gain expected at maturity, discounted back to present value terms by the prevailing interest rate. By discounting all the expected gains at the same interest rate, any connection between rate movements and the option payoffs is implicitly ignored. These limitations reflect the fact that the Black model can address movements in a single underlying asset rather than the entire term structure of interest rates.

The Garman-Kohlhagen Model

Garman and Kohlhagen (GK) devised a variation of the Black-Scholes model for European options that allowed pricing of European puts and calls on foreign currencies. This model requires

---

2 The binomial model is equivalent to the Black-Scholes model under the following conditions: there exist an infinite number of up/down movements in the reference asset from today until expiration; the magnitude of the movement and the probability of an up/down movement are defined by market parameters; the option is only exercisable at maturity. The Black-Scholes is thus a special subset of the binomial process.

six parameters: the domestic and foreign currency interest rates plus the four other standard parameters for option valuation under Black-Scholes. GK also developed an alternative formulation of the model, which can accommodate forward, rather than spot, foreign exchange rates.

BINOMIAL MODEL

Cox, Ross, and Rubinstein introduced a numerical approach to valuing options in 1979. This approach, known as the binomial model, is a flexible process for option pricing that allows an approximate solution to be found for any period in an option's life; this makes it quite suitable for valuing American options and other complex contracts.

We introduced a simple description of the binomial model in the last chapter: under the framework the life of the option is first divided into a large number of small time periods of equal length, and at the end of each discrete interval the price of the underlying asset is allowed to assume two new values. Using these time intervals and the assumption of price movements, a tree of prices is constructed from trade date to maturity. Starting at the tree's endpoints, where the option carries only the known intrinsic value, the values at all other points in the tree are computed. As these intervening computations are developed (backwards from maturity to trade date), the price of the option is derived. By computing the potential worth of the option at each node on the tree, we see that it is possible to account for the value of the option at any time—meaning valuation of early exercise contracts is possible.

Binomial Pricing in Practice

In order to illustrate how to price an option using the binomial framework we develop in this section a continuing example that incorporates each step in the process. We begin by noting that the binomial tree assumes that an asset price can move up or down from period to period:

- The probability that the spot asset price moves up over the next period is denoted by p.
- The probability that it moves down over the next period is therefore $(1 - p)$.

When prices move up, they move up by a certain amount:

■ 1 + the percentage up movement is denoted by u.

Prices move down by a certain amount, too:

■ 1 + the percentage down movement is given by d.

We can solve for p, $(1-p)$, u and d using current market conditions. The volatility of the asset price determines how far up and down the underlying price might move, while interest rates for each asset determine the relation between the forward price and current price.

We define the up and down movements in terms of volatility, adjusted for length of time between steps, via:

$$u = e^{\sigma\sqrt{t}} \tag{9.9}$$

$$d = e^{-\sigma\sqrt{t}} \tag{9.10}$$

The magnitude of the upward and downward movements is directly related to the volatility of the underlying. The greater the volatility, the greater the differential between up and down movements. We observe this characteristic through the data in Table 9.2.

We can state the future, or forward price, in terms of the current (or spot) price using present value factors. For

T A B L E 9.2

Upward/Downward Asset Price Movements

Percent Movements		
Volatility	Up	Down
5%	2.53%	−2.47%
10%	5.13%	−4.88%
15%	7.79%	−7.23%
20%	10.52%	−9.52%
25%	13.31%	−11.75%
30%	16.18%	−13.93%
35%	19.12%	−16.05%
40%	22.14%	−18.13%

instance, for an equity price or index we use the relevant dividend yield:

$$\text{Forward} = \text{Spot} * \frac{PVf_{\text{dividend yield}}}{PVf_{\text{interest rate}}} \qquad (9.11)$$

We define probability so that the weighted average of possible outcomes generates the forward price for each period. Using simple algebra we can solve for probability p as follows:

$$[p * \text{Spot} * u] + [(1-p) * \text{Spot} * d] = \text{Spot} * \frac{PVf_{\text{d}}}{PVf_{\text{i}}} \qquad (9.12)$$

where

$$p = \frac{\dfrac{PVf_{\text{d}}}{PVf_{\text{i}}} - d}{u - d} \qquad (9.13)$$

Thus, the probability of upward and downward moves is defined in terms of the differential between interest rates and dividend yields, adjusted by volatility.

Using the binomial methodology outlined above and the sample data reflected in Table 9.3, we can price a two-year at-the-money DAX call option (strike 2165).

The upward/downward percentage movements for each quarter, using (9.9) and (9.10), are equal to:

$$u = \exp(0.20\sqrt{0.25}) = 1.105171 = 110.5171\%$$
$$d = \exp(-0.20\sqrt{0.25}) = 0.904837 = 90.4387\%$$

T A B L E   9.3

Sample DAX Data

Spot DAX	2165.00
Maturity	2 years
Length of each interval	0.25 years
€ 2-year rate	6.25%
DAX dividend yield	4.0%
Volatility	20%

T A B L E 9.4

DAX Option Data

% Up Move	110.5171%
% Down Move	90.4837%
Probability of an Up Move	50.3178%
Probability of a Down Move	49.6822%

Using *PV* factors derived from two-year € interest rates and the DAX dividend yield, we obtain the following probabilities:

$$p = \frac{\dfrac{0.99005}{0.984496} - 0.904837}{1.105171 - 0.904837} = 50.3178\%$$

$$1 - p = 0.496819 = 49.6819\%$$

These results are summarized in Table 9.4.

Possible spot rates for the end of the first quarter, based on 20% volatility, are calculated as follows:

$$\text{Spot} * \%\text{UpMove} = 2165 * 1.105171 = 2392.70$$
$$\text{Spot} * \%\text{DownMove} = 2165 * 0.904837 = 1958.97$$

These form the first "nodes" of the binomial tree:

Quarter	1
	2392.70
2165.00	
	1958.97

The associated up/down probabilities for the first quarterly period are:

Probability	1
	50.3178%
100.00%	
	49.6822%

At the end of the first quarter the average of the two possible outcomes, weighted by their probabilities, must equal the forward DAX price calculated using the interest rate/dividend yield differential:

$$\text{Forward} = 2165.00 * \exp\left(\frac{\text{rate} - \text{dividend yield}}{4}\right) = 2177.21$$

$$\text{Forward} = (2392.70 * 0.3178\%) + (1958.97 * 49.6822\%)$$
$$= 2177.21$$

This must hold true since we solved for the probabilities of up and down moves to force them to return the forward DAX value.

The process used to calculate the forward value of the DAX at the end of the first quarter can be extended to derive a range of possible forward DAX values at every quarter-end over the next two years, as noted in Table 9.5. At each date, the weighted average of the possible forward values recombines into the forward DAX

T A B L E 9.5

DAX Values

Quarter	1	2	3	4	5	6	7	8
Forwards	2177.21	2189.49	2201.84	2214.26	2226.75	2239.32	2251.95	2264.65
								4818.30
							4359.77	
						3944.89		3944.89
					3569.48		3569.48	
				3229.80		3229.80		3229.80
			2922.44		2922.44		2922.44	
		2644.34		2644.34		2644.34		2644.34
	2392.70		2392.70		2392.70		2392.70	
2165.00		2165.00		2165.00		2165.00		2165.00
	1958.97		1958.97		1958.97		1958.97	
		1772.55		1772.55		1772.55		1772.55
			1603.87		1603.87		1603.87	
				1451.24		1451.24		1451.24
					1313.14		1313.14	
						1188.18		1188.18
							1075.11	
								972.80

F I G U R E 9.1

Range of Forward DAX Values

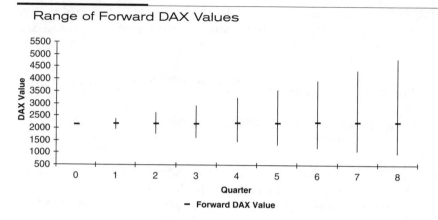

curve. Note that this lattice of values assumes the general form described in the last chapter.

We can depict the same information via the diagram in Figure 9.1.

Each point on the tree is associated with a specific probability based on the forward values and volatility described above. The probability of being at any point in the tree is determined by the number of possible paths needed to get to that point and the probability of each path occurring.

For quarter one there is only one path to each of the two possible points. The price can only move up or down. For quarter two the options increase, as follows:

Quarter	1	2
		1
	1	
1		2
	1	
		1

This means that there are two possible paths to get to the middle point in the tree at quarter two: the price can move up and then down; or, the price can move down and then up.

The probabilities associated with these possible paths are given as:

Quarter	1	2
		0.2532
	0.5032	
1		0.5000
	0.4968	
		0.2468

The probability of being at a specific point in the tree is the sum of the probabilities of each path to that point occurring, as in Tables 9.6 and 9.7.

Most of the weight, in terms of the number of possible paths and the probability of being at a point in the tree, falls in the "middle" of the tree. Very few paths, and very little probabilistic weight, are assigned to points at the high or low extremes of the tree.

T A B L E 9.6

Number of Possible Price Paths

Quarter	1	2	3	4	5	6	7	8
								1
							1	
						1		8
					1		7	
				1		6		28
			1		5		21	
		1		4		15		56
			3		10		35	
1		2		6		20		70
			3		10		35	
		1		4		15		56
			1		5		21	
				1		6		28
					1		7	
						1		8
							1	
								1

T A B L E 9.7

Probabilities of Price Paths

Quarter	1	2	3	4	5	6	7	8
								0.0041
							0.0082	
						0.0162		0.0325
					0.0323		0.0564	
				0.0641		0.0962		0.1122
			0.1274		0.1592		0.1672	
		0.2532		0.2532		0.2373		0.2215
	0.5032		0.3774		0.3145		0.2751	
1.0000		0.5000		0.3750		0.3125		0.2734
	0.4968		0.3726		0.3105		0.2717	
		0.2468		0.2468		0.2314		0.2160
			0.1226		0.1533		0.1609	
				0.0609		0.0914		0.1066
					0.0303		0.0530	
						0.0150		0.0301
							0.0075	
								0.0037

Let us next derive an option price by recombining through the tree, from expiry (quarter eight) to trade date. We begin by deriving the potential forward values at quarter eight and subtracting them from the strike to generate a measure of intrinsic value. The results are noted in Table 9.8.

T A B L E 9.8

DAX Values at Expiry

$4818.30 - 2165 = 2653.30$
$3944.89 - 2165 = 1779.89$
$3229.80 - 2165 = 1064.80$
$2644.34 - 2165 = 479.34$
$2165.00 - 2165 = 0.00$
$1772.55 - 2165 < 0.00$
$1451.24 - 2165 < 0.00$
$1188.18 - 2165 < 0.00$
$972.80 - 2165 < 0.00$

T A B L E 9.9

Price of DAX Option

	Quarter	1	2	3	4	5	6	7	8
									2653.30
								2184.96	A
							1768.38	C	1779.89
						1398.13		1402.53	B
					1069.33		1067.46		1064.80
				788.60		770.22		761.93	
Option			561.52		529.28		493.59		479.34
Premium		387.29		349.32		302.05		237.45	
259.72			223.11		178.13		117.63		0.00
		138.75		102.36		58.27		0.00	
			57.70		28.87		0.00		0.00
				14.30		0.00		0.00	
					0.00		0.00		0.00
						0.00		0.00	
							0.00		0.00
								0.00	
									0.00

Our next step is to move backwards through the tree by discounting each intrinsic value back one period, adjusting by the probability of an upward or downward move. For each of the prior quarters, results are computed by taking the *PV* or the probability-weighted average of up/down moves. For instance, in Table 9.9 node "C" is calculated from nodes "A" and "B." After moving backwards through the entire tree, we obtain a single value at time 0—this represents the price of the option. Table 9.9 summarizes the results.

The price of the European option using the binomial tree is 259.72. Note that if we were to use the same data in the Black-Scholes model, we would obtain a price of 262.10. If the tree presented above had more branches and nodes, its value would converge on the Black-Scholes value, demonstrating that the Black-Scholes is a special case of the binomial model.

A European option can also be priced using a binomial tree and the final period (e.g., expiration). To do so we perform the following steps:

- Calculate the intrinsic value at the final period. There is no more time value at this point so it is not a consideration.

T A B L E   9.10

European Option Pricing Using Terminal Values

	Forward Value	Intrinsic Value	Probability	Weighted Value
	4818.30	2653.30	0.0041	10.90
	3944.89	1779.89	0.0325	57.77
	3229.80	1064.80	0.1122	119.44
	2644.34	479.34	0.2215	106.18
	2165.00	0.00	0.2734	0.00
	1772.55	0.00	0.2160	0.00
	1451.24	0.00	0.1066	0.00
	1188.18	0.00	0.0301	0.00
	972.80	0.00	0.0037	0.00
Sum of Weighted Intrinsic Value				294.30
PV of Sum				259.72
Compared to Going through Tree				259.72

- Weight each intrinsic value by the probability associated with that point in the tree.
- Add up the weighted intrinsic values at maturity and discount the results back to the present.

This yields the value of the European option.

This process effectively condenses the method described earlier—but it can only be used to value European options. The results are summarized in Table 9.10.

The binomial tree can also be used to produce a range of possible future spot prices. We know that each possible spot price outcome has some associated probability of occurrence. We noted earlier that most of the outcomes are likely to be contained in the "middle" portion of the curve, with only small probabilities associated with extremely high or low values. This suggests that the distribution of values in the tree will approximate the normal probability function.

A distribution function is a way to describe a process that has uncertainty. In option pricing this obviously relates to the future value of the underlying asset. The distribution provides us with valuable information on the mean and standard deviation, which we can incorporate into the pricing function. Figure 9.2 illustrates the standard deviations of a normal distribution.

Normal Distribution

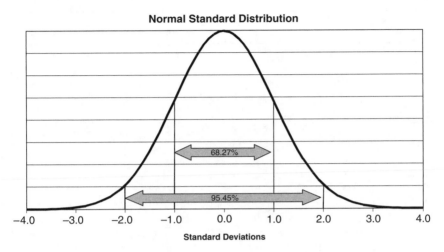

We can calculate the future spot price by using the normal score (i.e., number of standard deviations from the mean), volatility and time:

$$\text{Spot}_{\text{at time } t} = \text{Spot}_{\text{today}} * \exp(\text{normal score} * \text{vol} * \sqrt{t}) \quad (9.14)$$

For instance, for two standard deviations and 20% volatility this result is equal to:

$$\text{Spot}_t = 2165 * \exp(2 * 0.20 * \sqrt{2}) = 3811.82$$

By creating a normal score at each point in the tree we can produce a range of forward spot prices and calculate the option premium using either recombination or terminal pricing. The key to this process is to regard each node in the tree as a possible "state." The tree begins at time 0 in state 0 and then moves up or down. The "states" for each period are shown in Table 9.11.

For instance, at time 1 there are 2 states, 0 and 1; at time 5 there are 6 states, 0, through 5; and so on. Normal scores, which have a mean of 0 and standard deviation of 1, are created from ordinary series of numbers through the following simple formula:

$$\text{Normal Score} = \frac{(\text{Number} - \text{Mean})}{\text{Standard Deviation}} \quad (9.15)$$

T A B L E 9.11

Option Node States

Quarter	1	2	3	4	5	6	7	8
								8
							7	
						6		7
					5		6	
				4		5		6
			3		4		5	
		2		3		4		5
	1		2		3		4	
0		1		2		3		4
	0		1		2		3	
		0		1		2		3
			0		1		2	
				0		1		2
					0		1	
						0		1
							0	
								0

We can define the mean and standard deviation at each node in the tree as follows:

$$\text{Mean} = \text{Quarter} \div 2 \tag{9.16}$$

For instance, when quarter = 8, mean = 4.
Similarly,

$$\text{Standard Deviation} = \sqrt{p * (1 - p) * \text{Quarter}} \tag{9.17}$$

For Quarter 8 and $p = 0.5$, $SD = \sqrt{0.5 * 0.5 * 8} = \sqrt{2} = 1.414$

The normal scores for each node in the tree are highlighted in Table 9.12.

We can use these normal scores to derive the spot prices in the binomial tree, as in Table 9.13.

Not surprisingly, these spot prices match the ones derived in the earlier section.

The power of the binomial tree lies in its simplicity and ability to show exactly how the option premium is generated. As a result, it is particularly effective in valuing American or Bermudan

T A B L E 9.12

Normal Scores for Binomial Tree

Quarter	1	2	3	4	5	6	7	8
								2.8284
							2.6458	
						2.4495		2.1213
					2.2361		1.8898	
				2.0000		1.6330		1.4142
			1.7321		1.3416		1.1339	
		1.4142		1.0000		0.8165		0.7071
	1.0000		0.5774		0.4472		0.3780	
		0.0000		0.0000		0.0000		0.0000
	−1.0000		−0.5774		−0.4472		−0.3780	
		−1.4142		−1.0000		−0.8165		−0.7071
			−1.7321		−1.3416		−1.1339	
				−2.0000		−1.6330		−1.4142
					−2.2361		−1.8898	
						−2.4495		−2.1213
							−2.6458	
								−2.8284

T A B L E 9.13

Spot Prices in Binomial Tree

Quarter	1	2	3	4	5	6	7	8
								4818.30
							4359.77	
						3944.89		3944.89
					3569.48		3569.48	
				3229.80		3229.80		3229.80
			2922.44		2922.44		2922.44	
		2644.34		2644.34		2644.34		2644.34
	2392.70		2392.70		2392.70		2392.70	
		2165.00		2165.00		2165.00		2165.00
	1958.97		1958.97		1958.97		1958.97	
		1772.55		1772.55		1772.55		1772.55
			1603.87		1603.87		1603.87	
				1451.24		1451.24		1451.24
					1313.14		1313.14	
						1188.18		1188.18
							1075.11	
								972.80

options, or other complex options such as we have described in Part I. Note that we expand on the binomial model in Appendix II when we discuss pricing of correlated options.

TERM STRUCTURE MODELS

While valuing options on stocks, commodities, and currencies relies on the price of a single reference asset at a point in time, valuation of interest rate options depends on the shape of an entire yield curve—a more complex undertaking. Accordingly, significant efforts have been applied over the past two decades to the creation of term structure models. While these models can be described and classified in various ways, we do so by dividing them into one-factor term structure models, two-factor term structure models, and market models.

Each interest rate modeling approach has advantages and disadvantages. For instance, one-factor models (such as Rendleman-Bartter, Vasicek, and Cox-Ingersoll-Ross) are analytically tractable and relatively simple to implement, but may not always provide the most realistic view of the market. Two-factor models (including Ho and Lee and Heath-Jarrow-Morton) are complex to build and calibrate but may offer a more realistic view of the market once implemented. Market models, like two-factor models, conform more precisely to market views, but can be analytically difficult to create and calibrate. In practice, institutions may use a model based primarily on the type of options business being executed. Thus, a bank focused on exotics related to long-term securities may prefer a market model or a two-factor model, while an investment fund dealing primarily in short-dated options on short-dated securities may select a one-factor model.

One-Factor (Equilibrium) Term Structure Models

One-factor (or equilibrium) models define the term structure of interest rates by describing how the short-term rate will evolve through time. The process followed by the short rate is described by the model, which must be calibrated to the current market yield curve. Although one-factor models can be made to fit the current market yield curve very well, rarely is there a precise fit. As a result, prices for bonds or swaps may be slightly different from those observed in the market. Note that a one-factor model does not mean that all rates forming the yield curve are the same, or that they move by the same amount; in any short time frame all rates move in the same direction, but by different amounts.

One-factor models are typically built atop the basic geometric Brownian motion (GBM) equation:

$$dr = adt + \sigma dz \qquad (9.18)$$

where

a is the drift rate

σ is the standard deviation of rates,

and the path of rates dr is normally distributed with mean $(r_0 + at)$ and variance $\sigma 2t$

While this process is fairly easy to implement, it has several disadvantages: it allows for negative short-term rates, which is unrealistic; the drift rate of interest rates is constant, so that if $a > 0$ short-term rates can rise without any boundary (i.e., there is no mean reversion of rates (or return to long-term average levels), which is contrary to market experience); and, the volatility of the short-rate is the same whether rates are high or low, despite the fact that evidence suggests that short-rates are more volatile when they are higher.

To overcome these problems, enhancements have been introduced over the past years. One example is the Rendleman-Bartter model:

$$dr = a(r)dt + \sigma(r)dz \qquad (9.19)$$

This model is considered more realistic as the drift rate, a, and standard deviation, σ, are functions of the short-rate r. This means that interest rates cannot be negative, which is a far more realistic approach. However, the other drawbacks mentioned above remain.

The Vasicek model, given as:

$$dr = a(b - r)dt + \sigma(r)dz \qquad (9.20)$$

is considered to be a further refinement, because it does not permit negative rates and incorporates mean reversion into the process via the term $(b - r)$. However, the trade-off between simplicity and tractability begins to arise: while the Vasicek model may be more accurate than a standard GBM or Rendleman model, it is more difficult to calibrate.

Another one-factor approach is the Cox-Ingersoll-Ross model, given as:

$$dr = a(b - r)dt + \sigma \sqrt{(r)}dz \qquad (9.21)$$

This model attempts to overcome all of the disadvantages cited above, because it does not allow negative rates, it accommodates mean reversion, and it sets the variance of short-rate proportional to the square root of rates—so as short-rates rise, the volatility of short-rates rises. Once again, the increased level of realism translates into a more complex implementation process.

Two-Factor Term Structure Models

Two-factor models (or forward rate models) are more complex to calibrate and implement but can yield more stable and accurate results. The most important and useful two-factor models are so-called "no-arbitrage" models that are consistent with the market term structure. Unlike other interest rate models, no-arbitrage term structure models are intended to fit the market, making them more useful for market practitioners. They are, of course, more computationally rigorous than models based on short-rate evolution.

One example of the two-factor process is the Ho and Lee model, given as:

$$dr = \theta(t)dt + \sigma dz \qquad (9.22)$$

where $\theta(t) = Ft(0, t)+ \sigma^2 \, dt$, chosen to fit the initial term structure of the yield curve

The process is analytically tractable, but all spot and forward rates have the same standard deviation and rates do not mean revert.[3]

Another example is the Hull and White model (hybrid short/forward rate model):

$$dr = (\theta(t) - ar)dt + \sigma dz \qquad (9.23)$$

This is essentially an extended Vasicek/Ho and Lee approach with mean reversion and volatility structure determined by a and σ.

---

3 Various no-arbitrage extensions of Ho and Lee have appeared over the years
   (e.g., the original Cox, Ingersoll, Ross model has been recast in no-arbitrage form).

Various other models exist, e.g., Black-Karasinski, Heath-Jarrow-Morton, Brace-Garacek-Musiala, and so forth, each with particular advantages and disadvantages.[4]

LIBOR and Market Models

Market models take as inputs forward LIBOR (or swap) rates and their observable volatilities, and can be used to value caps, floors, swaptions, and more complex swap derivatives, like Bermudan swaptions and constant maturity spread-based coupons.

Market models evolve the entire LIBOR forward curve by assigning separate volatilities to each forward LIBOR point. A tree cannot be implemented under this process, because each node in the tree would have to hold an entire term structure of interest rates and volatilities, and the nodes would not recombine. Instead, market models are implemented using Monte Carlo simulation, which generates paths for the term structures. A major strength of market models is that they provide forward volatility term structures that resemble the market-observed volatility term structure.

Major option pricing models used in the market are summarized in Table 9.14 (a) and (b).

PRACTICAL APPLICATIONS OF PRICING MODELS

To demonstrate how certain option pricing models are used in practice we consider, in this section, certain practical applications. In particular, we consider the pricing of caps and floors, and then extend our discussion to the pricing of swaptions.

Pricing Caps and Floors

As noted in Chapter 2, caps and floors are somewhat different from conventional options on equities, currencies, and other asset

---

4 For instance, Black and Karasinski (BK) created a model in 1991 that incorporates mean reversion and, due to the fundamental assumption that the distribution of interest rates is lognormal, prevents interest rates from becoming negative. While appealing, this assumption also means that there is no closed-form solution for pricing options on zero coupon bonds, indicating that all options must be valued using a tree that runs through the maturity of the underlying zero coupon bond. BK can be fit to the market term structure as well as the market term structure of volatility.

T A B L E   9.14

(a) Features of Major Option Models

Model	Interest Rates	Foreign Exchange	Equities	Commodities (Futures)	Style
Black-Scholes			yes		E
Modified Black-Scholes			yes		E
Black	yes			yes	E
Garman-Kohlhagen		yes			E
Cox, Ross, Rubinstein	yes	yes	yes	yes	E, A
Cox, Ingersoll, Ross	yes				E, A
Ho-Lee	yes				E, A
Hull-White	yes				E, A
Black-Karasinski	yes				E, A, B
LIBOR Market Models	yes	yes			E, A, B, C

E = European; A = American; B = Bermudan; C = Complex Bermudan

references in that they are multiexercise products. Each cap and floor is comprised of a series of options (caplets, floorlets) exercisable on specific rate reset dates. These individual options are equal to calls or puts on the current forward rate for the forward periods referenced in the structure, and have to be priced individually. In fact, the total price paid for a cap or floor is the sum of the premiums for each of the individual caplets or floorlets. Each caplet/floorlet can be valued by examining the input variables we described in the last chapter, including strike, rate volatility, and time to expiration.

Market practitioners often price simple caps and floors using a variation of Black-Scholes (e.g., an extension of the LIBOR market model); this generates a price for each option on successive forward rates using market volatility quotes. Cap and floor strikes use the money market basis convention for the currencies in which they are priced ($, €, ¥ caps and floors are priced on an Actual/360 day basis, while £ caps and floors are priced on an Actual/365 day basis). To price any cap or floor against six-month LIBOR, we must compare the strike rate of the cap to each of the forward rates up to the tenor of the contract and calculate the individual price for each caplet or floorlet. The formula for calculating the at-the-money rate for any full-cap period is shown below in equation 9.24.

T A B L E   9.14

(b) Features of Major Option Models (cont.)

Model	Year	Origin	Advantages	Disadvantages
Black-Scholes	1973	Seminal model		Narrow assumptions limit usability
Modified Black-Scholes		Black-Scholes adaptation	Can value equity options with dividends	
Black	1976	Black-Scholes adaptation	Flexible enough to value any futures option	European options only
Cox, Ross, Rubinstein (binomial)	1979	Black-Scholes variation	Very flexible: American, European, any underlying	Numerically demanding, limitations when applied to interest rates
Garman-Kohlhagen	1983	Black-Scholes variation	Useful for foreign exchange options	
Cox, Ingersoll, Ross	1985	Term structure model	Uses market data; models the entire term structure of interest rates	Does not fit the observed market term structure
Ho-Lee	1986	Term structure model	Automatically fits the initial market term structure	
Hull-White	1990	Term structure model	Fits term structure of interest rates and volatility; mean reversion; formulas for bond options	Normal interest rates (can be negative)
Black-Karasinski	1991	Term structure model	Fits term structure of interest rates and volatility; mean reversion; lognormal interest rates	No formulas for bond options
LIBOR Market Models	1997 on	Term structure model	Models the forward LIBOR curve that the market is used to pricing; provides Black model formulas for interest rate options; handles future volatility term structures well; can price highly complex interest rate options	Implemented using Monte Carlo, making valuation of Bermudan and American options demanding; difficult to implement correctly

T A B L E 9.15

ATM Swap and Strike Data

	Period	Days	Discount Factor	Forward	ATM Strike Calculated	Actual ATM Strike
1	0 × 6					
2	6 × 12	184	0.986193	0.03377	0.0338	0.0338
3	12 × 18	181	0.969462	0.03948	0.0366	0.0366
4	18 × 24	186	0.950594	0.04489	0.0393	0.0393
5	24 × 30	179	0.929047	0.05195	0.0423	0.0423
6	30 × 36	185	0.905655	0.05863	0.0455	0.0454
7	36 × 42	182	0.879167	0.06889	0.0491	0.0491
8	42 × 48	182	0.84958	0.07683	0.0527	0.0527
9	48 × 54	182	0.817812	0.07787	0.0556	0.0554
10	54 × 60	184	0.786837	0.07676	0.0576	0.0575
11	60 × 66	181	0.757134			

$$ATM\ Cap\ Rate = \frac{\sum_{t=2}^{n} Forward\ rate_t * Days_t * Discount\ factor_t}{\sum_{t=2}^{n} Discount\ factor_t * Days_t} \qquad (9.24)$$

The at-the-money cap rate can be calculated by dividing the present value of the floating-rate cash flows by the forward period discount factors weighted by the number of days in each six-month period. Since we are applying the cap to six-month forward periods, the at-the-money price for the overall cap may be slightly different from the swap price quoted for the period. The difference is due only to the basis and market conventions used in quoting.

Let us assume that we are presented with the calculated ATM swap prices for various tenors in Table 9.15.

The table gives us the at-the-money price for each period out to five years. For instance, let us consider the period three caplet, which begins with the computation of a forward rate via:

$(((1/(DF\ period\ 4\ /\ DF\ period\ 3)) - 1) * 360)\ /$ days in period 3

This yields the following result:

$(((1\ /\ (0.950594\ /\ 0.969462)) - 1) * 360)\ /\ 181 = 3.95\%$

F I G U R E   9.3

Five-year Forward Rates

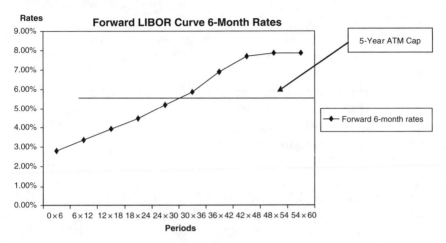

Inserting the forward rate into equation 9.24 gives us the at-the-money strike for an 18-month cap:

$$((0.0395 * 0.969462 * 181) + (0.0338 * 0.986193 * 184)) \,/$$
$$((0.969462 * 181) + (0.986193 * 184))$$
$$= 3.66\% = \text{ATM strike for an 18-month cap}$$

The next step in the pricing process is to calculate the premiums for each of the caplets comprising the cap. In this example we are pricing five-year at-the-money caps and floors using the forward rates in Figure 9.3. This involves computing the premiums for nine caplets and floorlets, and then summing to obtain the total costs.

The calculation of a caplet (or floorlet) on a forward period can be accomplished by using a modified version of Black-Scholes:

$$premium = P * DF_t * [FLRN(d_1) - SN(d_2)] * \frac{days}{360} \qquad (9.25)$$

where:

$$d_1 = \frac{ln\left(\dfrac{FLR}{S}\right) + \dfrac{\sigma^2 t}{2}}{\sigma\sqrt{t}}$$

$$d_2 = d_1 - \sigma\sqrt{t}$$

and

P	is nominal principal
FLR	is the current forward rate for the forward period on which the caplet is struck
DF_t	is the discount factor for the end of period t (i.e., the DF for the end of the period on which the caplet is being struck)
$N(..)$	is the normal standard distribution function
ln	is the natural logarithm function
S	is the strike price
Σ	is the annualized LIBOR volatility
t	is time to expiry

In the case of a caplet we are examining the possibility that the LIBOR set will exceed the six-month LIBOR rate for the forward period at expiry. As we might expect, volatility is a central to this determination: the higher the volatility, the more likely it is that the caplet will move in-the-money and, therefore, the higher the caplet's premium. We assume in our example that volatility for all forward LIBOR periods is 20%.

The Black-Scholes formula also requires a strike price and time to expiration (in years). In this example the at-the-money strike is 5.75% and the cap expiry is five years. However, the time to expiration on each individual caplet has to be calibrated. This is accomplished by considering the days in the year, 365, and the actual number of days to get to the expiry date of the caplet. Note that in this example there is a leap year effect (366 days) on the 18 × 24 and 24 × 30 forward periods, which must be incorporated. For instance, the time to expiry for the 54 × 60 month forward period is:

sum (days 0 × 6 period: days 48 × 54 period) /
average number of days in years to that point

The average number of days in the year to the 54–60 point is $(7 * 365) + (2 * 366)/9 = 365.22$. Note that time refers to actual days (i.e., 365 or 366) and is unrelated to the LIBOR day count (Actual/360) used to calculate interest.

Given this information we can compile the data in Table 9.17 and can then proceed with the next step in the calculation.

In order to make the computation process tenable, we use a spreadsheet to perform all required calculations. After inputting all

TABLE 9.16

Sample Caplet Inputs

	Period	Days	DF	Forward	Cap Strike	Volatility	Time to Expiry
1	0 × 6	182	0.986193				
2	6 × 12	184	0.969462	0.0338	0.0575	0.20	0.4986
3	12 × 18	181	0.950594	0.0395	0.0575	0.20	1.0027
4	18 × 24	186	0.929047	0.0449	0.0575	0.20	1.4966
5	24 × 30	179	0.905655	0.0519	0.0575	0.20	2.0055
6	30 × 36	185	0.879167	0.0586	0.0575	0.20	2.4959
7	36 × 42	182	0.84958	0.0689	0.0575	0.20	3.0028
8	42 × 48	182	0.817812	0.0768	0.0575	0.20	3.5014
9	48 × 54	182	0.786837	0.0779	0.0575	0.20	4.0000
10	54 × 60	184	0.757134	0.0768	0.0575	0.20	4.4987

of the data in Table 9.16 into a spreadsheet, we create additional columns that automatically determine the lognormal and normal distribution variables for $d1$ and $d2$. The results are reflected in Table 9.17.

If we add up the individual caplet prices across the full 5-year horizon, we obtain a cap price of 4.02%.

The formula for calculating a floor is virtually identical to the one for caps. The difference arises in deducting the forward rate times $N(d1)$ from the strike price times $N(d2)$, rather than vice versa; we notice that $d2$ and $d1$ must now be expressed as negative values. The equation for a floor, under the Black-Scholes framework, is thus:

$$Premium = P * DF_t * [SN - (-d_2) - FLRN(-d_1)] * \frac{days}{360} \quad (9.26)$$

Applying this change to the spreadsheet framework allows us to compute the value of the floorlets and, by extension, the floor itself. The results are shown in Tables 9.18 and 9.19.

A five-year at-the-money floor, with a strike of 5.75%, costs 4.02%, which is precisely equal to the price obtained on the five-year cap.

TABLE 9.17

Sample Caplet Pricing Data

	Period	Days	DF	Forward	Cap Strike	Vol	Time to Expiry	Cap Price	d(1)	d(2)	Normsdist (d1)	Normsdist (d2)
1	0 × 6	182	0.986193									
2	6 × 12	184	0.969462	0.0338	0.0575	0.20	0.4986	0.000000	-3.6986	-3.8398	0.000108	0.000062
3	12 × 18	181	0.950594	0.0395	0.0575	0.20	1.0027	0.000053	-1.7775	-1.9777	0.037747	0.023980
4	18 × 24	186	0.929047	0.0449	0.0575	0.20	1.4966	0.000484	-0.8897	-1.1343	0.186821	0.128326
5	24 × 30	179	0.905655	0.0519	0.0575	0.20	2.0055	0.001700	-0.2170	-0.5003	0.414093	0.308447
6	30 × 36	185	0.879167	0.0586	0.0575	0.20	2.4959	0.003554	0.2194	-0.0965	0.586849	0.461554
7	36 × 42	182	0.84958	0.0689	0.0575	0.20	3.0028	0.006669	0.6947	0.3481	0.756366	0.636114
8	42 × 48	182	0.817812	0.0768	0.0575	0.20	3.5014	0.009273	0.9617	0.5874	0.831894	0.721545
9	48 × 54	182	0.786837	0.0779	0.0575	0.20	4.0000	0.009463	0.9581	0.5581	0.830986	0.711601
10	54 × 60	184	0.757134	0.0768	0.0575	0.20	4.4987	0.009041	0.8930	0.4688	0.814076	0.680399

Nominal 1

Cap Price 5 years 4.02%

T A B L E 9.18

Sample Floorlet Pricing Data

	Period	Days	DF	Forward	Floor Strike	Volatility	Time to Expiry	Floor Price	d(1)	d(2)	Normsdist (d1)	Normsdist (d2)
1	0 × 6	182	0.986193	0.0338	0.0575	0.20	0.4986	0.011760	-3.6986	-3.8398	0.999892	0.999938
2	6 × 12	184	0.969462	0.0395	0.0575	0.20	1.0027	0.008666	-1.7775	-1.9777	0.962253	0.976020
3	12 × 18	181	0.950594	0.0449	0.0575	0.20	1.4966	0.006537	-0.8897	-1.1343	0.813179	0.871674
4	18 × 24	186	0.929047	0.0519	0.0575	0.20	2.0055	0.004201	-0.2170	-0.5003	0.585907	0.691553
5	24 × 30	179	0.905655	0.0586	0.0575	0.20	2.4959	0.003044	0.2194	-0.0965	0.413151	0.538446
6	30 × 36	185	0.879167	0.0586	0.0575	0.20	2.4959	0.003044	0.6947	0.3481	0.243634	0.363886
7	36 × 42	182	0.84958	0.0689	0.0575	0.20	3.0028	0.001778	0.9617	0.5874	0.168106	0.278455
8	42 × 48	182	0.817812	0.0768	0.0575	0.20	3.5014	0.001280	0.9581	0.5581	0.169014	0.288399
9	48 × 54	182	0.786837	0.0779	0.0575	0.20	4.0000	0.001361	0.8930	0.4688	0.185924	0.319601
10	54 × 60	184	0.757134	0.0768	0.0575	0.20	4.4987	0.001589				

| | | | | | | | Floor | | | | |
| Nominal | 1 | | | | | | 5 years | 4.02% | | | |

T A B L E 9.19

Summary Cap and Floor Prices: Five Years

	Period	Days	DF	Forward	Cap Strike	Volatility	Time to Expiry	Cap Price	Floor price
1	0 × 6	182	0.986193						
2	6 × 12	184	0.969462	0.0338	0.0575	0.20	0.4986	0.000000	0.011760
3	12 × 18	181	0.950594	0.0395	0.0575	0.20	1.0027	0.000053	0.008666
4	18 × 24	186	0.929047	0.0449	0.0575	0.20	1.4966	0.000484	0.006537
5	24 × 30	179	0.905655	0.0519	0.0575	0.20	2.0055	0.001700	0.004201
6	30 × 36	185	0.879167	0.0586	0.0575	0.20	2.4959	0.003554	0.003044
7	36 × 42	182	0.84958	0.0689	0.0575	0.20	3.0028	0.006669	0.001778
8	42 × 48	182	0.817812	0.0768	0.0575	0.20	3.5014	0.009273	0.001280
9	48 × 54	182	0.786837	0.0779	0.0575	0.20	4.0000	0.009463	0.001361
10	54 × 60	184	0.757134	0.0768	0.0575	0.20	4.4987	0.009041	0.001589
								Cap	Floor
Nominal	1						5 Years	4.02%	4.02%

T A B L E 9.20

Summary Cap and Floor Prices: Three Years

	Period	Days	DF	Forward	Cap Strike	Volatility	Time to Expiry	Cap Price	Floor price
1	0 × 6	182	0.986193						
2	6 × 12	184	0.969462	0.0338	0.0454	0.20	0.4986	0.000018	0.005782
3	12 × 18	181	0.950594	0.0395	0.0454	0.20	1.0027	0.000579	0.003410
4	18 × 24	186	0.929047	0.0449	0.0454	0.20	1.4966	0.001989	0.002235
5	24 × 30	179	0.905655	0.0519	0.0454	0.20	2.0055	0.004214	0.001266
6	30 × 36	185	0.879167	0.0586	0.0454	0.20	2.4959	0.006841	0.000865
7	36 × 42	182	0.84958	0.0689	0.0454	0.20	3.0028	0.010548	0.000459
8	42 × 48	182	0.817812	0.0768	0.0454	0.20	3.5014	0.013323	0.000327
9	48 × 54	182	0.786837	0.0779	0.0454	0.20	4.0000	0.013298	0.000383
10	54 × 60	184	0.757134	0.0768	0.0454	0.20	4.4987	0.012629	0.000495
								Cap	Floor
Nominal	1						3 Years	1.36%	1.36%

Note that if we buy a cap and sell a floor, both at-the-money, the premium paid matches the premium received and we have created a synthetic swap for the period. We can test this by entering the 4.54% at-the-money strike for three years into our cap and floor spreadsheet, and observe that the same results arise; Table 9.20

T A B L E 9.21

Summary Cap and Floor Prices: Three-year

Period	Days	DF	Forward	Cap Strike	Volatility	Time to Expiry	Cap Price	Floor price
1	0 × 6	182	0.986193						
2	6 × 12	184	0.969462	0.0338	0.0575	0.20	0.4986	0.000000	0.011760
3	12 × 18	181	0.950594	0.0395	0.0575	0.20	1.0027	0.000053	0.008666
4	18 × 24	186	0.929047	0.0449	0.0575	0.20	1.4966	0.000484	0.006537
5	24 × 30	179	0.905655	0.0519	0.0575	0.20	2.0055	0.001700	0.004201
6	30 × 36	185	0.879167	0.0586	0.0575	0.20	2.4959	0.003554	0.003044
7	36 × 42	182	0.84958	0.0689	0.0575	0.20	3.0028	0.006669	0.001778
8	42 × 48	182	0.817812	0.0768	0.0575	0.20	3.5014	0.009273	0.001280
9	48 × 54	182	0.786837	0.0779	0.0575	0.20	4.0000	0.009463	0.001361
10	54 × 60	184	0.757134	0.0768	0.0575	0.20	4.4987	0.009041	0.001589

							Cap	Floor
Nominal	1					3 Years	0.58%	3.42%

illustrates the results obtained from adding the first five caplets and floorlets.

We can continue analysis of the structure by keeping the strike at 5.75%. In this case a three-year floor struck at 5.75% is well in-the-money relative to the three-year at-the-money price of 4.54%, meaning that it has significant intrinsic value and a premium of 342 bps. The cap, on the other hand, is now out-of-the-money and only attracts a premium of 58 bps. These results are contained in Table 9.21.

The magnitude of volatility will also have an impact on prices. For instance, if we return to our original five-year at-the-money cap and floor and increase volatility from 20% to 25% for all forward periods, the price of the options increases to 4.55%, as noted in Table 9.22. Note that in this simple example we are assuming flat volatility across all maturities. In practice a term structure of volatility exists, with short maturity rates exhibiting greater volatility than long maturity rates.

Pricing Swaptions

To illustrate another practical application of the pricing process we can examine the valuation of a swaption under a modified version

T A B L E 9.22

Summary Cap and Floor Prices: Five-year, 25% Volatility

Period	Days	DF	Forward	Cap Strike	Volatility	Time to Expiry	Cap Price	Floor price
1	0 × 6	182	0.986193						
2	6 × 12	184	0.969462	0.0338	0.0575	0.25	0.4986	0.000001	0.011761
3	12 × 18	181	0.950594	0.0395	0.0575	0.25	1.0027	0.000165	0.008779
4	18 × 24	186	0.929047	0.0449	0.0575	0.25	1.4966	0.000875	0.006929
5	24 × 30	179	0.905655	0.0519	0.0575	0.25	2.0055	0.002352	0.004853
6	30 × 36	185	0.879167	0.0586	0.0575	0.25	2.4959	0.004366	0.003857
7	36 × 42	182	0.84958	0.0689	0.0575	0.25	3.0028	0.007492	0.002601
8	42 × 48	182	0.817812	0.0768	0.0575	0.25	3.5014	0.010063	0.002069
9	48 × 54	182	0.786837	0.0779	0.0575	0.25	4.0000	0.010286	0.002184
10	54 × 60	184	0.757134	0.0768	0.0575	0.25	4.4987	0.009919	0.002467
							Cap	Floor
Nominal		1					5 Years	4.55%	4.55%

of Black-Scholes. In this example we use the forward swap rate volatility as a key input; we also note that the forward swap rate is the price of the underlying and that the swaption rate is the strike. In pricing any swaption it is important to remember that a call swaption gains intrinsic value as the underlying rate rises above the swaption strike. A put swaption is gains value if rates fall below the strike price.

The modified Black-Scholes formula for a payer swaption is given as:

$$PS = P * \sum_{p=1}^{n} (DF_p * AF_p) * [FSRN(d_1) - SN(d_2)] \qquad (9.27)$$

where:

$$d_1 = \frac{ln\left(\dfrac{FSR}{S}\right) + \dfrac{\sigma^2 t}{2}}{\sigma\sqrt{t}}$$

$$d_2 = d_1 - \sigma\sqrt{t}$$

and all other terms are as defined earlier in the chapter.

Using this formula we can price a two- × three-year EURIBOR payer swaption. To do so we must first establish the at-the-money price for the swaption by calculating the forward starting three-year swap rate in two-year's time. We simplify the process by creating a spreadsheet with input and output as noted in Table 9.23.

The two- × three-year forward starting swap calculates to a fixed rate of 6.884%. This is the at-the-money strike rate for our two- × three-year payer swaption. The results are reflected in Table 9.24.

Thus, given an at-the-money strike rate of 6.884% (the same as that of a two- × three-year forward starting swap) and a volatility of 20%, the payer swaption carries a premium of 1.95%.

We note from this spreadsheet that using a higher strike price than the at-the-money forward rate of 6.884% leads to a lower premium because the payer swaption is out-of-the-money. Similarly, using higher volatility increases the swaption premium and lowering it decreases it. Table 9.25 illustrates the results from increasing the strike from 6.884% to 7.50%; the value of the swaption premium declines by 60 bps.

We can adjust the pricing formula to take account of the receiver swaption, and do so by subtracting the forward rate times $N(d1)$ from the strike rate times $N(d2)$, and ensuring that $d1$ and $d2$ are now negative. This yields the following formula:

$$RS = P * \sum_{p=1}^{n} (DF_t * AF_p) * [SN(-d_2) - FSRN(-d_1)] \qquad (9.28)$$

If we apply this formula to price a two- × three-year receiver swaption based on the curve data presented above, we obtain the results noted in Table 9.26.

Not surprisingly, the price of the receiver swaption is 1.95%, the same as the price obtained for the payer swaption.

To illustrate the price effect on a receiver swaption let us change the strike to 7.50%. Because the swaption is in-the-money, the premium rises, in this case to 2.91%. The results are summarized in Table 9.27.

T A B L E 9.23

EURIBOR Forward Swap Rates

Euribor Yield Curve

Period	Dates	Period Accrual Factors	Futures and Swap Prices	Discount Factor	Spot Rate (BEY)%	Forward Rate	Vanilla Swap—4 years		Forward LIBOR	
							PV Floating Cash Flows	PV Fixed Cash Flows	PV Floating Cash Flows	PV Fixed Cash Flows
1	04/01/2005	0.5028	2.80	0.9862	2.8000	2.80	138834	272883		
2	04/07/2005	0.5111	3.15	0.9695	3.1500	3.50	173456	272700		
3	04/01/2006	0.5028	3.40	0.9506	3.4066	3.92	187386	263033		
4	04/07/2006	0.5111	3.70	0.9290	3.7139	4.64	220256	261332		
5	04/01/2007	0.5028	3.98	0.9057	4.0034	5.17	235219	250598	235219	313458
6	04/07/2007	0.5111	4.30	0.8792	4.3391	6.03	270762	247301	270762	309334
7	04/01/2008	0.5056	4.65	0.8496	4.7122	6.97	299167	236381	299167	295674
8	04/07/2008	0.5139	5.00	0.8178	5.0918	7.77	326497	231293	326497	289310
9	05/01/2009	0.5056	5.28	0.7868	5.3990	7.87	313192	218924	313192	273839
10	06/07/2009	0.5056	5.50	0.7571	5.6424	7.85	300330	210659	300330	263501
	04/01/2010									

Principal 10,000,000

Vanilla Fixed	5 year	5.504				**Total PVs**	2,465,099	2,465,103	1,745,167	1,745,117
Forward Fixed	2-3 Year	6.884								

Basis 360

TABLE 9.24

Payer Swaption Results

Euribor Yield Curve

Period	Dates	Period Accrual Factors	Futures and Swap Prices	Discount Factor	Spot Rate	Forward Rate	DF × AF	Time to Expiry	Strike	Volatility	Payer's Swaption	d1	d2	NORMS DIST (d1)	NORMS DIST (d2)
1	04/01/2005	0.5028	2.80	0.9862	2.8000	2.80		0	0.06884						
2	04/07/2005	0.5111	3.15	0.9695	3.1500	3.50		0.4959	0.06884						
3	04/01/2006	0.5028	3.40	0.9506	3.4066	3.92		1.0000	0.06884						
4	04/07/2006	0.5111	3.70	0.9290	3.7139	4.64		1.4959	0.06884						
5	04/01/2007	0.5028	3.98	0.9057	4.0034	5.17	0.4553	2.0000	0.06884	0.20	1.95%	0.03506	−0.2478	0.5140	0.4022
6	04/07/2007	0.5111	4.30	0.8792	4.3391	6.03	0.4494	2.4959	0.06884						
7	04/01/2008	0.5056	4.65	0.8496	4.7122	6.97	0.4295	2.9918	0.06884						
8	04/07/2008	0.5139	5.00	0.8178	5.0918	7.77	0.4203	3.4891	0.06884						
9	05/01/2009	0.5056	5.28	0.7868	5.3990	7.87	0.3978	4.0055	0.06884						
10	06/07/2009	0.5056	5.50	0.7571	5.6424	7.85	0.3828	4.5041	0.06884						
	04/01/2010														

Principal 1

Sum of DF × AF   2.5350

Vanilla	Fixed	5 year	5.504
Forward	Fixed	2-3 Year	6.884
Basis		360

TABLE 9.25

Payer Swaption Results—2

Euribor Yield Curve

Period	Dates	Period Accrual Factors	Futures and Swap Prices	Discount Factor	Spot Rate	Forward Rate	DF × AF	Time to Expiry	Strike	Volatility	Payer's Swaption	d1	d2	NORMS DIST (d1)	NORMS DIST (d2)
1	04/01/2005	0.5028	2.80	0.9862	2.8000	2.80		0	0.075						
2	04/07/2005	0.5111	3.15	0.9695	3.1500	3.50		0.4959	0.075						
3	04/01/2006	0.5028	3.40	0.9506	3.4066	3.92		1.0000	0.075						
4	04/07/2006	0.5111	3.70	0.9290	3.7139	4.64		1.4959	0.075						
5	04/01/2007	0.5028	3.98	0.9057	4.0034	5.17	0.4553	2.0000	0.075		1.35%	−0.2679	−0.5508	0.3944	0.2909
6	04/07/2007	0.5111	4.30	0.8792	4.3391	6.03	0.4494	2.4959	0.075	0.20					
7	04/01/2008	0.5056	4.65	0.8496	4.7122	6.97	0.4295	2.9918	0.075						
8	04/07/2008	0.5139	5.00	0.8178	5.0918	7.77	0.4203	3.4891	0.075						
9	05/01/2009	0.5056	5.28	0.7868	5.3990	7.87	0.3978	4.0055	0.075						
10	06/07/2009	0.5056	5.50	0.7571	5.6424	7.85	0.3828	4.5041	0.075						
	04/01/2010														

Principal		1	
Vanilla	Fixed	5 year	5.504
Forward	Fixed	2-3 Year	6.884
Basis	360		

Sum of DF × AF   2.5350

TABLE 9.26

Receiver Swaption Results

Euribor Yield Curve

Period	Dates	Period Accrual Factors	Futures and Swap Prices	Discount Factor	Spot Rate	Forward Rate	DF × AF	Time to Expiry	Strike	Volatility	Payer's Swaption	d1	d2	NORMS DIST (d1)
1	04/01/2005	0.5028	2.80	0.9862	2.8000	2.80		0	0.06884					
2	04/07/2005	0.5111	3.15	0.9695	3.1500	3.50		0.4959	0.06884					
3	04/01/2006	0.5028	3.40	0.9506	3.4066	3.92		1.0000	0.06884					
4	04/07/2006	0.5111	3.70	0.9290	3.7139	4.64		1.4959	0.06884					
5	04/01/2007	0.5028	3.98	0.9057	4.0034	5.17	0.4553	2.0000	0.06884	0.20	1.95%	0.0351	-0.2478	0.4860
6	04/07/2007	0.5111	4.30	0.8792	4.3391	6.03	0.4494	2.4959	0.06884					
7	04/01/2008	0.5056	4.65	0.8496	4.7122	6.97	0.4295	2.9918	0.06884					
8	04/07/2008	0.5139	5.00	0.8178	5.0918	7.77	0.4203	3.4891	0.06884					
9	05/01/2009	0.5056	5.28	0.7868	5.3990	7.87	0.3978	4.0055	0.06884					
10	06/07/2009	0.5056	5.50	0.7571	5.6424	7.85	0.3828	4.5041	0.06884					
	04/01/2010													

Sum of DF × AF   2.5350

Principal		1
Vanilla Fixed	5 year	5.504
Forward Fixed	2-3 Year	6.884
Basis	360	

TABLE 9.27

Receiver Swaption Results—2

Euribor Yield Curve

Period	Dates	Period Accrual Factors	Futures and Swap Prices	Discount Factor	Spot Rate	Forward Rate	DF × AF	Time to Expiry	Strike	Volatility	Receiver Swaption	$d1$	$d2$	NORMS DIST ($d1$)	NORMS DIST ($d2$)
1	04/01/2005	0.5028	2.80	0.9862	2.8000	2.80		0	0.075						
2	04/07/2005	0.5111	3.15	0.9695	3.1500	3.50		0.4959	0.075						
3	04/01/2006	0.5028	3.40	0.9506	3.4066	3.92		1.0000	0.075						
4	04/07/2006	0.5111	3.70	0.9290	3.7139	4.64		1.4959	0.075						
5	04/01/2007	0.5028	3.98	0.9057	4.0034	5.17	0.4553	2.0000	0.075	0.20	2.91%	−0.2679	−0.5508	0.6056	0.7091
6	04/07/2007	0.5111	4.30	0.8792	4.3391	6.03	0.4494	2.4959	0.075						
7	04/01/2008	0.5056	4.65	0.8496	4.7122	6.97	0.4295	2.9918	0.075						
8	04/07/2008	0.5139	5.00	0.8178	5.0918	7.77	0.4203	3.4891	0.075						
9	05/01/2009	0.5056	5.28	0.7868	5.3990	7.87	0.3978	4.0055	0.075						
10	06/07/2009	0.5056	5.50	0.7571	5.6424	7.85	0.3828	4.5041	0.075						
	04/01/2010														

Principal		1				
Vanilla	Fixed	5 year	5.504		Sum of DF × AF	2.5350
Forward	Fixed	2-3 Year	6.884			
Basis		360				

CHAPTER EXERCISES

1. Put-call parity in the Black-Scholes pricing framework indicates that:
   a. $C - P = X - S(\exp(-rt))$
   b. $C - P = S(\exp(-rt)) - X$
   c. $C + S(\exp(-rt)) = X - P$
   d. $C - S(\exp(-rt)) = P - X$
   e. None of the above

2. The natural log of the daily returns of an asset price that trades at 47 on day one and 51 on day two is equal to:
   a. 3.75
   b. 3.65
   c. 3.85
   d. 3.95
   e. 4.05

3. Given asset volatility of 25% and a half-year time step, what is the upward move of an asset under the binomial framework?
   a. 118.34
   b. 117.89
   c. 123.32
   d. 119.26
   e. None of the above

4. Given spot prices today of $1,000, 25% asset volatility, two standard deviation statistical measurements and a time period of two years, what is the expected spot price in two years?
   a. 1,982
   b. 1,783
   c. 2,023
   d. 2,301
   e. 2,454

5. A disadvantage of the geometric Brownian motion for interest rates is that:
   a. It allows for negative rates
   b. Rates do not mean revert

   c. The volatility of rates is constant across maturity

   d. All of the above

   e. None of the above

6. Under the Black-Scholes framework the put price can be regarded intuitively as:

   a. (costs * weight of costs) − (benefits * weight of benefits)

   b. (costs * weight of costs) + (benefits * weight of benefits)

   c. (costs + benefits) * weight of benefits

   d. (costs − benefits) * weight of benefits

   e. None of the above

7. Which of the following is/are true?

   a. Swaptions can be priced using a Black-Scholes extension

   b. A two-factor interest rate model is more difficult to calibrate than a one-factor model

   c. The most accurate interest rate models include mean reversion

   d. All of the above

   e. None of the above

Hedging Option Portfolios

INTRODUCTION

Intermediaries, including banks, securities firms, and dedicated options dealers, which transact in the global options market must be able to operate in a prudent and efficient manner and manage their portfolio risks accurately. While the core of the process is built atop an internal risk-management and control framework, which we will consider in the next chapter, the starting point centers on measuring and managing option hedges. In this chapter we consider the essential elements of options hedging by focusing on option sensitivities—delta, gamma, vega, theta, and rho (i.e., the "Greeks")—and practical approaches to portfolio management. We will investigate the topic as it applies to both vanilla and exotic options.

OPTION SENSITIVITIES

We begin our discussion by presenting examples of option sensitivities using currency options; the entire framework is, of course, applicable across all asset underlyings. We know from Chapter 8 that an option is sensitive to several different parameters, including asset price, strike, volatility, time, and interest rates. For instance, in a currency option the major price determinant is the level of spot prices in relation to the strike price. This is illustrated in Figure 10.1, where a € call/$ put has a strike of 1.19; the dark

FIGURE 10.1

€/$ FX Option

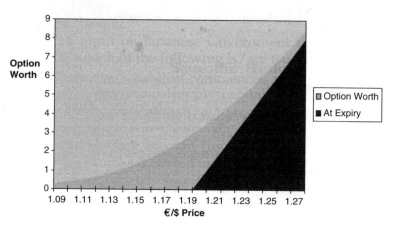

region reflects the intrinsic value that will arise if the option moves in-the-money, while the light region reflects time value. The option features maximum time value when spot €/$ is at the 1.1900 strike. When the option is well out-of-the-money we see that time value is considerably smaller; the same exists when the option is well in-the-money. This is true for both scenarios because time has very little residual impact on value when an option is already well in- or out-of-the-money. Intrinsic value, in contrast, is equal to zero when the option is at- or out-of-the-money, and grows as the option moves in-the-money. Intrinsic value dominates an option's value by the time the underlying has forced the contract well in-the-money. Spot rates clearly have a major effect on the price of the option.

However, because a currency option is also based on a forward rate, it carries a dimension of interest rate risk. For example, a €/$ option is exposed to both € and $ interest rates. If € rates increase and $ rates remain unchanged, the forward rate will decline as forward points increase. This change pushes the forward at-the-money price down, making a € call cheaper (i.e., less valuable). A € put becomes more valuable for the opposite reasons. Volatility also plays a role in the price of an option, with more volatile market conditions leading to higher option prices, and vice versa. We also recall that time to expiration has an impact on price, with longer time to expiration translating into greater value. Since an option's price is sensitive to each one of these parameters, it is clear that they must be understood, measured, and managed if an option portfolio is to remain profitable. Let us consider these sensitivities in more detail.

Delta

Delta measures option price sensitivity to changes in the underlying asset price and can be regarded as the probability that an option will be exercised. Mathematically, delta can be regarded as the slope of the line tangent to the option payoff function (recall that we have illustrated payoff profiles as being purely linear for simplicity; in fact, they have a slight degree of curvature, or convexity, hence the need for the tangent). Since slope measures the rate of change, it is easy to see how it can provide information on the price sensitivity of an option. Consider the payoff profile of a long call in Figure 10.2: the slope of the line tangent reveals the change in the price (profit) of the option for a unit change in the asset price. In this case, a one unit increase in the asset price leads to a 0.7 change in the option price, meaning the delta is $+0.7$ (i.e., $0.7/1$).

F I G U R E   10.2

Delta of Long Call Option

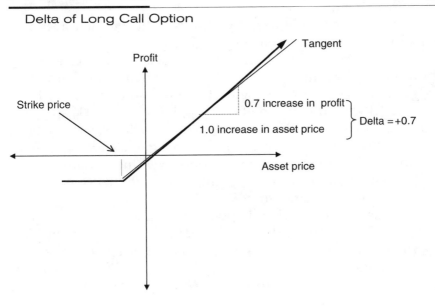

T A B L E 10.1

Sample Option Premiums and Deltas

| 3-Month Options –3 months to expiry | | | | | | |
Description	Call/Put	Strike	ATM Price	Volatility	Premium	Delta
EUR/USD	Call	1.1900	1.1900	10%	1.99%	49%
EUR/USD	Call	1.2200	1.1900	10%	1.00%	31%
EUR/USD	Call	1.2500	1.1900	10%	0.44%	16%
EUR/USD	Call	1.1600	1.1900	10%	3.46%	66%

Let us illustrate the practical use of delta through an example. Table 10.1 provides sample option prices (premiums) and deltas for three-month €/$ options at varying prices/strikes.

We can see from the results in the table that the farther out-of-the-money the option, the lower its delta. Thus, if the current market is 1.19 and the strike is 1.25, the delta is approximately 16%, suggesting that there is a 16% chance that the option will move in-the-money prior to expiry. When the underlying is precisely at the strike (e.g., both at 1.19) the delta is equal to approximately 50%, meaning there is an even chance of the option ending in- or out-of-the-money. As the underlying moves in-the-money, delta continues to increase, reflecting the increased likelihood that the option will expire with value.

Delta is commonly used by traders to hedge the directional risk of their option portfolios through a process known as delta hedging (this reverts to our brief hedging discussion in Chapter 8). For instance, if a bank sells a €1m 1.2500 call with a delta of 16%, it hedges by buying €160,000 against $ spot. Similarly, if the bank sells the 1.1900 call with a delta of 49%, it buys €490,000 spot as a hedge, and if it sells the 1.16 call with a delta of 66%, it buys €660,000. In all cases the bank will continue to increase the amount of € spot as the options move in-the-money. If the call buyer exercises when the options move in-the-money, the bank is able to deliver the required amount of €.

Let us consider what happens to delta as the spot rate changes. We can examine the behavior of four options by considering what happens when the spot rate moves to 1.2300; Table 10.2 contains the new prices and deltas of each one. Since the current spot rate has risen, each one of the calls is now worth more (i.e., all

T A B L E   10.2

Sample Option Premiums and Deltas — 2

3-Month Options –3 months to expiry						
Description	**Call/Put**	**Strike**	**ATM Price**	**Volatility**	**Premium**	**Delta**
EUR/USD	Call	1.1900	1.2300	10%	3.97%	71%
EUR/USD	Call	1.2200	1.2300	10%	2.41%	55%
EUR/USD	Call	1.2500	1.2300	10%	1.30%	37%
EUR/USD	Call	1.1600	1.2300	10%	5.93%	82%

of the premiums have risen). Consequently, the probability that the options will be exercised has also risen (i.e., all of the deltas have increased). The 1.1600 strike call has moved well in-the-money and now requires a delta hedge of 82%. Assuming that the bank already has €660,000 from the previous delta hedge of 66%, it must now buy an additional €160,000 at current spot to bring the total hedge to €820,000. Similarly, the 1.1900 call would require another €220,000 to bring it to a 71% delta hedge, while the 1.2500 call would require another €210,000 to bring it to a 37% delta hedge.

If the bank repeats this process for every change in spot (and delta), it creates a delta neutral portfolio: any gain on the option is offset by a loss on the spot, and vice versa, leading to the creation of a flat P&L profile. This is impractical, of course, and the bank will deliberately under- and overhedge options in the pursuit of profits. If the bank could neutralize the portfolio's delta perfectly (and if volatility did not change over the life of the option), then the position would make no profit or loss. Since a bank expects to generate profits, a pure delta neutral hedge is unlikely to be a worthwhile strategy.

If the spot rate moves again, to 1.1900, then the likelihood of exercise declines and the bank would sell some of the € previously purchased in order to bring the delta hedges back to previous levels. We can see that management of delta is a continuous process. Fortunately, the mathematical properties of delta mean that all of the options in a portfolio can be added together to create a single portfolio delta; the delta hedge is then applied against the total figure rather than each individual option. This, as we might imagine, is a considerable savings of time and expense for a portfolio that might have dozens, hundreds, or thousands of open put and call positions.

We can summarize certain useful characteristics regarding delta:

- Delta measures option premium change for any change in the underlying.
- Delta is equivalent to the cash portfolio needed to replicate the payoff of an option.
- For call options, an increase in the underlying creates a profit for the buyer, meaning the buyer's delta is positive; the same increase creates a loss for the seller, meaning the seller's delta is negative.
- For put options, an increase in the underlying creates a loss for the buyer, meaning the buyer's delta is negative; the same increase creates a profit for the seller (e.g., premium is retained), meaning the seller's delta is positive.
- Deltas for long call options vary between 0 and 1. Delta approaches 1 for deep in-the-money options and 0 for deep out-of-the-money options; the reverse is true for short call options.
- Deltas for long put options vary between 0 and –1. Delta approaches –1 for deep in-the-money options, and 0 for deep out-of-the-money options; the reverse is true for short put options.
- The Black-Scholes model defines the delta of an option as the normal distribution term associated with the underlying asset price. However, as the asset price changes, the normal distribution term changes. Delta is therefore a dynamic parameter that varies with the level of the underlying asset price.

Gamma

Gamma, the second major option sensitivity, measures the change in the delta for a change in the underlying asset price (first-order effect) or the change in an option price due to a change in the underlying asset price (second-order effect). In Figure 10.2 above, gamma captures the actual effect of the curvature embedded in the payoff profile (e.g., the nonlinear component that is not reflected by delta).

If we consider the normal distribution, the curve peaks where the price of the underlying is equal to the strike price (e.g., at-the-money). This suggests that the greatest change in delta (i.e., the highest gamma) occurs when an option is precisely at-the-money. This also makes intuitive sense, since the at-the-money point is characterized by the greatest uncertainty: an option can move in- or out-of-the-money with only the slightest shift in the underlying.

If gamma is small—meaning the option is well in- or out-of-the-money—delta changes very slowly and adjustments needed to keep a portfolio delta neutral are relatively small and infrequent. Conversely, if gamma is large (i.e., the option is at-the-money), delta is highly sensitive to a change in the underlying price and frequent adjustments to maintain delta neutrality are necessary.

Let us examine the gamma of various €/$ options to consider the pricing and hedging implications. Table 10.3 contains the gamma (and delta) of options with various strikes.

The options, with three months to expiry, have relatively small gammas—apart from the at-the-money 1.19 strike call, which features a much larger gamma. This means that its delta (and, by extension, its price) is much more sensitive to a change in the €/$ spot rate. In our example gamma is quoted as a percentage change in the delta for a 1.00% change in the spot rate. Assuming a spot rate of 1.1939 is used to price the 1.1900 at-the-money forward strike, a 1.00% change in the spot rate equals 1.2057. If we reprice the option at this new spot rate, delta moves from just below 50% to approximately 57%—a delta move of 7.88%, which would require rebalancing in order to preserve delta neutrality.

Let us now consider that the original three-month expiry has declined to one month (e.g., two months have passed) and that

T A B L E 10.3

Sample Option Gammas

3-Month Options –3 months to expiry							
Description	Call/Put	Strike	ATM Price	Volatility	Premium	Delta	Gamma
EUR/USD	Call	1.1900	1.1900	10%	1.99%	49%	7.88%
EUR/USD	Call	1.2200	1.1900	10%	1.00%	31%	7.06%
EUR/USD	Call	1.2500	1.1900	10%	0.44%	16%	5.00%
EUR/USD	Call	1.1600	1.1900	10%	3.46%	66%	6.84%

T A B L E   10.4

Sample Option Gammas — 2

| 3-Month Options –1 month to expiry | | | | | | | |
Description	Call/Put	Strike	ATM Price	Volatility	Premium	Delta	Gamma
EUR/USD	Call	1.1900	1.1900	10%	1.12%	49%	14.12%
EUR/USD	Call	1.2200	1.1900	10%	0.29%	19%	9.68%
EUR/USD	Call	1.2500	1.1900	10%	5.50%	4%	3.16%
EUR/USD	Call	1.1600	1.1900	10%	2.79%	79%	9.24%

the spot rate remains unchanged. Table 10.4 highlights the new gammas.

We note that the deltas of the out-of-the money options have declined considerably. This should make intuitive sense, as there is less time for the options to move in-the-money; price sensitivity of the options declines in tandem. The delta of the in-the-money option, however, has increased, as there is now a higher probability that the option will be exercised. The gamma of the at-the-money option has increased, while the gammas of the out-of-the-money options have declined. Although the gamma of the in-the-money option has increased, it is still not as high as the gamma of the at-the-money option. We can extend this example by noting the deltas and gammas of the options one day before expiration. The results are reflected in Table 10.5.

The out-of-the-money and in-the-money options have zero gammas. The out-of-the-money options now feature deltas of zero,

T A B L E   10.5

Sample Option Gammas — 3

| 3-Month Options –1 day to expiry | | | | | | | |
Description	Call/Put	Strike	ATM Price	Volatility	Premium	Delta	Gamma
EUR/USD	Call	1.1900	1.1900	10%	0.21%	50%	76.20%
EUR/USD	Call	1.2200	1.1900	10%	0.00%	0%	0.00%
EUR/USD	Call	1.2500	1.1900	10%	0.00%	0%	0.00%
EUR/USD	Call	1.1600	1.1900	10%	2.53%	97%	0.00%

while the in-the-money options have deltas approaching 100%. This again makes sense as there is virtually nothing that can occur to push either set of contracts in the opposite direction with one day to expiry. The at-the-money option, in contrast, features a very large gamma, meaning that even very small changes in spot will create a large change in delta. To illustrate this, consider the situation five minutes before expiry of the at-the-money 1.1900 strike option: when spot is at 1.1898 the 1.1900 call is worth nothing and its delta is 0; however, if spot moves to 1.1903 five seconds before expiry, the option is now in-the-money and its delta is 100%. It is easy to see through this rather extreme scenario the gamma effect of an at-the-money option nearing expiry. For the trader managing an options portfolio, high gamma means paying careful attention to changes in the underlying, as delta hedging will be required frequently; low gamma options in the portfolio require less hedging maintenance. The gamma relationships of time and moneyness are summarized in Figure 10.3.

F I G U R E 10.3

Gammas Related to Time and Moneyness

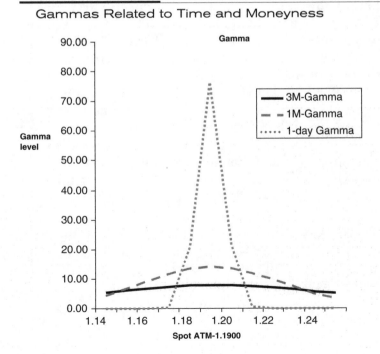

We can summarize the key characteristics of gamma as follows:

- Gamma is always positive for the buyer of options (calls and puts); it is always negative for the seller of options. Short gamma positions must be controlled very carefully as they can generate significant losses in a fast-moving and volatile market.
- Gamma means that the price of a call option changes more rapidly for rising prices than delta suggests, and falls less slowly for falling prices than delta suggests. Similarly, the price of a put option falls more slowly due to an increase in the underlying than delta suggests and increases more rapidly due to a drop in the underlying than delta suggests. This gives rise to a convexity effect.
- As an option nears maturity, gamma for at-the-money options becomes more sensitive because even small changes in the underlying can have a large impact on delta.

Vega

Vega, sometimes known as kappa or lambda, reflects the change in option price for a change in volatility. As volatility rises, the prices of puts and calls rise because the likelihood that a contract will move in-the-money (or further in-the-money) increases. Conversely, as volatility declines, the prices of puts and calls decline. In fact, if we set volatility equal to 0 in a pricing model, the premium returned will equal 0, as there is no chance of the market's moving.

We can again return to our €/$ call options to illustrate the impact of volatility on prices. Vega is typically measured as the price impact given an absolute change in volatility of some defined magnitude. For instance, if we increase the volatility of the calls from 10% to 15%, the prices of all of the options increase, as noted in Table 10.6.

Table 10.7 contains the actual vega computations for the portfolio of options. We note that vega, like gamma, is maximized for at-the-money options. The further out- or in-the-money the contract, the lower the vega, and the lower the sensitivity of the option price to changes in volatility. The application of the measurement is straightforward. Let us examine the 1.1900 call: if volatility moves from 10% to 11%, then the price of this option will rise from 1.99%

T A B L E 10.6

Sample Option Vegas

| 3-Month Options –3 months to expiry | | | | | | | |
Description	Call/ Put	Strike	ATM Price	Volatility	Premium	Volatility	Premium
EUR/USD	Call	1.1900	1.1900	10%	1.99%	15%	2.98%
EUR/USD	Call	1.2200	1.1900	10%	1.00%	15%	1.93%
EUR/USD	Call	1.2500	1.1900	10%	0.44%	15%	1.19%
EUR/USD	Call	1.1600	1.1900	10%	3.46%	15%	4.37%

T A B L E 10.7

Sample Option Vegas — 2

| 3-Month Options –3 months to expiry | | | | | | | | |
Description	Call/ Put	Strike	ATM Price	Volatility	Premium	Delta	Gamma	Vega
EUR/USD	Call	1.1900	1.1900	10%	1.99%	49%	7.88%	0.20%
EUR/USD	Call	1.2200	1.1900	10%	1.00%	31%	7.06%	0.18%
EUR/USD	Call	1.2500	1.1900	10%	0.44%	16%	5.00%	0.13%
EUR/USD	Call	1.1600	1.1900	10%	3.46%	66%	6.84%	0.17%

to 2.19% (i.e., 1.99% + 0.20%). If the bank has sold this option, it will now cost an extra 0.20% to buy it back. If the bank has bought the option, it can now sell it at a higher price and earn a profit.

Let us also note that vega decreases as time to expiry draws closer, because there is less chance for a contract to move in-the-money. Holding all other variables constant, we note in Table 10.8 the decrease in vega as time to maturity declines from three months to one month.

An additional element of volatility risk we must consider relates to the volatility smile, which is a measure of implied volatility versus strike level. The volatility smile arises because sentiment in the market may suggest that a spot rate is trending in one direction; it becomes especially important when pricing and revaluing out-of-the-money options. Assume, for example, that the current £/$ rate is 1.8300 and the market believes that £ may strengthen to

T A B L E 10.8

Sample Option Vegas — 3

3-Month Options –1 month to expiry								
Description	Call/ Put	Strike	ATM Price	Volatility	Premium	Delta	Gamma	Vega
EUR/USD	Call	1.1900	1.1900	10%	1.12%	49%	14.12%	0.11%
EUR/USD	Call	1.2200	1.1900	10%	0.29%	19%	9.68%	0.08%
EUR/USD	Call	1.2500	1.1900	10%	5.50%	4%	3.16%	0.03%
EUR/USD	Call	1.1600	1.1900	10%	2.79%	79%	9.24%	0.07%

1.7000 in the near term. If a £ buyer requests a quote from a bank on a one-month, out-of-the-money, put struck at 1.8000, the bank may believe that the strike will be reached very quickly (at which point it will begin losing money). The current level of at-the-money volatility does not compensate for the risk being taken in selling the option. In fact, if the market is correct, £/$ could move to 1.8000 in a matter of days, forcing the option in-the-money. Under this scenario the bank will seek to protect itself by increasing quoted volatility for the out-of-the-money contracts; this creates the appearance of a smile. Note that the same volatility differential must be applied when the portfolio is revalued (e.g., the full smile, rather than a pure straight-line at-the-money volatility quote) or a significant profit misstatement may occur. Figure 10.4 illustrates a sample volatility smile.

F I G U R E 10.4

Volatility Smile

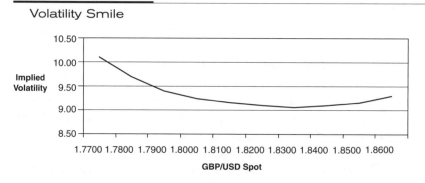

We summarize the key characteristics of vega as follows:

- Vega is the rate of change of the option value with respect to a change in the volatility of the underlying.
- Vega is always positive for buyers of options and negative for sellers of options.
- If vega is high, the option price is sensitive to changes in volatility; if vega is low, price is relatively insensitive to changes in volatility.
- Vega is highest for ATM options and has a profile similar to that of gamma.

Theta

Theta is the change in an option's value given the passage of time, all other variables remaining constant. This sensitivity is based on the fact that value decays with each passing day. Since a purchased option is a decaying asset (i.e., a portion of the premium paid is time value, which declines every day), theta is virtually always negative.[1]

Time value decays slowly at the start of the option's life and accelerates as maturity draws closer, since the likelihood of moving in-the-money (or further in-the-money) becomes increasingly remote. In fact, the approximation for time decay is given as the square root of time. If we consider a 90-day option, the first point on the time decay curve is $\sqrt{90}$, or 9.49; with 9 days to expiry the time decay point is $\sqrt{9}$, or 3; and so forth. This process yields the distinctive curve illustrated in Figure 10.5 (which assumes the appearance of the calendar spread profile we described in Chapter 6).

A bank wanting to square a long options position in its portfolio must attempt to do so as early as possible in order to preserve as much premium as possible. Theta works against the speculator buying options on an outright basis when the market is calm: if the spot rate and volatility remain unchanged (e.g., the market is calm), there will be no possibility of a gain to offset the inevitable loss from time decay. Not surprisingly, time decay benefits option sellers. This occurs because as an option moves through time, the rate of decay increases, allowing the seller to preserve more of the premium charged for selling the option.

---

1 There is an exception to this rule related to the likelihood of early exercise on a near-the-money American-style option; we shall, however, not consider this special case further.

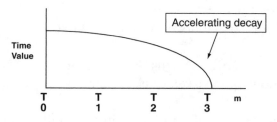

Time Decay

We can summarize the key characteristics of theta as follows:

- Theta is the rate of change of the option value with respect to the passage of time.
- Theta is always negative for buyers of options and positive for sellers of options.
- If theta is high, the option price is sensitive to the passage of time; if theta is low, price is less sensitive to the passage of time.
- Time decay accelerates as expiry of the option draws closer; short-term options feature very high thetas, meaning their value decays very rapidly.

Rho and Phi

Options are sensitive to changes in the risk-free interest rate; this sensitivity is measured via rho. In general, high interest rates lead to lower forward prices, which reduce the value of purchased calls and increase the value of purchased puts; the opposite relationship holds when rates decline. Currency options have an added level of interest rate exposure, as changes in either of the two underlying currency interest rates will affect the forward rate, and therefore the price of an option. When considering currency options we therefore distinguish between phi, which measures interest rate changes in the fixed currency, and rho, which measures interest rate changes in the variable currency.

Let us consider the €/$ relationship as an example. If € (the fixed currency) has a higher interest rate than $ (the variable currency), the forward points are deducted from the spot rate to calculate the forward rate. If the € rate rises, it will increase the interest

T A B L E   10.9

Key Option Risk Sensitivities

	Delta	Gamma	Vega	Theta	Rho
Long Call	Positive	Positive	Positive	Negative	Varies
Long Put	Negative	Positive	Positive	Negative	Varies
Short Call	Negative	Negative	Negative	Positive	Varies
Short Put	Positive	Negative	Negative	Positive	Varies

differential between the two currencies, increasing the size of the forward points and decreasing the forward price. € calls therefore become less valuable, because € can be bought in the market more cheaply. € puts, in contrast, will become more valuable. If $ rates rise, the forward rate rises, making € calls more valuable and € puts less valuable.

Table 10.9 summarizes the key sensitivities described above.

PORTFOLIO MANAGEMENT

Managing a portfolio of options is a complex process that is sometimes subject to competing forces. For instance, an intermediary that is actively quoting and trading options must consider the requirements of:

- Clients, who seek the best possible pricing
- Business managers, who want the portfolio to be profitable
- Financial officers, who want to ensure that options in the portfolio are being valued properly
- Risk managers, who want to know the nature and magnitude of the risks in the portfolio
- Senior managers, who want to ensure that risks are prudent and that exposure being taken is sufficiently profitable

We know by now that the value of a portfolio is subject to constant changes as underlying asset references change, new trades are executed, and existing trades expire or are exercised. This dynamism demands continuous review and management. To consider how this function works in practice, let us examine the management of a portfolio of currency options.

The management of a currency option portfolio is similar to that of a spot foreign exchange portfolio, except that several additional variables must be considered, including interest rate risk and volatility risk. The first step in managing an option portfolio is to identify the most liquid market instruments available to manage the risks generated by the book. This is normally some combination of spot positions, forwards, and money market deposits. Liquid market rates are used to calculate a pricing curve (i.e., discount function), which can be used to value all positions in the portfolio uniformly. Instrument cash flows (from each individual option trade) are mapped onto the dates of a pricing curve. This is normally done using interpolation methods (e.g., exponential interpolation or cubic splines), which have the effect of splitting the actual instrument cash flows among the dates on the pricing curve. Once the cash flows are mapped, the portfolio can be valued. Then, the portfolio's value sensitivity to currency, volatility, time, and interest rate changes is measured; this provides an estimate of the riskiness of the portfolio. This general process is summarized in Figure 10.6.

While all steps in the process are important, the mapping and valuation steps are rather mechanistic once a deal booking, cash flow mapping, and valuation framework has been established. The art and science of risk management is contained in the final step, which involves using the sensitivities described above to determine how best to manage the risks in the portfolio in order to maximize profits. Though we shall continue exploring the topic in the context of currency options, it is worth noting that the process is equally applicable to all other classes of options.

Option traders do not individually hedge every single option in their portfolios. Rather, they focus on the overall risks inherent in their portfolios, which include the natural hedges of purchased and sold options. A typical portfolio is generally quite diversified (e.g., long/short exposure to asset appreciation and depreciation). Some options are generated by client deals, others by proprietary views, and still others as a way of balancing the portfolio; these are supplemented by cash and forward market positions. The value of the portfolio is subject to constant change resulting from moves in underlying currency rates, interest rates, volatility, and time, and by the addition of new trades and exercise or expiration of existing trades. The portfolio can therefore be considered a dynamic pool of transactions that has to be managed on a continuous basis.

F I G U R E   10.6

General Portfolio Management Process

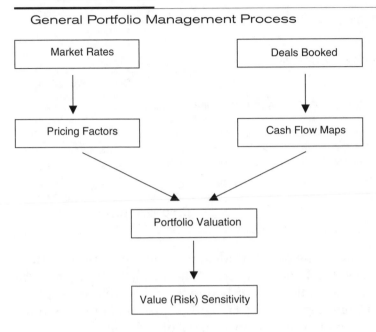

Managing a Portfolio of Vanilla Options

We know that each option trade a bank executes will either increase or decrease overall option portfolio exposure. The bank must therefore be attuned to overall portfolio delta, gamma, vega, theta, and rho in order to properly manage the net position. And, though portfolio analysis is clearly most important, traders usually know which individual options in their portfolios are the most important to monitor. In extreme scenarios, such as when a single large option at a given strike dominates the portfolio, a trader may prefer to hedge the option separately in order to manage the balance of the portfolio with greater ease.

Let us consider a very simple example of hedging a mini-portfolio of options and spot positions in €/$; again, the same principles apply to other asset classes. We begin by considering the delta hedges of the trades illustrated in Table 10.10.

Let us consider the first short at-the-money put option. If the buyer exercises the option, the buyer will pay the trader €10m, meaning the trade has positive delta. Thus, in order to hedge this

T A B L E 10.10

Delta Hedging a Portfolio

EUR/USD Trades	ATM Price			1.1900			
EUR Amount	Trade	Period	Strike	Volatility	Premium	Delta of the Position	Weighted Delta Position
10,000,000	Sell-Put	3-month	1.1900	10%	1.99%	49%	4,900,000
5,000,000	Sell-Call	3-month	1.2200	11%	1.19%	−32%	−1,600,000
10,000,000	Sell-Call	1-month	1.2500	12%	0.14%	−8%	−800,000
30,000,000	Buy-Call	1-week	1.1900	10%	0.56%	50%	15,000,000
15,000,000	Sell-Cash	Spot		0%	0.00%	−100%	−15,000,000
					Net Delta Portfolio		2,500,000

option individually, the bank's traders will sell the delta amount of the option, or €4.9m. To hedge the next short call, the trader focuses on the delta of –32%; the proper hedge would therefore hedge by purchasing €1.6m (e.g., 32% of €5m). The process is the same for the long at-the-money call with a delta of 50%: in this case the trader would sell €15m spot to hedge the position individually. Finally, if the trader wanted to square the cash position, it would buy back €15m. Naturally, since delta is additive, it is simpler for the trader to simply examine the net delta of the portfolio and arrange a single hedge transaction. Since the net portfolio delta is €2.5m (including the spot cash position), the trader needs only to arrange a single transaction where it sells €2.5m; this will generate a net portfolio delta of 0, meaning the portfolio is no longer exposed to small changes in the €/$ exchange rate. The portfolio hedge position can be created by:

- Selling €2.5m spot.
- Selling a €5m 50% delta call. This would create a delta hedge of –€2.5, bringing the net delta to zero. However, the trader would then need to examine the impact of gamma and vega generated by the overarching call.
- Buying a €10m 25% delta put. This would also create a delta hedge of – €2.5m. Again, the trader would need to analyze the impact on gamma and vega.
- Transacting any other combination of trades that results in a delta of – €2.5m.

At the conclusion, the bank's option trader has hedged the portfolio delta, but since €/$ is a dynamic variable, the hedges will have to be rebalanced continuously. In order to cope more precisely with this task, the trader uses gamma to understand the sensitivity of the portfolio deltas to changes in spot. To understand the practical effect of this process, let us consider the gamma of the portfolio as summarized in Table 10.11, which provides the change in delta for a 1.00% change in the spot rate.

A 1.00% percent move in the spot rate leads to a portfolio delta adjustment of €7.08m, which suggests a relatively high gamma. In fact, most of this change is due to the long €30m call with a one-week expiry. If spot rises by 1.00%, the delta on the one-week option moves from 50% to nearly 79%, which is equal to an individual delta sale of €8.637m. If spot moves down by 1.00% an equally large purchase of € will be required. We can see, therefore, that this option is responsible for most of this portfolio's gamma.

By way of contrast the first three-month €10m put has a much lower delta, suggesting a lower rebalancing requirement. If spot rates rise by 1.00% the put will be less valuable and its delta will decline. Having sold €4.9m to hedge this option originally, the trader now needs to buy back €788,000. If the spot rate declines, then the put becomes more expensive and the trader will sell an additional €788,000 to bring the delta hedge up to nearly 58% (e.g., 49% + 7.88%). The same logic can be applied to the other options in the portfolio. In practice, of course, the trader will attempt to balance gamma on a portfolio, rather than a trade-specific, basis.

Eliminating gamma from a portfolio is difficult. The only failsafe way to flatten gamma completely is to arrange an equal and opposite trade with the same characteristics, so that the risks of the two options net out. However, many traders preserve gamma in their portfolios as it creates more trading (i.e., potential profit) opportunities.

A trader must also manage the portfolio vega position, as changes in volatility have an immediate impact on P&L. As noted earlier, vega measures the change in the value of the option (or portfolio) for a 1.00% change in volatility. Returning to our portfolio example, we note specific vegas in Table 10.12 for each option and the entire portfolio. If volatility rises by 1.00%, then the long options will be worth more since they can be sold at a higher premium; short options, in contrast, will reflect a loss because it will

TABLE 10.11

Gamma Hedging a Portfolio

EUR/USD	Trades			ATM Price				Spot up 1% Delta	
EUR Amount	Call/Put	Period	Strike	Vol.	Premium	Delta	Gamma	Adj.	New Delta
10,000,000	Sell-Put	3-month	1.1900	10%	1.99%	49%	7.88%	7.88%	41.12%
50,000,000	Sell-Call	3-month	1.2200	11%	1.19%	-32%	6.56%	-6.56%	-38.56%
10,000,000	Sell-Call	1-month	1.2500	12%	0.14%	-8%	4.41%	-4.41%	-12.41%
300,000,000	Buy-Call	1-week	1.1900	10%	0.56%	50%	28.79%	28.79%	78.79%
15,000,000	Sell-Cash	Spot		0%	0.00%	-100%	0.00%	0	0
2,500,000	Sell-Cash	Spot		0%	0.00%	-100%	0.00%	0	0

T A B L E 10.12

Vega Hedging a Portfolio

EUR/USD	Trades			ATM Price	1.1900				
EUR Amount	Call/Put	Period	Strike	Volatility	Premium	Delta	Vega	Change in Value for a 1% Change in Volatility
10,000,000	Sell-Put	3-month	1.1900	10%	1.99%	49%	0.20%	-20,000
5,000,000	Sell-Call	3-month	1.2200	11%	1.19%	-32%	0.18%	-9,000
10,000,000	Sell-Call	1-month	1.2500	12%	0.14%	-8%	0.05%	-5,000
30,000,000	Buy-Call	1-week	1.1900	10%	0.56%	50%	0.06%	18,000
15,000,000	Sell-Cash	Spot		0%	0.00%	-100%	0.00%	0.00
2,500,000	Sell-Cash	Spot		0%	0.00%	-100%	0.00%	0.00
							Net	-16,000

cost more to buy them back. The reverse occurs if volatility falls. The portfolio in this example reflects a net loss of €16,000 for a 1% increase in volatility, and a net profit of €16,000 for a 1% decrease in volatility. Though this figure is relatively modest, the trader could neutralize the effects of volatility by buying options with enough vega to eliminate the exposure. Some care would need to be taken to consider the effects of the volatility smile, as a linear change in volatility may lead to different P&L impacts.

It is important to stress again that vega and gamma hedges will affect the delta position of the total portfolio and vice versa, so the total hedge must be rebalanced again. In practice it is not possible to hedge delta, then gamma, and then vega, as the portfolio will never be in balance; the correct sequence is to first balance vega, then gamma, and then delta, i.e., add delta hedge instruments, with no optionality, last.

Theta and rho can be managed in a similar fashion. Though they are less volatile measurements and generally have a smaller P&L impact, they must still be monitored and managed. This is particularly true of theta, which becomes very important as market volatility subsidies. A trader with long theta positions loses money steadily on a daily basis and may need to take some precautionary action (such as selling short-term options with a greater time decay) in order to manage loss levels.

Managing a Portfolio of Exotic Options

Most of the characteristics and procedures applicable to portfolio management of vanilla options are readily transferable to management of exotic options. However, since exotic options have some unique payoff characteristics that can alter their risk parameters, they must be considered during the portfolio management process. To illustrate this process we examine simple examples of barriers and digitals.

Barrier options may exhibit significant or minimal sensitivity to the key risk sensitivities—depending on the position of the barrier, strike, and underlying asset price. Consider, for instance, a position where a bank sells a €/$ 1.1900 call with a knock-out trigger at 1.1700. If the spot rate rises, the option will behave just like any other vanilla call option in the portfolio, and the bank's trader

FIGURE 10.7

(a) Delta of a Barrier (b) Gamma of a Barrier

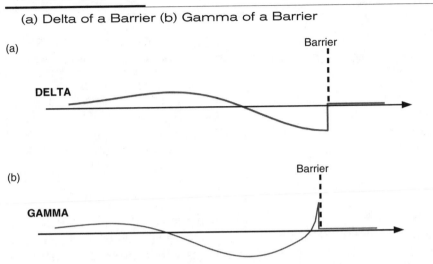

will cover the resulting delta above 50% in the manner described earlier. But as spot starts to move towards the trigger, the chances of the option being worth nothing accelerate. The trader will therefore notice that gamma becomes very large as the spot rate moves down; delta declines more quickly than normal, meaning the trader will have to adjust the delta hedge more frequently than on a vanilla option. One day prior to expiry, the delta and gamma profiles can assume those depicted in Figures 10.7(a) and 10.7 (b). The same process applies to an entire portfolio of barrier options; under this scenario the trader must be aware of all key barrier levels.

Reverse knock-ins create additional challenges. Table 10.13 illustrates the sensitivities for different time periods on a reverse knock-in € put with a strike at 1.1900 and a trigger at 1.1300. The table illustrates two spot scenarios: one with spot at 1.1900 (i.e., nearly ATM) and one with spot at 1.1350 (i.e., very close to the trigger).

If spot remains well above the trigger the option never comes into existence and hedging requirements are minimal. As time to expiry approaches and spot remains near 1.1938 (i.e., volatility is very low), the option is unlikely to knock-in and its value declines very quickly. If, however, the spot rate starts to move towards the trigger, instability increases. As option expiry draws nearer and spot approaches the knock-in barrier, delta and gamma increase significantly. As the results indicate, delta and gamma can increase

T A B L E   10.13

Sensitivities for a Reverse Knock-In Put Option

Time to Expiry	Current Spot	Premium	Delta	Gamma	Vega
3-months	1.1938	1.58%	50%	10.73%	0.27%
1-month	1.1938	0.45%	32%	18.45%	0.16%
1-day	1.1938	0%	0%	0%	0%
3-months	1.1350	5.51%	101%	5.16%	0.14%
1-month	1.1350	4.80%	146%	7.89%	0.08%
1-day	1.1350	2.13%	568%	904%	0.25%

above 100% because the option will come into existence in-the-money, with 600 FX points of intrinsic value (1.1900-1.1300). A delta of 568% one day prior to expiry suggests that the trader must purchase all of the intrinsic value immediately. Hedging this transaction instantaneously would, of course, be a formidable task, e.g., a €10m option would require a €56.8m spot hedge. Naturally, the prudent trader will hedge this position in small increments as the spot moves from 1.19 towards the barrier level. Nevertheless, the example illustrates the additional complexities that arise from risk-managing options that may or may not come into existence.

Similar challenges arise in managing a portfolio of digital options. As with barriers, the delta of the digital option increases more quickly than a vanilla option as the underlying reference moves closer-to-the-money. In fact, the delta hedge needs to be close to 100% as soon as the option is at-the-money. Gamma will be very large at this point, regardless of the time left to expiry. However, once the digital is in-the-money, gamma declines dramatically, meaning little in the way of delta-rebalancing requirements; the same occurs if the options moves, or remains, out-of-the-money.

Average price/strike options, in contrast, are easier to manage than vanilla options. As we know, the strike on an average strike option is the average of the spot prices over a period in time. This means that, as time passes, the average of the spot rates gains in influence, to the point where even large spot changes will not have much impact on the average. This makes it easier for the trader to delta hedge the option because there is a greater amount of certainty as to the maximum price path that can be traveled prior to expiry. Other structures, such as strangles, straddles, butterflies, and collars are commonly found in options portfolios and can easily be decomposed into their constituent parts and managed as part of the overall portfolio.

CHAPTER EXERCISES

1. A bank has just sold a €/$, 10 million € put with a delta of 45%. The position can be hedged by:
   a. Buying €4.5 million against $ spot
   b. Selling €4.5 million against $ spot
   c. Buying €5.5 million against $ spot
   d. Selling €5.5 million against $ spot
   e. None of the above

2. An option book manager is worried about imminent changes in currency volatility. Which tool might this manager use to measure this exposure in the trading book?
   a. Vega
   b. Theta
   c. Phi
   d. Gamma
   e. Rho

3. The sensitivity of an option's price to changes in spot is at its highest when the option is:
   a. At-the-money
   b. Out-of-the-money
   c. In-the-money
   d. Six months to expiry
   e. None of the above

4. Delta measures the sensitivity of an option's price with regard to a change in:
   a. Time
   b. Volatility
   c. Rates
   d. Underlying asset
   e. None of the above

5. Given an underlying asset of $100 and a strike price of $100, the delta of a long call is approximately equal to:

   a. − 0.25

   b. + 0.25

   c. − 0.50

   d. + 0.50

   e. + 0.10

6. The proper sequence by which to rebalance an option portfolio is:

   a. Vega, gamma, delta

   b. Delta, gamma, vega

   c. Vega, delta, gamma

   d. It does not matter

   e. None of the above

7. Given the following positions:
   Long call + $100,000 delta
   Long put − $250,000 delta
   Short call − $100,000 delta
   The necessary hedge to neutralize delta is to:

   a. Buy $250,000

   b. Sell $250,000

   c. Buy $100,000

   d. Sell $100,000

   e. None of the above

8. Which of the following is/are true?

   a. At-the-money options have maximum gamma

   b. Out-of-the-money options have minimum gamma

   c. In-the-money options have minimum gamma

   d. All of the above

   e. None of the above

9. The inclusion of a barrier option in a portfolio:

   a. Always creates greater delta and gamma instability

   b. May create greater delta and gamma instability

   c. Never creates greater delta and gamma instability

   d. Creates the same delta and gamma instability

   e. None of the above

Risk and Control Issues

INTRODUCTION

We have seen throughout the text that options are an essential element of modern financial markets, helping participants arrange and execute investment and risk management strategies. Understanding how to properly manage options from a control perspective is, therefore, vitally important, particularly given the pace of growth and change that has occurred in the marketplace over the past two decades. The control framework—whether for intermediaries or end-users—is broad in its scope and important in its detail. In this chapter we consider the essential elements of a framework designed to deal with risk and control of options activity, including credit and risk management controls, financial and internal audit controls, and legal and documentary controls. We also incorporate general discussion of regulatory risk and accounting requirements.

INTERNAL RISK MANAGEMENT

Institutions dealing actively with derivative products are aware of the need to build and maintain a proper internal control framework that permits prudent management of risks. A proper risk framework can create a more secure dealing environment, particularly when coupled with the financial and legal controls discussed in the sections below.

Internal risk management of options dealing forms part of the control process applicable to all risky products. While controlling options risk at a product level is important, it is one component of a broader set of business risks that must be considered in totality. This ensures that a firm is taking proper account of all of its risks, and that it derives the benefit of offsetting exposures.

Credit and Market Risks

Credit risk and market risk form the main focus of financial risk management. We can define credit risk as the risk of loss arising from a failure by a counterparty to perform on its contractual obligations. In terms of options business this means failure by a counterparty that has sold options to the firm to fulfill its obligations under the options contract. Thus, if Bank ABC buys an option contract from Bank XYZ (paying premium for the contract), and XYZ fails to perform as expected, ABC will suffer a credit loss. The amount of the loss will depend largely on the replacement value of the contract at the time of default. In some cases the loss may be relatively small: if ABC pays $100,000 in premium for a six-month option that is well out-of-the-money, and XYZ fails the day after the trade is booked, ABC loses $100,000 if the market has not moved. The loss in this instance relates to the time value of premium associated with the contract, because no intrinsic value exists. However, if the option moves $1m in-the-money and XYZ defaults one day prior to expiry, ABC will lose $1m. That is, it will cost ABC $1m to replace the contract based on the characteristics of the contract and the movement of the market. The option in this case is comprised solely of intrinsic value, because time value is negligible one day prior to expiry.

The computation of replacement values based on degree of future moneyness is generally accomplished through standard credit risk quantification models that value the underlying asset path through simulation processes and statistical confidence levels. The degree to which an underlying asset price might cause the option to move in-the-money has a direct bearing on the amount of potential credit exposure assigned to a trade.[1] Not surprisingly, options that have the potential of generating a large payout—including those with a large notional value, volatility

---

1 Those interested in a detailed examination of replacement cost estimates may wish to consult Banks (2003).

underlying or leveraged payout formula—can create significant exposures.

In the example given above, XYZ has no exposure to ABC: once it receives premium for the option, it owes future performance to ABC, and not vice versa. XYZ therefore generates no credit exposure when selling options. In fact, short options carry no credit risk except in two special cases: a put on a call (compound option), where the seller of the put may be exercised against and have to accept a long call position, and a currency option, where exercise by the buyer can lead to delivery risk on the currency component of the transaction (e.g., the overnight risk that arises in settling currency balances across time zones).

Market risk is the risk of loss arising from an adverse movement in any of the market variables that define an option's value. In fact, we've examined aspects of market risk through the Greek risk sensitivities analyzed in the last chapter. Thus, delta, gamma, vega, theta, and rho are essential market risk loss parameters, each of which can appear depending on whether a participant's portfolio is long or short puts or calls. We know, for instance, that if Bank ABC is net long volatility in its option portfolio (it will suffer losses as volatility declines, and gains as volatility rises). Similarly, if the bank's portfolio is net short delta, gains will accrue as the market declines and losses will mount as it rallies. If its portfolio is net long theta it will suffer daily time decay losses, and if it is net short theta it will generate profits (e.g., premium preservation). However, market risks extend beyond risk sensitivities to include parameters such as liquidity risk (the risk of loss arising from an inability to buy/sell an asset or contract at the mark-to-market price), correlation risk (the risk of loss arising from adverse changes in correlations between multiple assets/contracts), curve risk (the risk of loss from adverse changes in the shape of the term structure of interest rates or the volatility curve), basis risk (the risk of loss from adverse changes in the basis or differential, between two assets), and spread risk (the risk of loss from adverse changes in the differential between a risk-free and risky asset), among others.

The Risk Management Framework

Internal credit and market risk managers often serve as the "front line" of controls, enforcing a series of standards that are intended to keep a firm's risk operations in balance. Credit and market risk managers are involved in establishing limits and other controls for risky businesses. These may also include formal new product reviews that examine the structural nuances and risks of new option products or strategies; this is especially important for option-embedded securities and derivatives, which may feature very unique payoffs and risks.

The internal risk management process must, in the first instance, be driven by the institution's risk philosophy and tolerance, which are generally defined and set by the board of directors and enforced by executive management. The philosophy is a descriptor of the types of risks the firm is willing to take in order to achieve its end goals. The firm may be relatively focused in its risk taking or be very willing to assume a broad range of risks; the philosophy helps define this view. Tolerance, in turn, is the amount of capital the firm is willing and able to risk in its activities. In other words, it is the maximum amount it is willing to lose under extreme scenarios. The tolerance level is, itself, a function of the firm's financial resources, and its ability to generate a minimum level of risk-adjusted return on the capital it allocates in support of risky activities. Only once the philosophy and tolerance have been defined, and sanctioned, is a firm prepared to implement a practical daily risk management framework.

The market risk framework is typically based on a four-stage process that involves:

- Identifying all market risks impacting options (and other risky products); as noted above, these may include:
  - □ Delta, gamma, vega, theta, rho risks
  - □ Spread risk
  - □ Basis risk
  - □ Correlation risk
  - □ Curve risk
- Quantifying all risks arising from option trading (and from dealing in other risky business)
- Establishing meaningful risk limits for relevant market risk exposure classes that relate specifically to the institution's stated risk tolerance level and the potential returns it can earn
- Monitoring market exposures on a continuous basis to ensure that risks generated remain within limits, and making adjustments as necessary

In addition to setting meaningful delta, gamma, vega, theta, and rho portfolio limits that correspond to the firm's tolerance levels, the creation of maturity concentration limits is a prudent control measure. Recall that high gamma options with very short maturities can create significant hedging issues within the portfolio. Accordingly, placing a limit on the maximum amount of options that mature over a given short-term horizon (e.g., next one week, two weeks, three weeks) can help manage some of the inherent instability that might arise in the portfolio. For instance, if a €50m limit is placed on the portfolio, the trader must ensure that open deals maturing during the period remain at or below the limit. This may involve selling some positions or swapping long and short positions to square the book.

The credit risk management framework is based on a similar four-stage process:

- Identifying all credit risks related to options (and other risky transactions); these may include
  - □ Counterparty credit risk
  - □ Correlated credit risk
  - □ Sovereign risk
- Quantifying all risks arising from the options business, and developing algorithms that account for netting of multiple exposures with a single counterparty.
- Establishing limits related to the net credit exposures the institution is willing to assume, ensuring some relationship to the stated risk tolerance and the potential returns that can be earned; concentration limits are likely to be set by counterparty, ratings, industry, and country.
- Monitoring credit exposures on a continuous basis to ensure that risks generated in the business remain within limits.

Those that deal actively in options and other risky products must be able to quantify and monitor all of their exposures accurately and efficiently. This is typically done through a commercial or proprietary risk management system, which captures essential details regarding each trade, and which can also aggregate exposures across products and counterparties to provide proper portfolio views.

Market and credit risk processes should be reviewed for efficacy on a regular basis (e.g., every year). Once again, we emphasize the point that any risk control process must be applied to all risky instruments and transactions; options generally form only one component of an institution's financial dealing and, while aspects must be considered separately, the entire credit and market risk picture must be managed on a portfolio basis.

Figure 11.1 summarizes the internal risk management framework.

FIGURE 11.1

The Internal Risk Management Framework

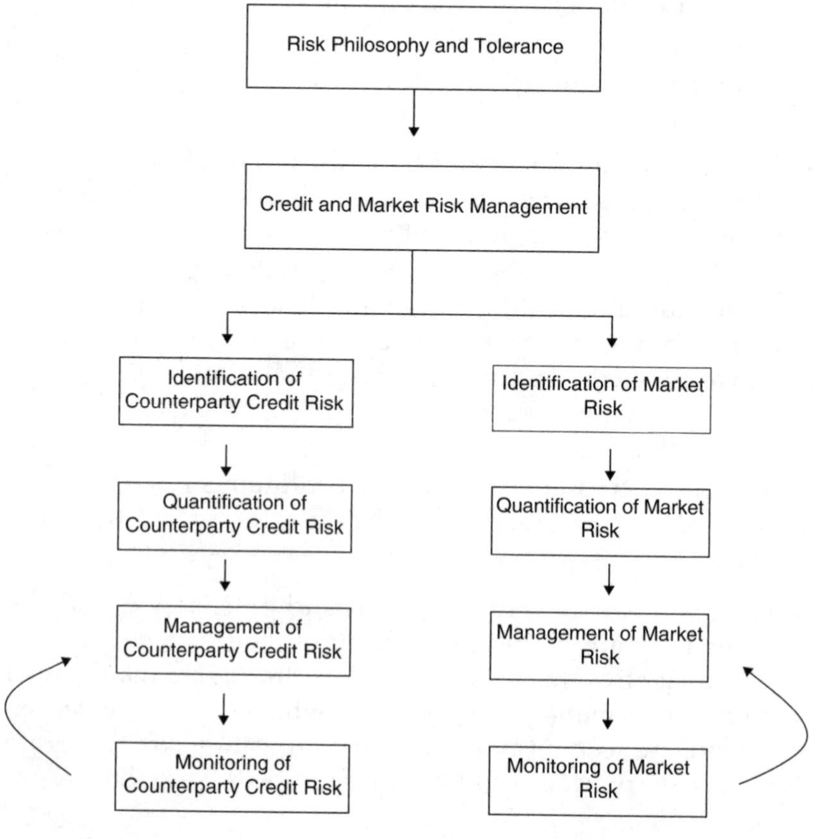

REGULATORY RISK REQUIREMENTS

In December 1995, the Bank for International Settlements (BIS) Supervisors Committee approved an amendment (i.e., the market risk amendment) to the Basel Accord setting forth capital requirements for exposure to general market risk for all positions held in an institution's trading account (and for all foreign exchange and commodity positions, regardless of account location), as well as for specific risk of debt and equity positions held in the trading account. The requirements of the U.S. rules implementing the market risk amendment became effective on a mandatory basis in 1998.

In 2004, the BIS implemented the Basel II Accord as a means of strengthening the counterparty risk component of the capital allocation process.[2] Under Basel II, participating institutions allocate capital in support of counterparty credit risks via the Internal Ratings Based (IRB) method, in either foundation or advanced form. The Basel II credit framework replaces the original framework promulgated in 1988.

Under the BIS framework national banking regulators specify three risks as related to derivatives:

- General market risk: the risk arising from changes in the reference asset's value due to broad market movements (e.g., changes in the general level of interest rates)
- Specific risk: the risk arising from changes in the reference asset's value due to factors other than broad market movements (e.g., changes in the reference asset's credit risk)
- Counterparty credit risk: the risk arising from the possibility that the counterparty may default on amounts owed on a derivative transaction

General Market Risk

A banking organization subject to the market risk amendment must use internal models to measure its daily value-at-risk (VAR) for covered positions in the trading account (and for foreign exchange and commodity positions located in any account). Capital charges are applied to general market risks. VAR is a

---

2 Additional elements of Basel II focus on operational risks, which we shall not consider further.

widely used portfolio risk management tool that uses asset correlations and volatilities, along with defined liquidation periods, to define potential market risk losses under specified statistical confidence levels.

Specific Risk

In general, a bank must apply capital to cover its specific risks. However, if it can demonstrate to regulators that its internal models accurately measure the specific risk of its equity and debt positions in the trading account (including those related to options), and this measure is included in its VAR-based capital charge, it can reduce or eliminate its specific risk capital charges (subject to the minimum specific risk charges prescribed in the amendment). Standard specific risk charges for an asset may be calculated by using the specific risk weighting factors that apply to the referenced asset. Matched positions (i.e., those that represent a perfect match between the derivative and an underlying exposure) do not incur specific risk charges; open positions (i.e., those that represent no effective hedge at all) attract the same standard specific risk charges as a cash position in the reference asset.

Counterparty Risk

Capital is applied to counterparty risks. The advent of the IRB framework allows the credit capital allocation process to be driven by a firm's internal models and is intended to bring regulatory and economic capital processes closer together. The IRB framework requires an institution to develop estimates of potential future credit exposures, default probabilities, and recovery rates. Those choosing not to develop their own credit exposure estimates can revert to risk factors supplied by the BIS; this is known as the IRB foundation methodology. Those that have models capable of computing credit exposures may do so under the advance methodology, but only once the models have been vetted by the relevant national regulator. Default probabilities and recovery rates are determined by each individual institution through proprietary or benchmarking methods. When these probabilities and recovery estimates are applied to BIS- or internally-generated potential future credit exposures, they yield an estimate of possible economic losses, which must then be supported by a prescribed amount of capital.

INTERNAL FINANCIAL AND AUDIT CONTROLS

The control infrastructure is supplemented and strengthened by oversight from other independent management groups, including those involved with financial control and internal audit.

Financial Controls

Internal financial controls exist in order to track and verify transactions that can impact a firm's balance sheet, income statement, and cash flow statement, including any options dealing forming part of a firm's operations. The duties of the financial professionals of a firm, with specific reference to options dealing (but easily extended into all other assets/contracts), cross important boundaries that affect the front, mid-, and back offices, as well as executive management and regulators. Specific minimum internal financial controls (that are independent of the business unit generating P&L) should include those that properly support internal management requirements and external reporting (e.g., Basel II compliance, Sarbanes-Oxley compliance, and so on):

- Ensuring mark-to-market pricing feeds for options come from an independent source that cannot be manipulated
- Establishing reserves for option positions that appear impaired (e.g., illiquid, exposed to rapidly deteriorating counterparties)
- Interpreting and implementing accounting policies related to the options dealing business, e.g., proper recognition of options serving as hedges (with attendant reduction in capital charges)
- Making certain that the technology platform/trade entry screens include the entire population of daily dealings, in order to avoid any breaks/fails/settlement problems or financial fraud
- Reconciling daily trading activity in order to generate a link between the firm's P&L and books and records
- Gathering independent pricing valuations of exotic options to ensure that the daily marking policy is equitable

- Creating independent risk management reports reflecting option activities; these may be applied to risk limits supplied by the market and credit risk management departments
- Preparing executive management/board-level revenue and risk reporting to demonstrate the trends of the business
- Preparing all regulatory risk reports required under national or international regulations

Internal Audit

Virtually all major institutions have some form of internal audit function to ensure the integrity of operations. The typical audit function examines business and control units on a regular cycle, testing activities against established policies and procedures to ensure proper compliance and control. Deficiencies, weaknesses, shortcomings, or other potential problems are flagged and elevated when internal auditors are performing their functions properly.

Given this function, it is clear that units that take positions in options must form part of the regular audit cycle. In addition, risk management and credit management units that control a firm's options dealing must be reviewed regularly. Auditors focusing on derivative books generally, and options books specifically, must ensure the market and credit risk limits mentioned above are effective in controlling exposures. They must also verify the nature, quality, and accuracy of the pricing values/marks that the independent financial control units derive/supply for the computation of daily P&L, position tracking, and books and records reconciliation. Any discrepancies must, of course, be resolved as a matter of urgency.

LEGAL CONTROLS

Dealing in options (and other derivatives) requires effective legal, control, and settlements procedures; this is particularly true for OTC transactions. In fact, legal documentation is at the center of control. Such documentation, which must have a legal basis in a local dealing jurisdiction, is designed to reflect the terms of trade between two counterparties and establishes the rights of each party. Most derivatives documentation is contracted under the International Swaps and Derivatives Association (ISDA) framework and applies to options, swaps, forwards, and other OTC contracts. Though market practitioners can employ other forms of documentation (including, for example, the German Rahmenverstrag and the Association Francaise de Banque forms), most active dealers use ISDA; accordingly, our focus in this section is on elements of the ISDA process.

ISDA, which was chartered in 1985, is the global trade association representing participants in the derivatives industry. The organization has routinely pioneered efforts to identify and reduce sources of risk in the derivatives and risk management business; notable accomplishments include:

- Developing the ISDA Master Agreement
- Publishing a wide range of related documentation materials covering a variety of derivative classes
- Obtaining legal opinions regarding the enforceability of netting and collateral arrangements
- Securing recognition of the risk-reducing effects of netting in determining capital requirements
- Promoting sound risk management practices
- Advancing the understanding and treatment of derivatives and risk management from both a public policy and regulatory capital perspective

These endeavors are consistent with its overall mission, which is to encourage the prudent and effective development of the OTC derivatives business by:

- Promoting practices conducive to the efficient conduct of the business, including the development and maintenance of derivatives documentation
- Promoting the establishment of sound risk management practices
- Fostering high standards of commercial conduct
- Advancing international public understanding of the business
- Educating members and others on legislative regulatory, legal, documentation, accounting, tax, operational, technological, and other issues affecting them

ISDA Documentation Framework

The general ISDA framework, which has been refined and expanded over the past two decades, is comprised of several component parts, any (or all) of which an institution may utilize as part of its legal procedures:

- Master Agreement
  - □ Printed form
  - □ Schedule

- Credit Support Documents
  - □ Credit Support Annex, Credit Support Deed
  - □ Margin Provisions

- Confirmations
  - □ Long Form
  - □ Short Form

- Definitions

The Master Agreement is comprised of the printed form, which is a multipage document of standard terms and conditions that is not intended to be altered by the two parties to the agreement, and the Schedule, which is the attachment that two parties negotiate and can enhance, alter, or customize at will (including inserting changes that alter the printed form). The Master Agreement serves as a mechanism to avoid separate, and lengthy, documentation of each individual transaction by establishing, and then repeatedly referencing, standard terms and conditions. The terms and conditions relate primarily to legal and credit issues. The 1992 Master Agreement, which replaced the 1987 agreement, was itself replaced in 2002 by a new version, which is 50% longer than the previous versions; the additional material in the 2002 version is part of the industry's continued effort to clarify and standardize as much as possible within the legal environment, while retaining the flexibility to accommodate innovation.

The framework also allows for use of Credit Support Documents, which are intended primarily to establish credit arrangements between two parties (e.g., the need for one or both parties to post collateral, actions to be taken in the event certain credit exposure thresholds are breached or a ratings downgrade occurs, and so forth). The primary credit documents include the Credit Support Annex, the Credit Support Deed (used primarily under English law), and the 2001 Margin Provisions.

Confirmations, the third element of the framework, serve as evidence of individual transactions, and can be negotiated in long form or short form. Long-form confirmations, as the name suggests, are detailed documents that contain all relevant aspects of the legal/credit terms of a transaction (much as the Master Agreement does), and are generally used when the product/market is relatively new and lacks dealing standards, or when a transaction is so customized that it requires specialized documentation. Short-form confirmations, in contrast, are relatively simple forms that serve primarily to document the economics of a new transaction; terms and conditions automatically reference the Master Agreement and associated Definitions. Short forms are used when the market is standardized and mature and when product definitions are well established. Not surprisingly, the mechanism is efficient and reduces costs and operational errors.

Definitions, the last major component of the framework, serve to describe standard terms and provisions for different product/market segments. Definitions are introduced under ISDA sponsorship when a market has reached such a state of maturity that standardization is possible; standard Definitions have been issued for bullion derivatives (1997), government bond options (1997), Euro derivatives (1998), FX and currency options (1998), commodity derivatives (1993, 2005), equity derivatives (1996, 2002), and credit derivatives (1999, 2003). Short-form confirmations generally rely on, and reference, Definitions as part of the documentary process.

The general ISDA framework[3] is illustrated in Figure 11.2.

In the section that follows we briefly review certain clauses of interest that are contained within the Master Agreement.

ISDA Master Agreement

The 2002 ISDA Master Agreement (Multicurrency Cross Border) updates the 1987 and 1992 documents, expanding the breadth of products covered (thus promoting cross-product netting), addressing new legal developments that have appeared over the past

---

3 Note that the ISDA framework also includes certain bridges (cross agreements) and protocols (master change documents); we shall not consider them in further detail.

FIGURE 11.2

The General ISDA Documentation Framework

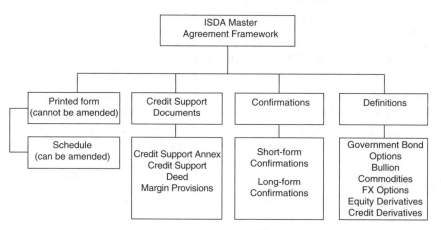

15 years, and clarifying important aspects of preceding versions. Key sections of note include:

Section 2: Obligations

Section 2(a) indicates that each transaction confirmation dictates payment terms of both parties, along with the timing and the method of payment. This section, which allows for physical deliveries, clarifies that the payment obligations are subject to the condition that no event of counterparty default has occurred and that no early termination date has been designated.

Section 2(c) provides that payments may be netted, as long as they are due on the same date, are payable in the same currency, and pertain to the same transaction. Subparagraph (ii) of this section enables parties to elect the option of netting two or more transactions, provided that they occur on the same payment date and in the same currency.

Section 3: Representations

Section 3 allows both parties and any credit support provider (e.g., guarantor, letter of credit issuer) to make representations that are automatically replicated each time a new swap transaction is arranged. Any misrepresentation comprises an event of default that enables the nondefaulting party to terminate the option (or swap) agreement.

Subparagraph (a) contains basic representations that both parties declare, including those referencing:

- Status
- Powers
- Lack of violation or conflict
- Consents
- Binding obligations

Other subparagraphs contain representations about the absence of certain events of default and potential events of default, absence of litigation, and the accuracy of information identified in the schedule.

Section 4: Agreements

Section 4 contains a list of agreements that both parties are obligated to adhere to as long as either party has obligations under the agreement; each party must:

- Furnish specified information
- Maintain dealing authorizations
- Comply with applicable laws
- Comply with tax agreements
- Pay stamp taxes/duties as applicable

Section 5: Events of Default and Termination Events

Section 5 contains a list of events that constitute an event of default or a termination event. This is critically important for proper management of counterparty risk, as parties to a transaction must be apprised of when a possible failure to pay will actually trigger legal actions.

Section 5(a): Events of Default

- Failure to pay or deliver. This event applies to the failure of a party to make a scheduled payment or delivery under Section 2, three days after notice.
- Breach of agreement; repudiation of agreement. This event can exist as an event of default only in limited circumstances and features a 30-day grace period following notice.
- Credit support default. This event provides that a credit support default can lead to an event of default under a derivative; it is not applicable if the derivative

counterparty's obligation under the transaction is not supported by another entity (guarantor).

- Misrepresentation. This event applies to misrepresentation made by either party or its credit support provider.
- Default under specified transaction. This event provides that if a party defaults on its obligation under a specified transaction, the nondefaulting party may elect to terminate the derivative.
- Cross default (obligation default). If specified in the schedule, this provision enables a party to declare the derivative to be in default if the other party or its credit support provider defaults on its obligation beyond an agreed threshold amount.
- Bankruptcy. This section applies to each party and any credit support provider, and specifies that if one party is subject to a variety of events associated with bankruptcy or insolvency, the other party may declare the derivative in default.
- Merger without assumption. If a party consolidates/ amalgamates or merges with, or into, another entity and the resulting entity fails to assume the obligations under the agreement or no longer benefits from a credit support document (guarantee), then the other party can terminate any transaction under the agreement.

Section 5(b): Termination Events
The following events constitute termination events under the Master Agreement:

- Illegality
- Force Majeure Event
- Tax Event
- Tax Event Upon Merger
- Additional Termination Events

Each one of these events permits one of the parties to the transaction(s) to end the agreement and settle outstanding amounts due/payable.

Section 6: Early Termination; Close-Out Netting
Section 6 represents the right to terminate following an event of default or a termination event. If either occurs, the nondefaulting/

affected party has the right to designate an early termination date (within 20 days of notice) by which the derivative(s) will end. Additionally, the parties have an opportunity to elect (in the Schedule) to have the derivative(s) terminate automatically and immediately upon the occurrence of certain events. This automatic termination election is designed to allow the nondefaulting party to exercise its termination rights outside of insolvency proceedings. In other words, it enables an early termination date to occur prior to the filing of insolvency proceedings. Note that it may be disadvantageous to select the automatic early termination election for derivatives that benefit from a credit support provider. The immediate termination of the derivative may not provide sufficient time to access and benefit from the credit support. The section also provides details on the effect of designation, calculations on payment date, payments[4] on early termination (depending on whether early

---

4 For example, an ISDA Master Agreement may prescribe the method that the Calculation Agent should use to value the asset when dealer quotations are not available or are not used. The dealer price is generally determined either by referring to a market quotation source or by polling a group of dealers, and reflects changes in the credit profile of the reference obligor and reference asset. If it is not feasible to specify the method of valuation (such as default probabilities, or option pricing), an alternative might be to require the Calculation Agent to use a method of valuing the class of the referenced credit along with a detailed report outlining valuation methodology—formulas, assumptions, and models. If periodic valuations are required in the agreement, valuation methods should be consistent over the duration of the contract.

A Market Quotation is defined as a quotation from a leading dealer in the relevant market (selected by the nondefaulting party) for an amount that would be paid to the nondefaulting party or by the nondefaulting party in consideration of an agreement between the leading dealer and the nondefaulting party to enter into a transaction that would have the effect of preserving the economic equivalent of all payment or delivery obligations under the transactions. If more than three Market Quotations are provided, the Market Quotation is defined as the average of the remaining quotations after the highest and lowest are disregarded.

Section 6(e)(iv) of the ISDA Master Agreement supports the enforceability of the Market Quotation close-out valuation method. It states that the parties agree that, if Market Quotation applies, the amount recoverable under the ISDA Master Agreement on termination is a reasonable pre-estimate of loss and not a penalty. Further, such amount is payable for the loss of bargain and the loss of protection against future risks. Other than as specifically provided, neither party will be entitled to recover any additional damages as a consequence of such losses.

Loss is calculated by reference to the nondefaulting party's total losses and costs in connection with the ISDA Master Agreement as at the early termination date. It includes loss of bargain, cost of funding, or, without duplication, loss or cost incurred as a result of its terminating, liquidating, obtaining, or re-establishing any hedge or related trading position. It does not include legal fees. If Market Quotation has been specified but cannot be determined or would not produce a commercially reasonable result, then loss is deemed to apply with respect to that particular transaction.

termination is via default or a termination event), and any set-off abilities. Close-out netting must be regarded as one of the chief benefits of the ISDA process as it allows an entire portfolio of options, swaps, and/or forwards between two parties to be condensed into a single net sum payable or receivable in the event of default. This eliminates the likelihood, in legal jurisdictions where netting is recognized, that a bankruptcy receiver will "cherry pick" only those contracts that have value to the defaulting party, while simultaneously dismissing those that are detrimental to the defaulting party.

Section 7: Transfer
Section 7 prevents both parties from transferring their obligations under the agreement to another party without the prior written consent of the other party.

Section 8: Contractual Currency
Section 8 indicates that payments under the Agreement will be made in the relevant currency specified in the Agreement for that payment (e.g., the "Contractual Currency"); in addition, it states that any shortfall or excess must be immediately rectified.

Other Sections
Sections 9 to 14 provide for rights and obligations with regard to multibranch dealings, expenses, and notices, and delineate governing law/jurisdiction and applicable definitions.

Confirmations and Definitions

Long-form confirmations are used for various classes of OTC derivatives, including options, when a full Master Agreement has not been negotiated or the specific derivative product remains in a relatively nascent stage (i.e., it lacks standard terms and definitions). For instance, a very exotic option on a new, or infrequently traded, asset class (e.g., catastrophe, inflation) does not feature standardized definitions. The long-form confirmation can be used with an ISDA Master Agreement or as a separate, stand-alone contract.

Consistent with ISDA's policy of introducing definitions under the ISDA framework when a product/market reaches a sufficient state of maturity, various standardized definitions exist and more are contemplated for the future. Once standard definitions exist, participants can migrate from long-form to short-form confirmations, reducing operational costs and time. As noted above, standardized definitions are available for bullion derivatives, government bond options, Euro derivatives, currency options, commodity derivatives, equity derivatives, and credit derivatives.

ACCOUNTING TREATMENT UNDER FAS 133 AND IAS 39

The accounting treatment of derivatives (including options) and structured/synthetic products with embedded derivatives has changed with the adoption of the Financial Accounting Standards 133 (FAS 133,[5] used in the U.S.) and International Accounting Standards 39 (IAS 39, used in regions/countries outside the U.S.). FAS 133 and IAS 39 are accounting rules intended to clarify the treatment of financial derivatives and structured securities (including those that are option-embedded) by linking them directly to the corporate financial statements. Though FAS 133 and IAS 39 contain differences, efforts at harmonization are underway. Our focus in this section is on the more comprehensive FAS 133 framework, though comments remain quite applicable for institutions adhering to IAS 39.

Accounting requirements set forth by Financial Accounting Standards Board (FASB) and International Accounting Standards Board (IASB) require derivatives/structured asset users to account for their derivatives via the income statement/balance sheet, rather than simply in the financial footnotes. This adds a degree of transparency to an institution's use of derivatives, but the framework is not completely precise, and is still subject to some degree of interpretation. It has also proven expensive for firms to implement.[6]

---

5 Prior to the introduction of FAS 133 in June 1999, U.S. institutions dealing in derivatives and derivative-related instruments obtained guidance from FAS 115 (Account for Investment in certain Debt and Equity Securities), FAS 52 (Foreign Currency Translation), FAS 80 (Accounting for Futures Contracts), and general advice from the Emerging Issues Task Force.

6 Some surveys have even suggested that the additional "onerous" reporting requirements, particularly for hedge accounting treatment, may discourage small-/mid-sized companies from pursuing hedging activities. If true, this may dampen business—particularly for exotic derivatives, where it may be more difficult to justify hedge treatment; however, this may only be a short-term reaction to the framework.

FAS 133 requires an entity to reflect at fair value all derivatives and derivative-related instruments through the income statement/balance sheet. If certain conditions are met regarding the nature of hedge risks[7] and the quality of the hedge,[8] then a derivative can qualify for hedge accounting treatment:

- Fair value hedge: A hedge against risk to changes in the fair value of an asset, liability, or commitment. If a derivative qualifies as a hedge of the exposure to changes in fair value of a recognized asset or liability, or an unrecognized commitment, then the gain or loss is recognized in earnings in the period of change, together with offsetting loss or gain on the hedge item. For example, the purchase of a put option as a hedge for an underlying equity position held available for sale may be considered a fair value hedge.

- Cash flow hedge: A hedge against risk to variability of future cash flows of an asset, liability, or commitment. If the derivative qualifies as a hedge of the exposure to variable cash flows of a forecasted transaction, the effective portion[9] of gain/loss is reported in other comprehensive income (outside earnings) and reclassified as earnings when the forecasted transaction affects earnings; the ineffective portion of gain/loss is reported in earnings immediately. For instance, the purchase of an interest rate option as a hedge for a planned purchase of an underlying bond to be held available for sale may be considered a cash flow hedge.

- Currency hedge: A hedge against risk of change in the fair value of an asset, liability, or commitment in a foreign currency. If a derivative qualifies as a hedge of a foreign currency exposure of a net investment in a foreign operation or security held available for sale, the effective portion of gain/loss is reported in other comprehensive income (outside earnings) and reclassified as earnings

---

7 Hedge risks are taken to include price risk, index risk, currency risk, interest rate risk, and default risk.

8 The actual conditions of hedge treatment can be complex to establish, and must generally be documented for ex-post audit or regulatory review.

9 The effective portion of a hedge is a function of cumulative change in fair value of the derivative to the cumulative change in the present value of expected cash flows of the forecast transaction.

when the foreign currency transaction affects earnings; the ineffective portion of gain/loss is reported in earnings immediately.

In order to qualify for hedge accounting treatment, the strategy must be documented prior to the booking of a transaction (with objectives and strategy well delineated); in addition, the ongoing effectiveness of the hedge must be evaluated (i.e., at least every quarter). Short option positions (outright or embedded) generally do not qualify for hedge accounting treatment (apart from premium received), as the option seller assumes more risk than the amount given up.

If a derivative is not designated as a hedge, the contract is carried at fair value, with any gain/loss recognized directly or indirectly in earnings in the period of change. This definition applies to most situations where an institution is dealing in synthetic and structured assets from an investment, speculation, or arbitrage perspective.

Conventional derivatives, including options and structured assets, must generally adhere to the FAS 133 guidelines above. This is, of course, a fundamental change. For instance, prior to FAS 133, instruments such as convertibles and structured notes were treated, from an accounting perspective, according to the predominant component of the package; the process began changing in the mid-1990s and was ultimately formalized via FAS 133. Thus, convertibles and other debt with nondetachable warrants with an equity component featuring little value at issuance were typically treated as debt. Securities with a detachable option and/or considerable equity value were split between debt and equity, with the debt component issued at a discount and amortized as additional interest expense, and the equity option component classified as an addition to permanent equity. FAS 133 formalized this requirement, which is now applicable regardless of the value of the equity option.[10]

---

10 It is important to note that equity hybrids with physical conversion/redemption that is outside the explicit control of the issuer be classified apart from equity—as a true hybrid between debt and equity. In effect, the option or warrant component is classed as "temporary equity" until it expires or is exercised; if exercise occurs, the shares become part of the issuer's equity account. Equity instruments that may be settled in cash or other assets (but not an issuer's new shares) cannot be treated in this fashion, and are thus subject to the FAS 133 accounting rules.

Under FAS 133 a derivative is defined in terms of its notional and underlying reference, and includes contracts that require no/small initial investment and which permit net settlement. This definition is applied to stand-alone derivatives and the embedded derivative component of a structured or synthetic asset. So, if a structured instrument is deemed to be a current, prospective, or currency hedge, it will receive hedge treatment; if it is considered a speculative position, the institution will be required to post any gain/loss to earnings in the period of change.[11]

Ultimately, financial and nonfinancial institutions that adhere to best practices established by regulators or their own boards of directors related to the entire range of internal controls will be well positioned to deal in synthetic and structured products. Such activities should, in turn, lead to additional growth and innovation, in what is already a very vibrant marketplace.

CHAPTER EXERCISES

1. The credit risk exposure of an option contract is influenced by:
   a. Volatility
   b. Time
   c. Current intrinsic value
   d. All of the above
   e. None of the above

2. Credit risk limits are typically established to:
   a. Control the maximum amount of counterparty losses
   b. Eliminate all credit losses

---

11 The exception would arise if the entire package were already being carried at fair value for trading securities, in which case gains/losses in the combined package would be recognized in earnings during the period of change. Thus, the embedded derivative should be recorded at fair value, and the host should be considered an investment in a discount bond with a yield that is distinct from that stated on the instrument (meaning that the host is likely to have a value that is different from the initial fair value). For instance, a $1m convertible bond with a coupon of 6% and an embedded call option that is worth a theoretical $100,000 suggests a $900,000 host bond with a yield of 7.4%, (recorded through coupon and discount amortization). Note that the yield is a function of the initial book value and not a function of rates and credit spreads.

    c. Reduce gamma exposure

    d. All of the above

    e. None of the above

3. Credit risk appears with short options:

    a. Never

    b. Always

    c. With select compound and currency options

    d. When combined with long options

    e. None of the above

4. Which of the following is not a form of market risk?

    a. Delta risk

    b. Sovereign risk

    c. Basis risk

    d. Theta risk

    e. Gamma risk

5. Which of the following form part of the conventional risk management process?

    a. Risk monitoring

    b. Risk identification

    c. Risk quantification

    d. Definition of tolerance

    e. All of the above

6. FAS 133 accounting rules allow options (and other derivatives) to be accounted for as:

    a. Speculative (no hedge) position

    b. Currency hedge

    c. Cash flow hedge

    d. Fair value hedge

    e. All of the above

7. Which of the following is/are not considered part of the regulatory risk framework?

    a. General market risk

    b. Specific market risk

    c. Detailed market risk

    d. Counterparty credit risk

    e. All are part of the regulatory framework

8. Which of the following is/are not part of the ISDA framework?

   a. Master Agreement
   b. Definitions
   c. Credit Support Documents
   d. Confirmations
   e. Attachments

Option-Adjusted Spreads

Option-adjusted spread (OAS) methodology offers a way to incorporate interest rate volatility assumptions explicitly into the pricing of bonds with embedded interest rate options, e.g., callable and puttable bonds, MBS. The cash flows of these bonds depend on whether the options are exercised, which in turn depends on the path of future interest rates; OAS analysis takes into account the uncertainty of a bond's cash flows brought about by the possibility that the embedded option may be exercised. This appendix shows how to develop a spreadsheet tool to compute the option-adjusted spread that equates the market price and the model-derived price of an option-embedded security. We shall focus our discussion on callable bonds, but it should be clear that the same analysis applies to all other embedded securities.

OAS INPUTS

Two inputs are needed to perform an OAS analysis: an interest rate tree model and the characteristics of the underlying bond.

The interest rate tree model simulates the expected future behavior of the yield curve. The tree models future forward (short) rates, and it is constructed to conform to the level and volatility of the zero-coupon yield curve. The result of the modeling process (in this case, the Black Derman Toy model) is a binomial tree showing the range of possible future short rates. At each node, the tree

F I G U R E A1.1

Binomial Interest Rate Tree Model

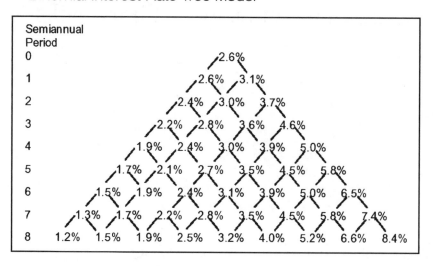

splits, with a period of six months between each node. The tree is constructed in this way in order to price a bond with semiannual payments. Figure A1.1 depicts a binomial interest rate tree that is essentially an extension of the binomial framework we have discussed in Chapters 8 and 9.

The binomial tree illustrated in the figure depicts the possible changes in interest rates over a four-year horizon (e.g., eight six-month periods). Period 0 is the present. In our example the semi-annual interest rate of 2.6% is used to discount cash flows that will occur six months from Period 0 (Period 1). The Period 1 interest rates are used to discount one-year cash flows (Period 2) back to Period 1. The Period 0 interest rate is used to discount the one-year cash flows from Period 1 back to the present (Period 0). The same process is used to discount cash flows at any node back to the present. The same tree can be adapted to a spreadsheet by arranging the interest rates into a right triangle. Figure A1.2, labeled Spreadsheet 1, arranges the interest rate in cells B2 to Kl 1.

The second input we require relates to the underlying bond characteristics. This supplies important details regarding the optionality of the security being analyzed. In this example, the

F I G U R E A1.2

Short Rates

	B	C	D	E	F	G	H	I	J	K
1										
2	Period				Interest Rate Tree - Short Rates					
3	0	2.6%								
4	1	2.6%	3.1%							
5	2	2.4%	3.0%	3.7%						
6	3	2.2%	2.8%	3.6%	4.6%					
7	4	1.9%	2.4%	3.0%	3.9%	5.0%				
8	5	1.7%	2.1%	2.7%	3.5%	4.5%	5.8%			
9	6	1.5%	1.9%	2.4%	3.1%	3.9%	5.0%	6.5%		
10	7	1.3%	1.7%	2.2%	2.8%	3.5%	4.5%	5.8%	7.4%	
11	8	1.2%	1.5%	1.9%	2.5%	3.2%	4.0%	5.2%	6.6%	8.4%

F I G U R E A1.3

Callable Bond Characteristics

	B	C	D	E
15	Years	4		
16	Freq	2		Spread
17	Periods	8		
18	Face	100	spread	
19	CoupRate	7.0%		
20	Coupon	3.50	M Price	101

bond has four years to maturity and pays interest semiannually, and is callable at the end of Year three. It has a coupon of 7% and a market price is 101. Figure A1.3 summarizes the key characteristics. The spreadsheet therefore indicates that:

- The bond has a maturity of four years (cell C15).
- The bond will pay interest on a semiannual basis, or a frequency of two payments per year (C16).
- The total number of period for the bond is equal to the product of the two previous entries C17 (= C15 * C16).
- The face or par value of the bond is set at 100 (C18).
- The bond has a coupon rate of 7.00% (C19).

- The dollar value of the coupon payment per period is computed in C20 (= C 19/C16 * C18).
- The market price of the callable bond, 101, is reflected in E20.

The estimate of the bond's spread is shown in E18. The spread button, above E18, activates the Excel Solver function. Once the bond's cash flows are modeled, Solver will calculate the bond's spread to the zero-coupon yield curve and display the resulting E18.

ESTIMATING THE OAS

In order to determine the OAS of a callable bond, several steps must be completed in sequence:

- Assume that the callable bond is a noncallable bond. Construct a price tree for the bond based on the interest rate tree. Discount the cash flows of the bond back to the present (Period 0) using the interest rate tree.
- Construct a price tree for the bond, less accrued interest. This tree will be needed later in the analysis to determine whether the bond should be called.
- Set the model-generated price of the bond (Period 0) equal to the market price of the bond (E20) by adding a positive spread to each interest rate in the tree. The Solver function will determine the appropriate spread. This spread is the incremental return of the bond over the zero-coupon yield curve assuming that the bond is noncallable.
- Adjust the bond's cash flows to incorporate the call feature of the bond. Note that the bond being analyzed in our example can be called once, at the end of the third year (Period 6).
- Repeat Step 3. Set the model-generated price of the bond (Period 0) equal to the market price of the bond (E20) by adding a positive spread to each interest rate in the tree. Solver will determine the appropriate spread. This is the option-adjusted spread of the callable bond.

We follow these steps in the tables below to generate the desired result.

FIGURE A1.4

Price Tree of Underlying Straight (Noncallable) Bond

	B	C	D	E	F	G	H	I	J	K
22	Period				Price Tree - Underlying Straight Bond					
23	0	103.13			(Spot Rate + 0 Spread)					
24	1	108.10	103.63							
25	2	109.17	105.46	100.99						
26	3	109.69	106.80	103.26	98.95					
27	4	109.58	107.50	104.92	101.74	97.85				
28	5	108.77	107.36	105.60	103.41	100.70	97.37			
29	6	107.44	106.61	105.56	104.24	102.59	100.55	98.02		
30	7	105.65	105.28	104.81	104.22	103.47	102.53	101.35	99.89	
31	8	103.50	103.50	103.50	103.50	103.50	103.50	103.50	103.50	103.50

Step 1

Spreadsheet 2 in Figure A1.4 depicts the discounted cash flows of the straight bond. The tree is constructed using the following formulas:

Cell	Formula	Copied to
C23	= 0.5 * ((C24)/(1 + C3 + SPREAD) + (D24)/(1 + C3 + SPREAD))	
C24	= 0.5 * ((C25/(1 + C4 + SPREAD) + COUPON) + (D25/(1 + C4 + SPREAD) + COUPON))	C25:C30, D24:D30, E25:E30, F26:F30, G27:G30, H28:H30, I29:I30, J30.
C31	= C18 + COUPON	D31:K31

The model-generated price of 103.13 is contained in cell C23.

Step 2

Spreadsheet 3, in Figure A1.5, depicts the price tree for the underlying straight bond, less accrued interest. This tree is needed in order to see which paths result in the bond being called. The price at which a bond can be called is quoted excluding accrued interest. This tree

F I G U R E A1.5

Price Trees of Underlying Straight Bond Less Accrued Interest

	B	C	D	E	F	G	H	I	J	K
33	Period	Price Tree - Underlying Straight Bond - less Accrued Interest								
34	0	103.13			(Spot Rate + 0 Spread)					
35	1	104.60	100.13							
36	2	105.67	101.96	97.49						
37	3	106.19	103.30	99.76	95.45					
38	4	106.08	104.00	101.42	98.24	94.35				
39	5	105.27	103.86	102.10	99.91	97.20	93.87			
40	6	103.94	103.11	102.06	100.74	99.09	97.05	94.52		
41	7	102.15	101.78	101.31	100.72	99.97	99.03	97.85	96.39	
42	8	100.00	100.00	100.00	100.00	100.00	100.00	100.00	100.00	100.00

is constructed by subtracting the coupon payment from every cell in the bond price tree, with the exception of cell C34. The formulas are:

Cell	Formula	Copied to
C34	= C23	
C35	= C24-COUPON	C36:C42, D35:D42, E36:E42, F37:F42, G38:G42, H39:H42, 140:142, J41:J42, K42

Step 3

The next step is to equate the model-determined price of the bond (103.13) to its market value (101). The model-determined price is higher than the market price because the bond's cash flows were discounted back to the present using the zero-coupon yield curve (risk-free interest rates). Solver iteratively adds a larger spread to the interest rate tree until the model-determined price of the bond is equal to its market price. To perform this function, click on the Tools menu, choose Solver and click on Solve. The target and variable cells have already been identified.

Note that a more direct approach is to click on the Solver button on the spreadsheet. Spreadsheet 4, Figure A1.6, depicts the successful result of calculating the spread. Click OK to keep the Solver solution. The spread (incremental return) of the bond over the yield curve is 30.3 bp.

F I G U R E   A1.6

Solver Results

	B	C	D	E	F	G	H
15	Years	4					
16	Freq	2		Spread			
17	Periods	8					
18	Face	100	spread	0.00303			
19	CoupRate	7.0%					
20	Coupon	3.50	M Price	101			
21							

Solver Results [×]

Solver found a solution. All constraints and optimality conditions are satisfied.

Reports: Answer / Sensitivity / Limits

○ Keep Solver Solution
○ Restore Original Values

[OK]   [Cancel]   [Save Scenario...]   [Help]

(right margin, partly obscured): raight / pread)   96.60 / 00.00 / 02.24

| 31 | 8 | 103.50 | 103.50 | | 103.50 | 103.50 | 103.50 | 103.50 |

F I G U R E   A1.7

Price Trees of Straight Bond, Discounted

	B	C	D	E	F	G	H	I	J	K
22	Period	Price Tree - Underlying Straight Bond								
23	0	101.00	(Spot Rate + 30.3 Basis Point Spread)							
24	1	106.17	101.79							
25	2	107.46	103.82	99.44						
26	3	108.23	105.39	101.90	97.67					
27	4	108.39	106.34	103.79	100.66	96.83				
28	5	107.86	106.47	104.73	102.57	99.89	96.60			
29	6	106.83	106.01	104.97	103.66	102.03	100.00	97.49		
30	7	105.35	104.98	104.51	103.92	103.18	102.24	101.07	99.62	
31	8	103.50	103.50	103.50	103.50	103.50	103.50	103.50	103.50	103.50

Spreadsheet 5, in Figure A1.7, depicts the price tree for the bond when its cash flows are discounted at the spot rate plus 30.3 bp. Notice that the model-generated price of the bond (101) is now equal to its market price (101).

Spreadsheet 6, Figure A1.8, shows the same price tree (discounted at the spot rate plus 30.3 bp) but subtracts accrued

FIGURE A1.8

Straight Bond Less Accrued Interest, Discounted

	B	C	D	E	F	G	H	I	J	K
33	Period	Price Tree – Underlying Straight Bond – less Accrued Interest								
34	0	101.00			(Spot Rate + 30.3 Basis Point Spread)					
35	1	102.67	98.29							
36	2	103.96	100.32	95.94						
37	3	104.73	101.89	98.40	94.17					
38	4	104.89	102.84	100.29	97.16	93.33				
39	5	104.36	102.97	101.23	99.07	96.39	93.10			
40	6	103.33	102.51	101.47	100.16	98.53	96.50	93.99		
41	7	101.85	101.48	101.01	100.42	99.68	98.74	97.57	96.12	
42	8	100.00	100.00	100.00	100.00	100.00	100.00	100.00	100.00	100.00

interest so that the prices are stated consistently with market convention.

Step 4

Up to this point, the spread of the bond has been calculated assuming that the bond is noncallable. The bond's cash flows must now be altered to take into account the issuer's option to call the bond at the end of Year three (Period 6).

To determine if it is advantageous for the issuer to call the bond at Period 6, we must examine the previous tree, which shows the bond value, less accrued interest, at every node. The call price is 100. If the bond value at any node in Period 6 is greater than 100, the issuer will exercise the right to call the bond. The issuer will pay the investor 100 for an asset whose value is greater than 100. In Period 6, the issuer will call the bond at four nodes in the range C40:F40 (103.33, 102.51, 101.47, and 100.16).

Calling the bond alters the cash flows. To reflect this, the value of cells C29:F29 must be changed to 103.5 (the 100 call price plus the final semiannual coupon of 3.5). Since the investor no longer receives coupon or principal payments after the bond is called, the value in subsequent nodes (cells C30:F31) is set to zero. This is shown in Figure A1.9.

Step 5

Based on the adjusted cash flows, the model-predicted price (100.43) no longer equates to the bond's market price (101). The

F I G U R E   A1.9

Price Tree of Callable Bond

	B	C	D	E	F	G	H	I	J	K
22	Period				Price Tree - Callable Bond					
23	0	100.43			(Spot Rate + 30.3 Basis Point Spread)					
24	1	105.29	101.49							
25	2	106.17	103.31	99.33						
26	3	106.44	104.54	101.68	97.65					
27	4	106.04	105.01	103.37	100.62	96.83				
28	5	105.00	104.53	103.94	102.49	99.89	96.60			
29	6	103.50	103.50	103.50	103.50	102.03	100.00	97.49		
30	7	0.00	0.00	0.00	0.00	103.18	102.24	101.07	99.62	
31	8	0.00	0.00	0.00	0.00	103.50	103.50	103.50	103.50	103.50

spread based on the assumption that the bond is not callable is now too high. Step 3 is repeated to calculate the spread of the bond, taking into account the fact that the bond is called at four of the nodes at the end of Year three (Period 6). This value is the option-adjusted spread of the bond. As in Step 3, Spreadsheet 8 (Figure A1.10) depicts the successful result of using Solver to

F I G U R E   A1.10

Option-Adjusted Spread

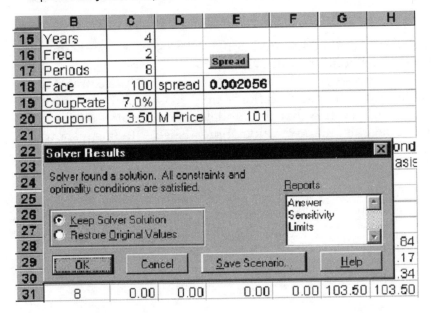

	B	C	D	E	F	G	H
15	Years	4					
16	Freq	2		Spread			
17	Periods	8					
18	Face	100	spread	0.002056			
19	CoupRate	7.0%					
20	Coupon	3.50	M Price	101			
21							

Solver Results   [X]

Solver found a solution. All constraints and optimality conditions are satisfied.

Reports:
Answer
Sensitivity
Limits

( ) Keep Solver Solution
( ) Restore Original Values

OK   Cancel   Save Scenario...   Help

| 31 | 8 | 0.00 | 0.00 | 0.00 | 0.00 | 103.50 | 103.50 |

FIGURE A1.11

Discounted Values of Callable Bond

Spreadsheet 9: Callable Bond Discounted at Spot Rate Plus OAS

	B	C	D	E	F	G	H	I	J	K
22	Period	Price Tree - Callable Bond								
23	0	101.00			(Spot Rate + 20.6 Basis Point Spread)					
24	1	105.77	101.99							
25	2	106.55	103.71	99.77						
26	3	106.72	104.84	102.03	98.04					
27	4	106.23	105.20	103.60	100.92	97.16				
28	5	105.10	104.63	104.04	102.67	100.15	96.84			
29	6	103.50	103.50	103.50	103.50	102.21	100.17	97.66		
30	7	0.00	0.00	0.00	0.00	103.27	102.34	101.16	99.71	
31	8	0.00	0.00	0.00	0.00	103.50	103.50	103.50	103.50	103.50

Spreadsheet 10: Callable Bond Discounted at Spot Rate Plus OAS, Less Accrued Interest

	B	C	D	E	F	G	H	I	J	K
33	Period	Price Tree - Callable Bond – less Accrued Interest								
34	0	101.00			(Spot Rate + 20.6 Basis Point Spread)					
35	1	102.27	98.49							
36	2	103.05	100.21	96.27						
37	3	103.22	101.34	98.53	94.54					
38	4	102.73	101.70	100.10	97.42	93.66				
39	5	101.60	101.13	100.54	99.17	96.65	93.34			
40	6	100.00	100.00	100.00	100.00	98.71	96.67	94.16		
41	7	0.00	0.00	0.00	0.00	99.77	98.84	97.66	96.21	
42	8	0.00	0.00	0.00	0.00	100.00	100.00	100.00	100.00	100.00

calculate the option-adjusted spread. The spread, or incremental return, of the bond over the yield curve is 20.6 bp.

Spreadsheet 9 (Figure A1.11) depicts the price tree for the callable bond when its cash flows are discounted at the T spot rate plus 20.6 bp. Notice that the model-generated price of the bond now equals its market value. Spreadsheet 10 (also shown in Figure A1.11) shows the same price tree minus accrued interest.

Pricing Options with Correlation

Certain options we have considered in the book feature payoffs that are based on the comovements, or correlations between two or more assets. The value of the option depends ultimately on the price paths that all reference assets take during the life of the contract. Pricing options that feature correlation, such as basket, spread, or quanto options, require additional modeling work. In this appendix we present some essential points regarding the pricing of options with correlation.

INTRODUCTION TO CORRELATION

The degree to which correlation factors into pricing considerations depends on the type of product. In some options, such as baskets and spreads, the correlation implications are first order—that is, they have a significant impact on the value of the contract. In others, such as quantos or outside barriers, the impact may only be secondary.

To illustrate the role of correlation, let's first imagine a simple basket of two shares, A and B. The market value of both A and B is 100 and ATM call options on the basket would be struck at 200. Should a call option on the basket cost the same as a pair of separate call options on both shares struck at 100? We can imagine that A and B might have values of 150 and 50, respectively, at the expiry of the option, meaning that the individual calls would be worth 50 and 0, respectively. Together they would be worth 50. The call on the basket, however, is worth nothing. The value of the basket has not changed and still equals the strike of 200. Generally, the price volatility of a basket is less than that of any of the assets in the basket. The correlation of the assets is normally less than +1 and greater than −1.

If there is any chance that the price movements of the underlying assets might offset each other to any degree, the value of the option on the basket must be less than the sum of the values of the separate options on the underlying assets. The value of basket options thus depends on the volatility of the underlying assets separately and the correlation between them.

Modeling correlation is a complex task that is fraught with problems. This is particularly true when historical data is considered, since correlations have a tendency to decouple, particularly during times of market stress. In fact, correlation is a statistical description of past movements: if there is causal relationship linking two assets together, there is no guarantee that the correlation observed today will be the same tomorrow. This means correlation results can vary widely.

However, even when two assets appear to have some relationship, other complications surface, such as timing of data collection. It would be ideal, for instance, to be able to record price data of multiple assets at the same time. However, this is rarely possible, as markets may trade at different times and be subject to different trading rules and parameters.

Consider, for instance, Figure A2.1, which shows the price movement between U.S. and German government bond futures traded on CBOT and LIFFE; since the time zones are different, the one-day offset price is also computed. It is relatively easy to see that even the one-day offset price will have an impact on the price correlation between the two assets.

As a result of data challenges such as these, some practitioners use weekly data to measure historical correlation, as the distortions of asynchronous closing times and time zone differences are relatively small over weekly data periods.

If historical correlation describes the past and there is no certainty that past relationships will be duplicated in the future, how can correlation be used to price and hedge options? The usual practice is to assume correlation will run against the market maker, who causes the market maker to quote a wider bid/offer spreads. Sellers of options on multiple asset underlyings thus build in a cushion of protection. However, this type of approach is not necessarily optimal as competition for business intensifies.

F I G U R E A2.1

U.S. Government and Bund Prices

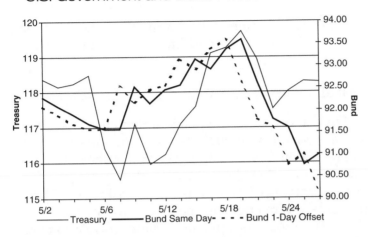

CORRELATION AND EXOTIC OPTIONS

We recall from Part I of the book, that a basket option is a mini-portfolio of assets included in a single contract, with a value that is determined by adding up the individual components according to their weights. A spread option represents the difference between two or more assets, and its value is determined by subtracting, rather than adding, the assets. A quanto option, which converts an underlying asset in a foreign currency back into a home currency, can be regarded as a form of a basket option. Each one of these exotics is impacted by correlation and will help us explore issues related to the effect of correlation on option value.

Pricing a Basket Option: Correlation and Volatility

To help consider the framework we introduce a basket call option comprised of the DAX index and the CAC 40 index; each index comprises 50% of the value of the basket. For the moment we ignore currency risk by assuming that all flows are in the investor's home currency of euros.

   To begin, we assume that there is no correlation between the DAX and the CAC; the price of the options can be considered individually. We also assume that the volatility of each option is 20%.

However, the volatility of the basket is not a simple summation of the two volatilities, but a weighted average of the variance of each position.

The correct result is obtained by squaring the volatility (Vol^2), which produces variance, and then adding up the weighted variances (50% in this example):

$$\text{Volatility of the Portfolio} = \sqrt{0.5 \times 0.20^2 + 0.5 \times 0.20^2} = 20\% \quad (A2.1)$$

Since the DAX and CAC are equally weighted in the basket and have the same volatility of 20%, the portfolio volatility must also be 20%. However, if CAC volatility is 25%, rather than 20%, the volatility of the portfolio rises to 22.64%.

With portfolio volatility in hand we next consider correlation (ρ), which measures the relationship between two variables – in this case the DAX and CAC. As a practical matter correlation has a maximum value of +1 (perfect positive correlation, meaning the price movement of one asset is matched precisely by the price movement of the second asset), and a minimum value of –1 (perfect negative correlation, meaning the two assets move in precisely the opposite manner). Correlation of 0 means that the two assets are independent, or uncorrelated: the price movement of one asset has no bearing on the price movement of the second asset. In our example, if DAX/CAC correlation is equal to +1, movements in the two indexes are perfectly matched.

In order to price a basket option we must therefore have access to the relevant correlations. With correlations in hand, we can create a binomial tree as noted below; all nodes in the tree represent possible forward prices based on assumed correlations.

Correlation also helps determine the variance of a basket of assets. The relationship between the volatility of a basket and the correlation between the assets in the basket can be calculated using a correlation matrix. The solution of a correlation matrix can be described via:

$$\text{Variance}_{\text{portfolio}} = \text{Vol}^2 = \sum_{a=1}^{n} (\%_a^2 * \text{Vol}_a^2)$$

$$+ \sum_{a=1}^{n} \sum_{a \neq b=1}^{n} (\%_a * \%_b * \text{Vol}_a * \text{Vol}_b * \rho_{a,b}) \quad (A2.2)$$

This formula indicates that the variance of a portfolio is equal to the sum of all the assets in the portfolio of the squared portfolio weight (%) of each asset times the squared volatility (vol) of each asset, plus the sum across every unique pair of assets in the portfolio of the portfolio weight of the first asset in the pair ($\%_a$) times the portfolio weight of the other asset ($\%_b$) times the volatility of the first asset (Vol_a) times the volatility of the other asset (Vol_b) times the correlation of the two assets ($\rho_{a,b}$).

Let us assume that our DAX/CAC basket option features 50% weights and 20% volatilities, along with a 0.50 correlation. The volatility of the basket, using (A2.2) is equal to:

$$Vol^2 = (0.5^2 * 0.2^2) + (0.5^2 * 0.2^2) + (0.5 * 0.5 * 0.2 * 0.2 * 0.5)$$
$$+ (0.5 * 0.5 * 0.2 * 0.2 * 0.5)$$

$$Vol^2 = 0.03$$

$$Vol = 17.32\%$$

This indicates that the volatility of the basket (17.32%) is less than the sum of the volatilities of each asset in the basket (20%). This is an important result that helps reveal how basket (and spread) options can help reduce volatility.

We can examine the sensitivity of volatility by altering correlation assumptions between the two indexes, as in Table A2.1 and Figure A2.2.

Pricing a Basket Option: The Binomial Tree

In order to take the next step in pricing the basket option we must construct a binomial tree that includes both the DAX and CAC. Let us assume that we already have the DAX tree in hand (e.g,. drawing from our example in Chapter 9). We must now create a CAC tree.

We begin by noting that, at expiration, there are nine possible DAX outcomes. For each possible DAX outcome there are nine possible CAC outcomes. This means that the total number of possible solutions is 81 (i.e., 9 * 9). As the number of underlying assets in a basket increases and/or the number of steps in the tree increases, the number of possible outcomes needs to value the option increases. This makes calculating basket (and other correlation) options extremely computer intensive.

We recall from Chapter 9 that we were able to create a binomial solution using normal scores. Let us refer to each normal score in the process that follows as a variable U. U has mean 0 and variance 1. Let us further assume that U is a representation of the DAX spot prices. We can similarly develop normal scores for CAC, which we term V; this will allow us to create a binomial tree of

T A B L E   A2.1

DAX and CAC volatility and correlation

Correlations	Volatility
−100%	0.00%
−90%	4.47%
−80%	6.32%
−70%	7.75%
−60%	8.94%
−50%	10.00%
−40%	10.95%
−30%	11.83%
−20%	12.65%
−10%	13.42%
0%	14.14%
10%	14.83%
20%	15.49%
30%	16.12%
40%	16.73%
50%	17.32%
60%	17.89%
70%	18.44%
80%	18.97%
90%	19.49%
100%	20.00%

CAC spot prices. We note further that U and V are created independently. As a result, they are uncorrelated, meaning that the binomial trees for the DAX and CAC are uncorrelated. By indicating that U and V are uncorrelated we mean that if we select numbers randomly from each distribution, the correlation between the two will equal 0, as summarized in Figure A2.3.

However, we suspect that the DAX and CAC must have some relationship. We must therefore transform U and V in a way that introduces the proper correlation. To do so we introduce W and Z, which are U and V with normal scores (i.e., "normalized"). Since W and Z are normalized they have a mean of 0 and variance 1, along with correlation of ρ.

We related W to the DAX index, meaning that $W = U$. Z, in turn, is created from both U and V. When Z is transformed back into a

F I G U R E   A2.2

DAX and CAC Volatility and Correlation

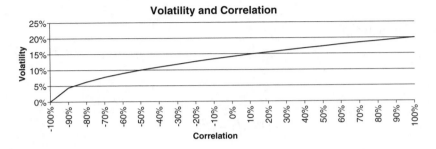

F I G U R E   A2.3

U and *V* with Zero Correlation

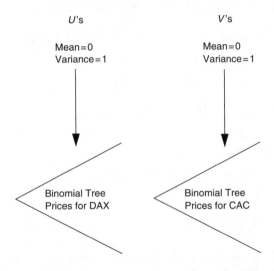

binomial tree of spot prices for the CAC, the DAX tree and CAC tree will have correlation equal to ρ. More specifically, Z is created by:

$$\rho * U + \sqrt{1 - \rho^2} * V \qquad (A2.3)$$

The binomial tree for the DAX and CAC are created from W and Z can then be computed as follows:

$$\text{DAX} : \text{Forward}_t = \exp(\text{normal score } W * \text{vol} * \sqrt{t}) * \text{Spot}$$
$$\text{CAC} : \text{Forward}_t = \exp(\text{normal score } Z * \text{vol} * \sqrt{t}) * \text{Spot}$$

Z and W can be obtained by solving a series of linear equations:

$$W = A * U + B * V$$
$$Z = C * U + D * V$$

Solve for A,B,C,D

$$A = 1$$
$$B = 0$$
$$C = \rho$$
$$D = \sqrt{1 - \rho^2}$$

This process essentially means we choose U and V independently. W and Z are also chosen, but not randomly: whichever U and V are selected determines which W and Z must be selected. The correlation we assume between the variables determines the selection, as summarized in Figure A2.4.

The process can be summarized as follows: W and Z have mean of 0 and variance of 1:

$$\text{Variance}_W = 1^2 * \text{Variance}_U + 0 * \text{Variance}_V = 1$$
$$\text{Variance}_Z = \rho^2 * \text{Variance}_U + \left(\sqrt{1 - \rho^2}\right)^2 * \text{Variance}_V = 1$$

W and Z have correlation of ρ:

$$\text{Correlation} = A * C * \text{Variance}_U + B * D * \text{Variance}_V$$
$$= 1 * \rho + 0 = \rho$$

All of the cross-product terms cancel because U and V are not correlated.

Using W and Z the spot prices in the binomial tree for the DAX and CAC can be created—with 81 outcomes, as noted above. We assume for purposes of this example that the correlation between the two variables is 0.5.

Since we have already computed the DAX tree in Chapter 9, we must now compute that CAC tree, and do so using the data supplied in Tables A2.2 and A2.3.

The data above allows us to create the CAC binomial tree of forward values illustrated in Table A2.4.

The probability weights are shown in Table A2.5.

Up to now we have assumed that the CAC forward values and probabilities are completely independent of the DAX forward

FIGURE A2.4

U and V with Correlation

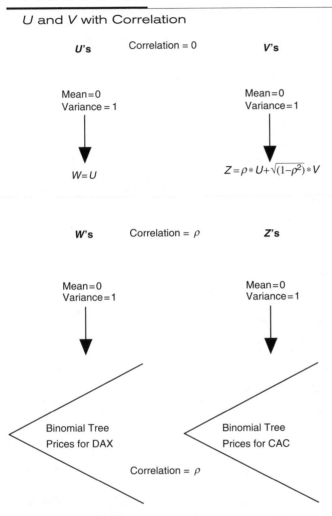

$$Z = \rho * U + \sqrt{(1-\rho^2)} * V$$

values and probabilities. The CAC tree is created in the same way as the DAX tree, but neither has influence over the other. This obviously changes as we introduce some degree of correlation. If we assume correlation of 0.5 between the two indexes, we force the two trees to have some relationship. We can then preserve the DAX values and recast the CAC values in terms of DAX, or vice versa. We shall use the former, though the choice has no impact on the ultimate price of an option.

Before constructing the combined tree, we can examine the two variable distribution (DAX and CAC under various correlation

T A B L E A2.2

CAC Index Data

Spot CAC	1965.00
Maturity	Two years
Length of each interval	0.25 years
€ rate:	7.15%
Dividend yield	4.0%
Volatility	20%

T A B L E A2.3

CAC Option Data

% Up Move	110.5171%
% Down Move	90.4837%
Probability of an Up Move	51.4485%
Probability of a Down Move	48.5515%

T A B L E A2.4

CAC Binomial Tree of Forward Values

CAC 40: Binomial Tree of Forward Values								
Quarter	**1**	**2**	**3**	**4**	**5**	**6**	**7**	**8**
								4373.19
							3957.02	
						3580.46		3580.46
					3239.74		3239.74	
				2931.44		2931.44		2931.44
			2652.47		2652.47		2652.47	
		2400.06		2400.06		2400.06		2400.06
	2171.66		2171.66		2171.66		2171.66	
1965.00		1965.00		1965.00		1965.00		1965.00
	1778.01		1778.01		1778.01		1778.01	
		1608.81		1608.81		1608.81		1608.81
			1455.71		1455.71		1455.71	
				1317.18		1317.18		1317.18
					1191.83		1191.83	
						1078.41		1078.41
							975.79	
								882.93

T A B L E A2.5

CAC Probability Weights

CAC 40: Probability of Being in Each Position (weighted by number of possible paths)								
Quarter	1	2	3	4	5	6	7	8
								0.0049
							0.0095	
						0.0185		0.0371
					0.0360		0.0630	
				0.0701		0.1050		0.1224
			0.1362		0.1701		0.1784	
		0.2647		0.2645		0.2477		0.2310
	0.5145		0.3855		0.3210		0.2807	
1.0000		0.4996		0.3744		0.3117		0.2725
	0.4855		0.3638		0.3029		0.2648	
		0.2357		0.2355		0.2206		0.2057
			0.1144		0.1429		0.1500	
				0.0556		0.0833		0.0971
					0.0270		0.0472	
						0.0131		0.0262
							0.0064	
								0.0031

scenarios: 0, 0.5, and 1.0); this helps us understand how the distribution changes in the face of correlation changes. Figure A2.5 begins with a correlation of 0.

This graph shows the probability of any given pair of values from the two indexes. Like a normal distribution for a single variable, the peak in the middle reflects greater probability that the DAX will be zero standard deviations away from its current forward value and the CAC will be zero standard deviations away from its current forward value. When correlation is equal to zero, the graph shows a typical normal distribution when viewed from either perspective.

Figure A2.6 introduces correlation: the second variable (CAC) is now dependent on the first variable (DAX), at a level of 0.5.

The slight rise in the surface of the distribution is due to the positive correlation: there is a slightly higher likelihood of seeing CAC values with positive standard deviations if the DAX value standard deviation is positive. The same is true for lower DAX

F I G U R E   A2.5

DAX and CAC Correlation = 0

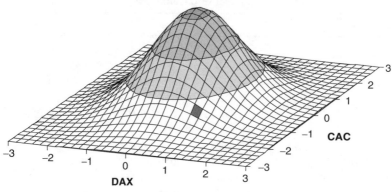

Two-Variable Distribution
Correlation = 0

F I G U R E   A2.6

DAX and CAC Correlation = 0.5

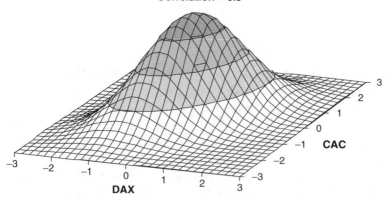

Two-Variable Distribution
Correlation = 0.5

values: the probability of a lower CAC value being paired with a lower DAX value is also greater. In other words, the movements in the DAX and CAC influence each other.

The most extreme version of this example occurs with correlation of 1.0, where the value of the CAC is entirely dependent on the value of the DAX. In this case there is effectively only 1 distribution, as noted in Figure A2.7.

F I G U R E   A2.7

DAX and CAC Correlation = 1.0

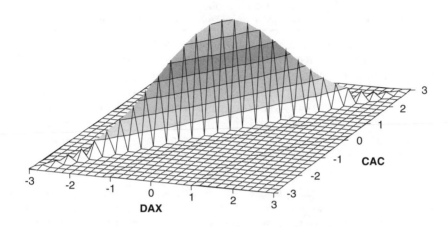

Reverting to the construction of the combined binomial tree, we know the following: since we will preserve the original nine DAX values and there are nine possible CAC values for *each* possible DAX value, the tree must yield 81 possible CAC forward prices. The process involved in developing the tree is as follows:

1. Calculate the intrinsic value of the basket option at all 81 possible levels at expiry.
2. Adjust this value by the probability of occurrence (where the relevant probability is the product of the separate DAX and CAC probabilities).
3. Sum the probability-weighted intrinsic values and compute the present value.

We recall that we are valuing a DAX/CAC basket call with a strike of 4130 (2165 + 1965). The results are summarized in Table A2.6.

We can summarize key elements of the table as follows:

- Basket option at strike of 4130: 474.58
- DAX option at strike of 2165: 259.72
- CAC-40 option at strike of 1965: 251.79
- CAC + DAX separate options: 511.51

T A B L E   A2.6

DAX/CAC Combined Results

State		Spot Prices				DAX+		Weighted
DAX	CAC	DAX	CAC 40	Prob DAX	Prob CAC-40	CAC	Intrinsic	Intrinsic
8	8	4818.30	5860.96	0.0041	0.0049	10679.25	6549.25	0.1321
8	7	4818.30	4928.86	0.0041	0.0371	9747.15	5617.15	0.8554
8	6	4818.30	4145.00	0.0041	0.1224	8963.29	4833.29	2.4312
8	5	4818.30	3485.80	0.0041	0.2310	8304.10	4174.10	3.9627
8	4	4818.30	2931.44	0.0041	0.2725	7749.73	3619.73	4.0537
8	3	4818.30	2465.24	0.0041	0.2057	7283.53	3153.53	2.6662
8	2	4818.30	2073.18	0.0041	0.0971	6891.47	2761.47	1.1016
8	1	4818.30	1743.47	0.0041	0.0262	6561.77	2431.77	0.2616
8	0	4818.30	1466.20	0.0041	0.0031	6284.49	2154.49	0.0273
7	8	3944.89	5303.21	0.0325	0.0049	9248.10	5118.10	0.8155
7	7	3944.89	4459.82	0.0325	0.0371	8404.70	4274.70	5.1422
7	6	3944.89	3750.55	0.0325	0.1224	7695.44	3565.44	14.1663
7	5	3944.89	3154.08	0.0325	0.2310	7098.97	2968.97	22.2643
7	4	3944.89	2652.47	0.0325	0.2725	6597.36	2467.36	21.8260
7	3	3944.89	2230.64	0.0325	0.2057	6175.52	2045.52	13.6605
7	2	3944.89	1875.89	0.0325	0.0971	5820.78	1690.78	5.3278
7	1	3944.89	1577.56	0.0325	0.0262	5522.44	1392.44	1.1830
7	0	3944.89	1326.67	0.0325	0.0031	5271.56	1141.56	0.1144
6	8	3229.80	4798.54	0.1122	0.0049	8028.34	3898.34	2.1466
6	7	3229.80	4035.41	0.1122	0.0371	7265.21	3135.21	13.0335
6	6	3229.80	3393.64	0.1122	0.1224	6623.44	2493.44	34.2365
6	5	3229.80	2853.93	0.1122	0.2310	6083.73	1953.73	50.6308
6	4	3229.80	2400.06	0.1122	0.2725	5629.86	1499.86	45.8500
6	3	3229.80	2018.36	0.1122	0.2057	5248.16	1118.16	25.8056
6	2	3229.80	1697.37	0.1122	0.0971	4927.17	797.17	8.6808
6	1	3229.80	1427.43	0.1122	0.0262	4657.23	527.23	1.5480
6	0	3229.80	1200.42	0.1122	0.0031	4430.22	300.22	0.1040
5	8	2644.34	4341.90	0.2215	0.0049	6986.24	2856.24	3.1058
5	7	2644.34	3651.39	0.2215	0.0371	6295.73	2165.73	17.7790
5	6	2644.34	3070.69	0.2215	0.1224	5715.03	1585.03	42.9771
5	5	2644.34	2582.34	0.2215	0.2310	5226.68	1096.68	56.1228
5	4	2644.34	2171.66	0.2215	0.2725	4816.00	686.00	41.4115
5	3	2644.34	1826.29	0.2215	0.2057	4470.63	340.63	15.5238
5	2	2644.34	1535.85	0.2215	0.0971	4180.18	50.18	1.0792

(Continued)

T A B L E A2.6 (*Continued*)

State		Spot Prices				DAX+		Weighted
DAX	CAC	DAX	CAC 40	Prob DAX	Prob CAC-40	CAC	Intrinsic	Intrinsic
5	1	2644.34	1291.59	0.2215	0.0262	3935.93	0.00	0.0000
5	0	2644.34	1086.19	0.2215	0.0031	3730.52	0.00	0.0000
4	8	2165.00	3928.72	0.2734	0.0049	6093.72	1963.72	2.6354
4	7	2165.00	3303.91	0.2734	0.0371	5468.91	1338.91	13.5658
4	6	2165.00	2778.48	0.2734	0.1224	4943.48	813.48	27.2228
4	5	2165.00	2336.60	0.2734	0.2310	4501.60	371.60	23.4706
4	4	2165.00	1965.00	0.2734	0.2725	4130.00	0.00	0.0000
4	3	2165.00	1652.50	0.2734	0.2057	3817.50	0.00	0.0000
4	2	2165.00	1389.69	0.2734	0.0971	3554.69	0.00	0.0000
4	1	2165.00	1168.68	0.2734	0.0262	3333.68	0.00	0.0000
4	0	2165.00	982.82	0.2734	0.0031	3147.82	0.00	0.0000
3	8	1772.55	3554.85	0.2160	0.0049	5327.40	1197.40	1.2693
3	7	1772.55	2989.50	0.2160	0.0371	4762.06	632.06	5.0584
3	6	1772.55	2514.07	0.2160	0.1224	4286.62	156.62	4.1401
3	5	1772.55	2114.24	0.2160	0.2310	3886.80	0.00	0.0000
3	4	1772.55	1778.01	0.2160	0.2725	3550.56	0.00	0.0000
3	3	1772.55	1495.24	0.2160	0.2057	3267.79	0.00	0.0000
3	2	1772.55	1257.45	0.2160	0.0971	3030.00	0.00	0.0000
3	1	1772.55	1057.47	0.2160	0.0262	2830.02	0.00	0.0000
3	0	1772.55	889.29	0.2160	0.0031	2661.85	0.00	0.0000
2	8	1451.24	3216.56	0.1066	0.0049	4667.80	537.80	0.2815
2	7	1451.24	2705.02	0.1066	0.0371	4156.26	26.26	0.1037
2	6	1451.24	2274.82	0.1066	0.1224	3726.07	0.00	0.0000
2	5	1451.24	1913.05	0.1066	0.2310	3364.29	0.00	0.0000
2	4	1451.24	1608.81	0.1066	0.2725	3060.05	0.00	0.0000
2	3	1451.24	1352.95	0.1066	0.2057	2804.19	0.00	0.0000
2	2	1451.24	1137.78	0.1066	0.0971	2589.03	0.00	0.0000
2	1	1451.24	956.84	0.1066	0.0262	2408.08	0.00	0.0000
2	0	1451.24	804.67	0.1066	0.0031	2255.91	0.00	0.0000
1	8	1188.18	2910.46	0.0301	0.0049	4098.64	0.00	0.0000
1	7	1188.18	2447.60	0.0301	0.0371	3635.78	0.00	0.0000
1	6	1188.18	2058.35	0.0301	0.1224	3246.52	0.00	0.0000
1	5	1188.18	1731.00	0.0301	0.2310	2919.17	0.00	0.0000
1	4	1188.18	1455.71	0.0301	0.2725	2643.88	0.00	0.0000

(*Continued*)

T A B L E   A2.6 (Continued)

| State | | Spot Prices | | | | DAX+ | | Weighted |
DAX	CAC	DAX	CAC 40	Prob DAX	Prob CAC-40	CAC	Intrinsic	Intrinsic
1	3	1188.18	1224.20	0.0301	0.2057	2412.38	0.00	0.0000
1	2	1188.18	1029.51	0.0301	0.0971	2217.69	0.00	0.0000
1	1	1188.18	865.78	0.0301	0.0262	2053.96	0.00	0.0000
1	0	1188.18	728.09	0.0301	0.0031	1916.27	0.00	0.0000
0	8	972.80	2633.50	0.0037	0.0049	3606.29	0.00	0.0000
0	7	972.80	2214.68	0.0037	0.0371	3187.48	0.00	0.0000
0	6	972.80	1862.47	0.0037	0.1224	2835.27	0.00	0.0000
0	5	972.80	1566.27	0.0037	0.2310	2539.07	0.00	0.0000
0	4	972.80	1317.18	0.0037	0.2725	2289.98	0.00	0.0000
0	3	972.80	1107.70	0.0037	0.2057	2080.50	0.00	0.0000
0	2	972.80	931.54	0.0037	0.0971	1904.34	0.00	0.0000
0	1	972.80	783.39	0.0037	0.0262	1756.19	0.00	0.0000
0	0	972.80	658.80	0.0037	0.0031	1631.60	0.00	0.0000
						TOTAL PRICE	**474.58**	

This suggests that the basket option results in a 7% premium reduction versus the purchase of the options separately. This savings is due, of course, to the assumed 0.5 correlation between the DAX and the CAC. With this framework in place, it is simple to recalculate the value of the basket for varying levels of correlation, as noted in Table A2.7. Not surprisingly, as correlation moves towards +1.0, the value of the basket approaches the sum of the individual index premiums. As it moves towards –1.0, it declines commensurately.

Pricing a Spread Option

The general methodology outlined above can also be used to price a spread option on the DAX and CAC index; this is logical, since a spread option is simply the differential between the indexes rather than a summation. To illustrate the process, we consider a call on the spread between the DAX and CAC with a strike of 200 (the current market value). That is, the option will finish in-the-money if the DAX finishes at least 200 points higher than the CAC.

T A B L E   A2.7

Correlation Scenarios for DAX/CAC Pricing

Correlation	Basket Premium
−100%	149.46
−90%	215.90
−80%	251.19
−70%	280.23
−60%	305.25
−50%	327.17
−40%	346.18
−30%	363.44
−20%	380.95
−10%	396.65
0%	410.72
10%	423.96
20%	437.57
30%	451.11
40%	463.28
50%	474.58
60%	484.85
70%	494.87
80%	503.81
90%	510.00
95%	510.10
100%	511.51

Once again, 81 different states need to be evaluated in order to derive the price of the option. However, instead of adding up the DAX and CAC values (as above) the CAC value is subtracted from the DAX. The resulting difference is compared against the strike of 200 to generate a payoff, i.e., spread option value = MAX(0, DAX − CAC − 200). Based on this process the price of the DAX/CAC spread option is seen to be 205.08; the full results are contained in Table A2.8.

As above, we can also compute the sensitivity of the option to changes in correlation; the results of this exercise are shown in Table A2.9.

Note that in this case the premium increases as the correlation declines, which is the reverse of the basket option. This result arises

T A B L E A2.8

Pricing of DAX/CAC Spread Option

| State | | Spot Prices | | DAX-CAC Intrinsic Value | |
DAX	CAC	DAX	CAC 40	Unweighted	Weighted
8	8	4818.30	5860.96	0.00	0.00
8	7	4818.30	4928.86	0.00	0.00
8	6	4818.30	4145.00	473.30	0.24
8	5	4818.30	3485.80	1132.50	1.08
8	4	4818.30	2931.44	1686.86	1.89
8	3	4818.30	2465.24	2153.06	1.82
8	2	4818.30	2073.18	2545.12	1.02
8	1	4818.30	1743.47	2874.83	0.31
8	0	4818.30	1466.20	3152.10	0.04
7	8	3944.89	5303.21	0.00	0.00
7	7	3944.89	4459.82	0.00	0.00
7	6	3944.89	3750.55	0.00	0.00
7	5	3944.89	3154.08	590.81	4.43
7	4	3944.89	2652.47	1092.41	9.66
7	3	3944.89	2230.64	1514.25	10.11
7	2	3944.89	1875.89	1869.00	5.89
7	1	3944.89	1577.56	2167.33	1.84
7	0	3944.89	1326.67	2418.22	0.24
6	8	3229.80	4798.54	0.00	0.00
6	7	3229.80	4035.41	0.00	0.00
6	6	3229.80	3393.64	0.00	0.00
6	5	3229.80	2853.93	175.87	4.56
6	4	3229.80	2400.06	629.74	19.25
6	3	3229.80	2018.36	1011.44	23.34
6	2	3229.80	1697.37	1332.43	14.51
6	1	3229.80	1427.43	1602.37	4.70
6	0	3229.80	1200.42	1829.38	0.63
5	8	2644.34	4341.90	0.00	0.00
5	7	2644.34	3651.39	0.00	0.00
5	6	2644.34	3070.69	0.00	0.00
5	5	2644.34	2582.34	0.00	0.00
5	4	2644.34	2171.66	272.68	16.46
5	3	2644.34	1826.29	618.05	28.17

(*Continued*)

T A B L E A2.8 (*Continued*)

State		Spot Prices		DAX-CAC Intrinsic Value	
DAX	CAC	DAX	CAC 40	Unweighted	Weighted
5	2	2644.34	1535.85	908.49	19.54
5	1	2644.34	1291.59	1152.74	6.68
5	0	2644.34	1086.19	1358.15	0.93
4	8	2165.00	3928.72	0.00	0.00
4	7	2165.00	3303.91	0.00	0.00
4	6	2165.00	2778.48	0.00	0.00
4	5	2165.00	2336.60	0.00	0.00
4	4	2165.00	1965.00	0.00	0.00
4	3	2165.00	1652.50	312.50	17.58
4	2	2165.00	1389.69	575.31	15.27
4	1	2165.00	1168.68	796.32	5.70
4	0	2165.00	982.82	982.18	0.83
3	8	1772.55	3554.85	0.00	0.00
3	7	1772.55	2989.50	0.00	0.00
3	6	1772.55	2514.07	0.00	0.00
3	5	1772.55	2114.24	0.00	0.00
3	4	1772.55	1778.01	0.00	0.00
3	3	1772.55	1495.24	77.31	3.43
3	2	1772.55	1257.45	315.11	6.61
3	1	1772.55	1057.47	515.08	2.91
3	0	1772.55	889.29	683.26	0.46
2	8	1451.24	3216.56	0.00	0.00
2	7	1451.24	2705.02	0.00	0.00
2	6	1451.24	2274.82	0.00	0.00
2	5	1451.24	1913.05	0.00	0.00
2	4	1451.24	1608.81	0.00	0.00
2	3	1451.24	1352.95	0.00	0.00
2	2	1451.24	1137.78	113.46	1.17
2	1	1451.24	956.84	294.41	0.82
2	0	1451.24	804.67	446.58	0.15
1	8	1188.18	2910.46	0.00	0.00
1	7	1188.18	2447.60	0.00	0.00
1	6	1188.18	2058.35	0.00	0.00

(*Continued*)

T A B L E A2.8 (Continued)

State		Spot Prices		DAX-CAC Intrinsic Value	
DAX	CAC	DAX	CAC 40	Unweighted	Weighted
1	5	1188.18	1731.00	0.00	0.00
1	4	1188.18	1455.71	0.00	0.00
1	3	1188.18	1224.20	0.00	0.00
1	2	1188.18	1029.51	0.00	0.00
1	1	1188.18	865.78	122.40	0.10
1	0	1188.18	728.09	260.09	0.02
0	8	972.80	2633.50	0.00	0.00
0	7	972.80	2214.68	0.00	0.00
0	6	972.80	1862.47	0.00	0.00
0	5	972.80	1566.27	0.00	0.00
0	4	972.80	1317.18	0.00	0.00
0	3	972.80	1107.70	0.00	0.00
0	2	972.80	931.54	0.00	0.00
0	1	972.80	783.39	0.00	0.00
0	0	972.80	658.80	113.99	0.00
			Spread Option		**205.08**

because for small (or negative) correlation, an increase in the DAX means that the CAC is more likely to fall. This means that the spread widens and the option becomes more valuable.

Extending the Model

The model presented above is based on two variables, DAX and CAC. We can, however, extend the process to accommodate additional reference assets. We recall that with two variables we were only concerned with one correlation value. With three variables the number of correlations increases to three (e.g., variables #1, #2, #3, and resulting correlations of #1 versus #2, #1 versus #3, and #2 versus #3). To begin, we start with three normal scores that are not correlated (we denominate these T,U,V). These scores are used to create the binomial tree for all three underlying variables. We then transform (T,U,V) into three normal scores, which are correlated

T A B L E A2.9

Correlation Scenarios for DAX/CAC Pricing

Correlation	Spread Option
−100%	422.80
−90%	418.95
−80%	405.56
−70%	392.05
−60%	377.41
−50%	364.03
−40%	350.99
−30%	336.91
−20%	322.31
−10%	306.62
0%	289.86
10%	272.35
20%	257.88
30%	242.15
40%	224.62
50%	205.08
60%	183.56
70%	158.95
80%	130.43
90%	94.14
95%	68.98
100%	23.99

with each other (X,Y,Z). Once in possession of X, Y, and Z, the correlated binomial trees can be created.

An option with three variables must be evaluated over all 279 possibilities in an eight-step tree (i.e., 9^3); this is obviously considerably more than our 81-step, two-asset, tree, suggesting that even greater computing power is required. We can, or course, extend the model to N variables, which will contain $((N * (N - 1))/2)$ correlations. It is not difficult to imagine that pricing a basket or spread option with dozens of reference assets can become computationally intensive. Fortunately, there exist certain closed-form solutions that replicate the binomial tree methodology; these processes are, however, outside the scope of our introductory discussion.

Note: Table A2.10 contains a list of normal function variables.

T A B L E   A2.10

Normal Function Variables

| State | | Normal Function | | | |
DAX	CAC	U	V	W	Z
8.0000	8.0000	2.8284	2.8284	2.8284	3.8637
8.0000	7.0000	2.8284	2.1213	2.8284	3.2513
8.0000	6.0000	2.8284	1.4142	2.8284	2.6390
8.0000	5.0000	2.8284	0.7071	2.8284	2.0266
8.0000	4.0000	2.8284	0.0000	2.8284	1.4142
8.0000	3.0000	2.8284	−0.7071	2.8284	0.8018
8.0000	2.0000	2.8284	−1.4142	2.8284	0.1895
8.0000	1.0000	2.8284	−2.1213	2.8284	−0.4229
8.0000	0.0000	2.8284	−2.8284	2.8284	−1.0353
7.0000	8.0000	2.1213	2.8284	2.1213	3.5101
7.0000	7.0000	2.1213	2.1213	2.1213	2.8978
7.0000	6.0000	2.1213	1.4142	2.1213	2.2854
7.0000	5.0000	2.1213	0.7071	2.1213	1.6730
7.0000	4.0000	2.1213	0.0000	2.1213	1.0607
7.0000	3.0000	2.1213	−0.7071	2.1213	0.4483
7.0000	2.0000	2.1213	−1.4142	2.1213	−0.1641
7.0000	1.0000	2.1213	−2.1213	2.1213	−0.7765
7.0000	0.0000	2.1213	−2.8284	2.1213	−1.3888
6.0000	8.0000	1.4142	2.8284	1.4142	3.1566
6.0000	7.0000	1.4142	2.1213	1.4142	2.5442
6.0000	6.0000	1.4142	1.4142	1.4142	1.9319
6.0000	5.0000	1.4142	0.7071	1.4142	1.3195
6.0000	4.0000	1.4142	0.0000	1.4142	0.7071
6.0000	3.0000	1.4142	−0.7071	1.4142	0.0947
6.0000	2.0000	1.4142	−1.4142	1.4142	−0.5176
6.0000	1.0000	1.4142	−2.1213	1.4142	−1.1300
6.0000	0.0000	1.4142	−2.8284	1.4142	−1.7424
5.0000	8.0000	0.7071	2.8284	0.7071	2.8030
5.0000	7.0000	0.7071	2.1213	0.7071	2.1907
5.0000	6.0000	0.7071	1.4142	0.7071	1.5783
5.0000	5.0000	0.7071	0.7071	0.7071	0.9659
5.0000	4.0000	0.7071	0.0000	0.7071	0.3536
5.0000	3.0000	0.7071	−0.7071	0.7071	−0.2588
5.0000	2.0000	0.7071	−1.4142	0.7071	−0.8712

(Continued)

T A B L E A2.10 (*Continued*)

| State | | Normal Function | | | |
DAX	CAC	U	V	W	Z
5.0000	1.0000	0.7071	−2.1213	0.7071	−1.4836
5.0000	0.0000	0.7071	−2.8284	0.7071	−2.0959
4.0000	8.0000	0.0000	2.8284	0.0000	2.4495
4.0000	7.0000	0.0000	2.1213	0.0000	1.8371
4.0000	6.0000	0.0000	1.4142	0.0000	1.2247
4.0000	5.0000	0.0000	0.7071	0.0000	0.6124
4.0000	4.0000	0.0000	0.0000	0.0000	0.0000
4.0000	3.0000	0.0000	−0.7071	0.0000	−0.6124
4.0000	2.0000	0.0000	−1.4142	0.0000	−1.2247
4.0000	1.0000	0.0000	−2.1213	0.0000	−1.8371
4.0000	0.0000	0.0000	−2.8284	0.0000	−2.4495
3.0000	8.0000	−0.7071	2.8284	−0.7071	2.0959
3.0000	7.0000	−0.7071	2.1213	−0.7071	1.4836
3.0000	6.0000	−0.7071	1.4142	−0.7071	0.8712
3.0000	5.0000	−0.7071	0.7071	−0.7071	0.2588
3.0000	4.0000	−0.7071	0.0000	−0.7071	−0.3536
3.0000	3.0000	−0.7071	−0.7071	−0.7071	−0.9659
3.0000	2.0000	−0.7071	−1.4142	−0.7071	−1.5783
3.0000	1.0000	−0.7071	−2.1213	−0.7071	−2.1907
3.0000	0.0000	−0.7071	−2.8284	−0.7071	−2.8030
2.0000	8.0000	−1.4142	2.8284	−1.4142	1.7424
2.0000	7.0000	−1.4142	2.1213	−1.4142	1.1300
2.0000	6.0000	−1.4142	1.4142	−1.4142	0.5176
2.0000	5.0000	−1.4142	0.7071	−1.4142	−0.0947
2.0000	4.0000	−1.4142	0.0000	−1.4142	−0.7071
2.0000	3.0000	−1.4142	−0.7071	−1.4142	−1.3195
2.0000	2.0000	−1.4142	−1.4142	−1.4142	−1.9319
2.0000	1.0000	−1.4142	−2.1213	−1.4142	−2.5442
2.0000	0.0000	−1.4142	−2.8284	−1.4142	−3.1566
1.0000	8.0000	−2.1213	2.8284	−2.1213	1.3888
1.0000	7.0000	−2.1213	2.1213	−2.1213	0.7765
1.0000	6.0000	−2.1213	1.4142	−2.1213	0.1641
1.0000	5.0000	−2.1213	0.7071	−2.1213	−0.4483
1.0000	4.0000	−2.1213	0.0000	−2.1213	−1.0607

(*Continued*)

T A B L E A2.10 (*Continued*)

State		Normal Function			
DAX	CAC	*U*	*V*	*W*	*Z*
1.0000	3.0000	−2.1213	−0.7071	−2.1213	−1.6730
1.0000	2.0000	−2.1213	−1.4142	−2.1213	−2.2854
1.0000	1.0000	−2.1213	−2.1213	−2.1213	−2.8978
1.0000	0.0000	−2.1213	−2.8284	−2.1213	−3.5101
0.0000	8.0000	−2.8284	2.8284	−2.8284	1.0353
0.0000	7.0000	−2.8284	2.1213	−2.8284	0.4229
0.0000	6.0000	−2.8284	1.4142	−2.8284	−0.1895
0.0000	5.0000	−2.8284	0.7071	−2.8284	−0.8018
0.0000	4.0000	−2.8284	0.0000	−2.8284	−1.4142
0.0000	3.0000	−2.8284	−0.7071	−2.8284	−2.0266
0.0000	2.0000	−2.8284	−1.4142	−2.8284	−2.6390
0.0000	1.0000	−2.8284	−2.1213	−2.8284	−3.2513
0.0000	0.0000	−2.8284	−2.8284	−2.8284	−3.8637

MBS Prepayment and Valuation

MBS are unique securities that must be valued by examining all critical parameters that influence the degree of mortgage prepayment that exists in a given mortgage pool. In this section we provide a brief introduction to prepayment modeling and MBS valuation.[1]

PREPAYMENTS

The most interesting, and complex, risk associated with mortgages (and, by extension, MBS) relates to cash flow uncertainty driven by prepayments of borrowed principal. Prepayments, in turn, are a function of refinancings, home sales, partial/accelerated prepayments, and defaults. In a typical fixed-rate, level-pay mortgage, the borrower is obliged to make regular (i.e., monthly or quarterly) payments of principal and interest (we ignore, for simplicity, mortgages that allow for increasing, balloon, or bullet payments of principal). However, interest rates may decline over time, inducing the borrower to repay the original mortgage and refinance through a new one with a lower interest rate (evidence suggests that refinancing becomes attractive when rates have declined by at least 100 bps below the original rate). Alternatively, the borrower may choose to sell the underlying property, repaying the original mortgage in the process. Or, the borrower may wish to make greater principal

---

1 Portions of this discussion are drawn from Banks (2005).

payments during a given month(s) in order to build equity more rapidly. In the worst case, the borrower may be unable to continue paying the mortgage and declare a default. Each one of these payment/prepayment actions creates cash flow uncertainties that make the valuation of MBS a nontrivial task. Note that adjustable rate mortgages (ARMs) can be impacted by the same variables, as well as the changing value of the interest rate component (which may be readjusted on a monthly, quarterly, semiannual, or annual basis). From an MBS investor's perspective, mortgage cash flows can be viewed as the sum of projected monthly interest less servicing fees, projected monthly scheduled principal repayments, and projected monthly additional principal prepayments.

Most prepayment activity is due to home sales when rates are stable. As rates rise, refinancing opportunities disappear and housing turnover slows, meaning that prepayments decline. Conversely, as rates fall, refinancing commences and housing turnover increases, leading to prepayment acceleration; we consider this at greater length below.

Refinancing, fueled primarily by declining interest rates, remains the single largest driver of prepayments and is the central focus of any prepayment model. This means, of course, that projected prepayment experience is extremely dependent on assumptions regarding future interest rates. Refinancing can be considered the equivalent of a call option on interest rates owned by the borrower; the option cannot, unfortunately, be modeled in a standard option-pricing framework due to the behavioral inefficiencies that characterize the housing market. That said, there is sufficient empirical evidence to suggest how refinancing patterns arise during a given cycle, and these results can be incorporated into a model. For instance, most cycles feature a burnout period, meaning that after a burst of refinancings, further refinancing activity tends to slow; each marginal decrease in rates yields less refinancing activity. Friction costs and barriers have declined in recent decades, making the refinancing process simpler, cheaper, and more efficient; the advent of online refinancing technologies, for instance, has allowed a greater number of borrowers to refinance during a particular cycle, meaning that the number of "lagging" refinancers has declined. Refinancing incentives and mortgage product availability must also feature in the model. These can be supplemented by other, less tangible, forces—media coverage of the rate environment and refinancing opportunities, promotional campaigns sponsored by lending institutions, "psychological" rate barriers that might drive activity, and so forth. The micro and macro construction of the pool must also be considered. The market features many types of mortgages and rates, some of which promote refinancing action more readily and efficiently than others. In addition, the diversity of borrowers in any given pool leads to a broad range of refinancing options. Slow refinancers will eventually comprise a larger proportion of a seasoned pool as the fast refinancers depart, which will again impact on prepayment speeds and valuation. Refinancings cannot, of course, be viewed in isolation: even if rates are declining to the point where borrowers can achieve real savings, an associated deterioration in housing prices can impact behavior.

Housing sales, the second most significant driver of prepayments and therefore a vital modeling input, can be impacted by overall market turnover, regional/local turnover, seasoning, and lock-in/prepayment penalties. Each of these variables, in turn, can be directly or indirectly influenced by other variables. For instance, overall and regional turnover may be affected by new housing starts and new home sales, economic growth, employment, taxes, interest rates, housing price inflation, and propensity for "trading up." Seasonal or cyclical effects must also be considered in the model.

Actual prepayment levels are determined by comparing actual principal cash flows received with those that are scheduled or expected; any difference between the two represents a prepayment, and is generally expressed in terms of the outstanding balance of the mortgage. In order to assess the potential impact of prepayment risk on mortgages the industry has come to rely on certain simplifying assumptions designed to serve as a proxy for prepayment behavior. The most fundamental computation is based on the single monthly mortality (SMM) gauge, which is a monthly prepayment indicator that computes the fraction of a pool's balance that prepays during the month. The constant prepayment rate (CPR) model serves as an annualized version of the SMM. The CPR assumes no difference in seasoning (i.e., the amount of time a loan has been outstanding), meaning that an assumed prepayment rate of 2% applies to a loan that has been outstanding for six months or five years; this assumption is considered unrealistic in light of available historical data.

In the mid-1980s the U.S. Public Security Association (PSA) introduced a variation on the SMM/CPR approach to account for seasoning characteristics. The PSA, in examining historical data, determined that prepayment patterns change based on loan life: specifically, new loans have lower prepayment rates than seasoned ones. The PSA model adjusts the CPR by the age of the loan. The base case PSA model, known as 100% CPR, assumes 0% prepayment for new loans, 0.2% prepayment for the first month, increasing by 0.2% per month for the next 30 months, and then converting to a flat 6% per year thereafter. This 100% benchmark can then be increased (e.g., to 150% or 200%) to reflect faster prepayment scenarios, or decreased (e.g., to 50% or 75%) to reflect slower prepayments. Figure A3.1 highlights various PSA CPR speeds.

It is common in MBS valuation to perform scenario analyses to determine interest rate sensitivity of the CPR and, by extension, the sensitivity of the WAM and yield. For instance, Figure A3.2 illustrates a hypothetical CPR curve for changes in interest rates; this curve, which can be constructed from historical prepayment data, can then be used to generate possible MBS values.

Ultimately, an effective prepayment model must take account of all of the variables that can impact prepayments in order to provide an indication of possible future prepayment speeds, as noted in Figure A3.3, so that a specific MBS can be properly valued. In some instances models are atomized to project each individual risk variable independently; these must, of course, be internally

F I G U R E A3.1

PSA CPR Speeds

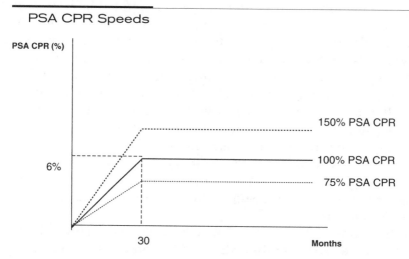

F I G U R E A3.2

Effect of Interest Rate Scenarios on CPR

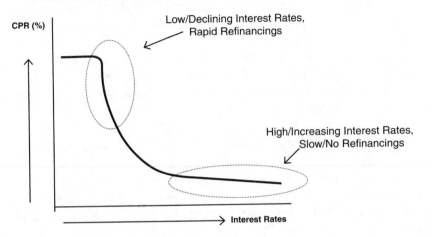

F I G U R E A3.3

Prepayment Projections from Model

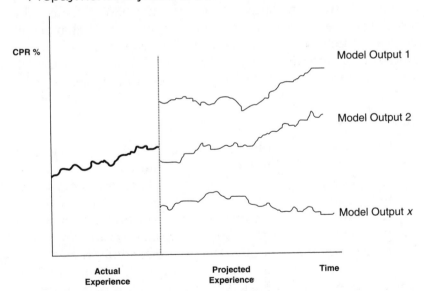

consistent so that the inputs and outputs among each independent submodel provide rational explanations of behavior (e.g., the effects of housing turnover from one submodel must be consistent with the effects of refinancing behavior from a second submodel).

By creating this additional level of detail an intermediary or investor can gain additional insight into future prepayments and security value. Importantly, the efficacy of a model can be back-tested by running simulations against actual prepayment experience.

Different types of MBS have different prepayment characteristics and sensitivities. Thus, in creating a workable model, attention must be given to the type of security being analyzed/traded; there is no single model that can properly compute prepayments and valuations across multiple types of instruments without some adjustment for the specifics of the asset/pool. For instance, GNMA pools tend to feature higher LTVs than commercial pools. High LTVs dampen prepayment speeds, leading to different values than commercial pools with lower LTVs. However, as GNMA loans season (and assuming housing market stability), LTVs drop and prepayments rise compared to commercial pools. Various others differences exist between other classes of MBS.

The modeling of prepayments must be viewed as a dynamic process, with parameters that change over time as market, borrower, and investor characteristics change. For instance, the introduction of new mortgage products, fundamental changes in interest rate structure, or differences in borrower behavior can all combine to permanently alter prepayments. A model that fails to take account of these changes will soon be of limited use.

VALUATION

The prepayment risks described above are a fundamental input in the valuation process. Indeed, intermediaries and investors attempt to model prepayment behavior so that they can use the output to value an MBS more accurately. There are various ways of valuing MBS; some are elemental and simplistic but easy to implement, while others are computationally rigorous, though may ultimately prove to be more accurate. The potential value/return of an MBS can be analyzed through a simple static yield computation or the more complex option adjusted spread (OAS) process which we have described in Appendix I.

The static yield calculation is a cash flow yield derived from assumptions about prepayment speeds; it assumes that the investor will reinvest at the yield to maturity rate and that the MBS is held until the final payoff date based on the prevailing prepayment

assumption. The reinvestment assumption is critical, as prepayments (and thus reinvestments) occur every month or quarter; if
cash flows differ from the assumption, then the cash flow yield will
differ as well. Under a static cash flow yield process the yield
spread of an MBS is equal to the difference between the cash flow
yield and the yield to maturity of the risk free benchmark (e.g., a
Treasury bond); this, however, fails to account for the term structure of the benchmark and expected interest rate volatility, which
will impact prepayments and cash flows.

We can extend the OAS concept to the option-embedded MBS.
The OAS values an MBS by comparing the security to a miniport-
folio of zero-coupon risk free benchmarks that have certain
projected cash flows; the portfolio can be adjusted to reflect MBS
default risk and cash flow uncertainty. The resulting spread makes
the present value of projected cash flows from MBS, discounted at
spot rate and spread, equal to the market price. As noted, the OAS
process begins with the computation of a yield curve spread as a
measure of the return of principal over multiple periods, with each
MBS cash flow discounted by the appropriate risk-free benchmark
and spread using forward rates. However, the yield curve spread
still assumes constant rates and cash flows, so it is only appropriate for current scenarios. In the second step, the OAS model
computes the yield curve spread through a series of forward rates
and then captures the effects of rate volatility to suggest a possible
path of future rates. Specifically, the OAS model creates random
interest rate paths based on model parameters, and each path is
used to project prepayment rates and MBS cash flows. Once
computed, the values are discounted to generate an estimate of
the average present value. The cost of the embedded option is
simply the difference between the OAS and the yield curve spread,
and can be interpreted as a measure of the investor's cost of rate
volatility.

Regardless of the valuation model used, securities feature
price compression, or negative convexity—a state where price
appreciation is lower, and price depreciation is greater, than on a
standard positive convexity-fixed income security. Negative
convexity arises as a result of the prepayment option the MBS
investor grants the mortgage borrower. For instance, in a falling
rate environment the upside price potential of an MBS is limited: if
borrowers refinance in the lower-rate environment, MBS investors
holding securities that are prepaying very rapidly must contend

with the prospect of having to reinvest in a lower-rate environment, and thus suffer from contraction, or reinvestment, risk. Conversely, in a rising-rate environment the price of an MBS will decline, but at a greater rate than conventional fixed income securities: rising rates slow prepayments and increase the amount invested in the pool at below-market rates; lack of prepayments means investors do not receive accelerated prepayment cash flows and cannot therefore reinvest at new, higher rates—thus suffering from extension risk.

Answers to Chapter Exercises

CHAPTER 1 EXERCISES

1. The buyer of a put option has the:
   a. Obligation to sell an asset
   b. Right to sell an asset
   c. Obligation to buy an asset
   d. Right to buy an asset
   e. None of the above

   Answer: b. The buyer of a put option pays the seller a premium in exchange for the right, but not the obligation, to sell an asset at a defined strike price.

2. The seller of a call option has the:
   a. Obligation to sell an asset
   b. Right to sell an asset
   c. Obligation to buy an asset
   d. Right to buy an asset
   e. None of the above

   Answer a. The seller of call option accepts a premium from the buyer and thus commits to selling the buyer a specified amount of the asset at the defined strike price if the contract is exercised.

3. Which of the following is/are true?
   a. A European option can be exercised only at maturity
   b. An American option can be exercised at any time
   c. A Bermudan option can be exercised at any time
   d. a and b
   e. a and c

   Answer: b. A European option can be exercised only at maturity, while an American option can be exercised at any point up to, and including, maturity. A Bermudan option can only be exercised on specified dates up to, and including, maturity.

4. Which of the following is/are true of exchange-traded options?
   a. Contracts are generally less liquid than OTC options
   b. Contracts are not customizable
   c. Contracts carry more credit risk than OTC options
   d. a and c
   e. b and c

   Answer: b. Exchange-traded contracts are not customizable and must always adhere to the standards established by the sponsoring exchange. The standardization makes exchange contracts more, rather than less, liquid that similar OTC counterparts, while the use of the clearinghouse mechanism reduces, rather than increases, credit risk.

5. Which of the following represent advantages of the OTC options market over the exchange-traded options market?
   a. OTC contracts are standardized and therefore more liquid than exchange contracts
   b. OTC contracts feature less counterparty risk than exchange contracts
   c. OTC contracts are customizable and therefore more flexible than exchange contracts
   d. OTC contracts have more price transparency than exchange contracts
   e. All of the above

   Answer: c. OTC contracts are customizable, meaning they can be tailored to the precise requirements of the parties to the trade. OTC contacts are not standardized, they feature more credit risk than exchange options, and they are generally less transparent because prices do not flow through a formal exchange mechanism.

6. Options are available on which of the following asset classes?
   a. Inflation
   b. Wheat
   c. Equity baskets
   d. Credit spreads
   e. All of the above

   Answer: e. Options can be bought and sold on a broad range of asset underlyings, including inflation, wheat, equity baskets, and credit spreads. "Esoteric" or new asset classes, such as inflation, are traded through the OTC market rather than the exchange market.

7. Options can be used to:
   a. Generate a speculative profit
   b. Hedge an existing or anticipated risk position
   c. Monetize value in an underlying asset position
   d. All of the above
   e. None of the above

   Answer: d. Options are regularly used to accomplish a range of goals, including speculative profit creation, risk hedging, and value monetization.

8. If the seller of an exchange-traded futures call option is exercised against, the seller must:
   a. Accept cash
   b. Deliver cash
   c. Accept a futures contract
   d. Deliver a futures contract
   e. None of the above

   Answer: d. A seller of a futures call option accepts premium in exchange for providing a futures contract should the buyer exercise the option.

CHAPTER 2 EXERCISES

1. In a positive yield curve environment, caplets priced at the long end of the yield curve will be:
   a. Cheaper than caplets at the short end of the curve
   b. Equally priced
   c. More expensive than caplets at the short end of the curve
   d. More out-of-the-money than caplets at the short end of the curve
   e. None of the above

   Answer: c. Caplets on the long end of the yield curve are likely to have intrinsic value as well as more time value than the shorter maturity caplets and will therefore be more expensive.

2. The payoff of a call option is equal to:
   a. Max (0, asset price – strike price)
   b. Max (0, strike price – asset price)
   c. Max (asset price – strike price, strike price – asset price)
   d. Max (0, –asset price – strike price)
   e. None of the above

   Answer: a. The payoff of a call is the maximum of 0 (meaning there can be no negative result apart from premium paid) and the differential between the strike and the asset price.

3. In covered call writing, the option seller:
   a. Never owns the asset
   b. May own the asset
   c. Always owns the asset
   d. Owns the call
   e. None of the above

   Answer: c. If an option seller is truly engaging in a covered call writing program, it must always own the underlying asset so that it can deliver should the buyer exercise.

4. The payoff of a put option is equal to:
   a. Max (0, asset price – strike price)
   b. Max (0, strike price – asset price)
   c. Max (asset price – strike price, strike price – asset price)

  d. Max (0, −asset price − strike price)

  e. None of the above

Answer: b. The payoff of a put is the maximum of 0 (meaning there can be no negative result apart from premium paid) and the differential between the asset price and the strike.

5. As an option's time to expiry increases:
   a. Time value increases
   b. Time value decreases
   c. Intrinsic value increases
   d. Intrinsic value decreases
   e. Time value and intrinsic value increase

Answer: a. As an option's time to expiration increases, the time value component of the option's premium also increases. This occurs because additional time provides the option buyer with a greater opportunity of having the underlying reference asset move in-the-money (or further in-the-money).

6. An option that is in-the-money and has not yet reached its expiry date:
   a. Has no intrinsic value
   b. Has no time value
   c. Has intrinsic value
   d. Has time value
   e. Has intrinsic value and time value

Answer: e. An in-the-money option, by definition, has intrinsic value as it can be exercised for immediate gain. An option that has not yet expired has some amount of time value. Accordingly, the total value of the in-the-money option consists of intrinsic and time value.

7. If the NASDAQ equity index is at 2,000 when an institution buys a 2,100 strike call struck what is the payoff of the call if the NASDAQ ends at 2,050 at option expiration?
   a. $2{,}000 - 2{,}100 = -100$
   b. $2{,}100 - 2{,}000 = 100$
   c. $2{,}100 - 2{,}050 = 50$
   d. $2{,}050 - 2{,}100 = -50$
   e. None of the above

Answer: e. None of the above. Although the payoff of the index call is equal to the ending value less the strike (2050 – 2100), the call payoff is floored at 0 because the buyer can never face a negative payoff.

8. Given a put on Japanese Government Bonds (JGB) struck at 100.5, which of the following is/are true?
   a. The seller's liability commences as soon as JGB prices fall below 100.5
   b. The seller's liability commences as soon as JGB prices rise above 100.5
   c. The buyer's price commences as soon as JGB prices rise above 100.5
   d. None of the above
   e. All of the above

Answer: a. The liability of the option seller begins to accrue once the price of the JGB falls below the 100.5 strike; while the price remains above 100.5 the seller has no liability.

9. The maximum loss on a long call is equal to:
   a. The maximum downside price of the asset
   b. The maximum upside price of the asset
   c. The premium received
   d. The premium paid
   e. None of the above

Answer: d. The owner of a long call can never lose more than the premium paid to secure the contract. This represents the essential unilateral characteristic of an option.

10. Which is/are false?
    a. Buyers of options have limited potential for loss (i.e., premium paid) and virtually unlimited potential for gains.
    b. Sellers of options have limited potential for gains (i.e, premium received) and virtually unlimited risk of losses.
    c. Option buying strategies are less risky than option selling strategies, though they involve an up-front cost.
    d. Option selling strategies are riskier than option buying strategies, though some of the risk is defrayed by the up-front income (and more risk can be mitigated through hedging).

e. Those who anticipate rising values in the underlying asset should buy puts or sell calls.

Answer: e. Institutions who anticipate an asset value will increase should buy calls or sell puts, rather than buy puts or sell calls.

11. If a company buys a two-year LIBOR cap struck at 6.00%, the three caplets pay off how many bps if LIBOR sets at 6.00%, 6.25%, and 5.75% during each sequential period?
    a. 0 bps, 25 bps, 25 bps
    b. 0 bps, 25 bps, −25 bps
    c. 0 bps, 25 bps, 0 bps
    d. 0 bps, 0 bps, 25 bps
    e. 25 bps, 0 bps, 0 bps

Answer: c. Based on a 6.00% cap, the first and third rate sets (6.00% and 5.75%) do not push the individual caplets in-the-money, suggesting the payoff for those two caplets will be equal to 0. When the rate set for the second caplet reaches 6.25%, the second caplet provides a 25 bps payoff.

12. A synthetic long asset position is created from:
    a. Long call and long put
    b. Long call and short put
    c. Short call and long put
    d. Short call and short put
    e. Short call and long call

Answer: b. The synthetic long asset position features elements of the long call (e.g., profit as the market rallies) and the short put (e.g., loss as the market trades off). When combined, the two options produce the long asset payoff profile.

CHAPTER 3 EXERCISES

1. Which of the following is/are true? Given a current bond price of 105, a strike price of 103, and a barrier of 102, a down and in put option:
    a. Is created without intrinsic value when the barrier is triggered.

b. Is extinguished without intrinsic value when the barrier is triggered.

c. Is created with intrinsic value when the barrier is triggered.

d. Is created without intrinsic value when the barrier is triggered.

e. None of the above.

Answer: c. An option is created ("in") when the barrier of 102 is reached; since this is a put with a strike of 103, the differential of 103-102 represents the intrinsic value that is created once the barrier is triggered.

2. Given a ladder call on Japanese Government Bonds (JGBs) with a strike of 100 and rungs at 102, 104, and 106, what will the final payoff be if the price path during the life of the option reaches a maximum of 105 and a minimum of 99?

a. $106 - 105 = 1$

b. $105 - 100 = 5$

c. $104 - 100 = 4$

d. $104 - 99 = 5$

e. $105 - 99 = 6$

Answer: c. The rung at 104 is the maximum lock-in point attained during the life of the trade, meaning the payoff is equal to $104 - 100$; though the peak price was 105, no rung existed at the 105 mark to provide an additional lock-in point.

3. Given a strike price of 100, a current bond price of 98, a sensitivity of $10,000 per bond point and a digital payoff $150,000, what is the payoff on a digital option if bond price at maturity is 104?

a. $40,000

b. $60,000

c. $120,000

d. $150,000

e. None of the above.

Answer: d. Since the option is a digital, the degree of moneyness has no impact on the payout once the strike is reached; the payoff is thus $150,000.

4. Which of the following instruments can help reduce uncertainty regarding the terminal price/rate of a reference bond?
   a. Up and in call option
   b. Digital put option
   c. Power put option
   d. Average price call option
   e. None of the above

   Answer: d. The average price structure reduces uncertainty regarding the terminal price of the bond by making the payoff a function of an average period that can span days, weeks, or months.

5. What are the major advantages of barrier options?
   a. The specific control the user has in incorporating a market view
   b. The relative ease with which they can be hedged
   c. The greater liquidity they feature versus European options
   d. The relatively cheap cost compared to European options
   e. a and d

   Answer: e. Barriers allow users to express very specific market views at a cost that compares favorably to that of European options.

6. All of the following are true of barrier options except:
   a. Barriers can more accurately take a customer's view and specific risk management needs into account.
   b. The seller of a barrier option assumes less risk than the seller of a standard option.
   c. As the spot price of an asset approaches the barrier, a knock-in option premium approaches the standard European option premium.
   d. As the spot price of an asset approaches the barrier, the knock-out option approaches the standard European option premium.
   e. As the spot price of an asset approaches the barrier, the knock-out option approaches the standard American option premium.

   Answer: d. As the spot price of an asset approaches the barrier, the knockout option approaches zero, due to the increased probability that the option will disappear.

7. Speculators use barrier options because:
   a. They do not have strong opinions about future market prices and can use barrier options as an inexpensive means of "guessing."
   b. They can gain greater leverage.
   c. They can set barriers at significant support or resistance levels.
   d. a and b
   e. b and c

   Answer: e. Option purchasers can gain greater leverage for the same amount of cash due since they pay smaller premiums than they do for European or American options. They can also customize barriers to appear or disappear at significant support or resistance levels.

CHAPTER 4 EXERCISES

1. Consider the following convertible bond issued by Company JKL:

Nominal value	$1,000
Conversion price	$78
Stock price at issuance	$61
Current share price	$63
Bond market price	$95

   a. Calculate the conversion ratio.

   $$= \frac{\text{nominal value}}{\text{conversion price}}$$

   $$= \frac{1,000}{78} = 12.82$$

   b. Calculate the conversion premium.

   $$= \left(\frac{\text{conversion price}}{\text{stock price at issuance}} \right) - 1$$

   $$= \left(\frac{78}{61} \right) - 1 = 28\%$$

c. Calculate the conversion value.

$$= \text{(conversion ratio)} \times \text{(current share price)}$$
$$= 12.82 \times 63 = 808$$

d. Calculate the parity.

$$= \left(\frac{\text{conversion ratio} \times \text{current share price}}{\text{nominal value}} \right) \times 100$$

$$= \left(\frac{12.82 \times 63}{1000} \right) \times 100 = 80.77$$

e. Calculate the premium.

$$= \left(\frac{\text{current bond market price}}{\text{parity}} \right) - 1$$

$$= \left(\frac{95}{80.77} \right) - 1 = 17.6\%$$

2. A convertible bond is a package of:
    a. Short bond and short investor call option
    b. Long bond and long investor call option
    c. Long bond and short investor call option
    d. Short bond and long investor call option
    e. None of the above

    Answer: b. The convertible is comprised of a long bond and the investor's right to exercise the embedded option to convert into shares once the conversion price (strike price) is reached. Since the investor owns the right, the investor is long the call.

3. The convertible bond conveys which of the following benefits?
    a. Increase in an issuer's cost of funds and decrease in an investor's returns
    b. Minimum value in an investor's returns and decrease in the issuer's cost of funds
    c. Increase in dividends and capital appreciation
    d. Increase in shareholder dilution
    e. None of the above

    Answer: b. A convertible bond generates a minimum investment return for investors in the form of bond value while simultaneously providing the issuer with a lower cost of funds from the sale of the embedded equity option.

4. Which of the following is/are true of a convertible bond?
   a. Dilution always occurs
   b. Dilution never occurs
   c. Dilution may occur
   d. Dilution will vary
   e. None of the above

Answer: c. While dilution will always occur if conversion occurs, conversion is not guaranteed to occur; that is, if the stock price does not exceed the conversion price, the bond will not be converted and no share dilution will occur.

5. A callable bond is a package of:
   a. A long bond and a long issuer call
   b. A long bond and a long investor call
   c. A short bond and a short issuer call
   d. A short bond and a short investor call
   e. None of the above

Answer: a. The callable bond is a combination of a long bond and a long issuer call on prices. The issuer has the right to call the bond back from investors, meaning the issuer is long the option; in exchange, the issuer pays investors a premium through a higher coupon.

6. The theoretical value of a callable bond is equal to:
   a. Noncallable bond + call option
   b. Callable bond – call option
   c. Noncallable bond – call option
   d. Callable bond + call option
   e. None of the above

Answer: c. The theoretical value of a callable bond must equal the difference between a noncallable bond and the call option that the issuer owns as part of the package. If the relationship does not hold true, arbitrage opportunities will arise.

7. A puttable bond is a package of:
   a. A long bond and a short issuer call
   b. A long bond and a short investor call
   c. A long bond and a long investor call
   d. A long bond and a short investor put
   e. A long bond and a long investor put

   Answer: e. The puttable bond is a combination of a long bond and a long investor put on prices. The investor has the right to put the bond back to the issuer, meaning it is long the option; in exchange, it pays the issuer via a lower coupon.

8. A collared FRN features:
   a. A long issuer floor and a short issuer cap
   b. A long investor floor and a short investor cap
   c. A long issuer floor and a long investor cap
   d. A short issuer floor and a long investor cap
   e. None of the above

   Answer: d. A collared FRN can be created when an issuer sells a floor and buys a cap; the combination reduces the premium normally payable on the cap.

9. In a credit-spread-linked credit-linked note with an embedded call option on credit spreads, the principal/coupon is:
   a. Increased as spreads widen
   b. Increased as spreads tighten
   c. Decreased as spreads widen
   d. Decreased as spreads tighten
   e. None of the above

   Answer: b. The embedded call option on credit spreads provides investors with an enhanced principal/coupon profile as credit spreads tighten.

CHAPTER 5 EXERCISES

1. Which of the following trades would represent the cheapest hedge for a borrower who thought interest rates were going to fall but needed protection if rates rose over the next two to five years?

    a. Pay fixed on a forward starting swap

    b. Buy a standard payer swaption

    c. Buy a five-year, no-call three-year Bermudan swaption with semiannual exercises

    d. Buy a three-year cap forward starting in two years

    e. All would be approximately equivalent

Answer: b. If the borrower believes interest rates are going to fall and is interested primarily in purchasing a "cheap" disaster hedge, the most inexpensive product is a standard payer. The optionality does not lock in the borrower's costs (as in a standard swap) and the relative lack of flexibility makes it cheaper than the Bermudan or cap alternatives.

2. A borrower who has issued a callable bond with an exercise date in three years wants to monetize the value of that bond. Which of the following would be suitable?

    a. Sell a standard payer's swaption

    b. Sell a standard receiver's swaption

    c. Sell a Bermudan payer's swaption

    d. Sell a Bermudan receiver's swaption

    e. None of the above

Answer: b. Since the embedded call has just one exercise date then the cheaper standard receiver swaption will be the most appropriate trade. If rates fall, the receiver swaption will be exercised, as will the embedded call in the bond. The net effect is that the borrower continues paying the bond's original fixed rate but has had use of the receiver swaption premium to reduce funding costs.

3. A long payer swaption:

    a. Grants the buyer the right to receive fixed rates

    b. Obligates the buyer to receive fixed rates

    c. Grants the buyer the right to pay fixed rates

    d. Obligates the buyer to pay fixed rates

    e. None of the above

Answer: a. A purchased payer swaption grants the buyer the right, but not the obligation, to pay fixed rates and receive floating rates on an underlying swap. Since the swaption is an option, it is a unilateral optionable contract, not an obligation.

4. Which of the following is/are true?
   a. A payer swaption is equal to a put swaption
   b. A payer swaption is equal to a call swaption
   c. A receiver swaption is equal to a payer swaption
   d. a and b
   e. b and c

   Answer: d. A payer swaption is the same as a put swaption, i.e., it allows the buyer the right to pay fixed rates to the seller. A receiver swaption is equivalent to a call swaption, allowing the buyer the right to receive fixed rates.

5. Which of the following is/are true?
   a. A receiver swaption with a high strike is more valuable than one with a low strike
   b. A payer swaption with a low strike is more valuable than one with a high strike
   c. A swaption with a longer time to maturity is more valuable than one with a shorter time to maturity
   d. All of the above
   e. None of the above

   Answer: d. A receiver with a high strike is more valuable than one with a low strike as it allows the buyer the right to receive an above market rate; similarly, a payer swaption with a low strike allows the buyer the right to pay a below market rate. Swaptions with longer time to maturity have more time value, and are thus more valuable.

6. Assume the following market/product scenarios:
   Current LIBOR = 5.00%
   Payer swaption strike = 4.00%
   Receiver swaption strike = 3.00%
   Which of the following is/are true?
   a. The payer swaption will be exercised
   b. The payer swaption will not be exercised
   c. The receiver swaption will not be exercised
   d. a and c
   e. b and c

Answer: d. The payer swaption will be exercised, as the payer swaption strike of 4% is below the current LIBOR set of 5%, making it economical for the buyer to pay the lower strike rate. Conversely, the receiver swaption will not be exercised as the buyer can receiver higher LIBOR in the current market environment.

7. A six-year, no-call-year Bermudan swaption with annual exercise allows for how many exercise opportunities?
   a. 6
   b. 5
   c. 4
   d. 3
   e. 2

Answer: d. The Bermudan swaption can be exercised 3 times, as follows: end of year 3, into a 3-year swap, end of year 4, into a 2-year swap, and end of year 5, into a 1-year swap.

8. A seven-year callable swap that is callable in three years is equal to:
   a. A seven-year swap and a three-year receiver swaption on a four-year swap
   b. A seven-year swap and a three-year payer swaption on a four-year swap
   c. A seven-year swap and a four-year receiver swaption on a three-year swap
   d. A seven-year swap and a four-year payer swaption on a four-year swap
   e. None of the above

Answer: a. The seven-year swap, callable in three-years, is simply a vanilla seven-year swap and a swaption that allows the buyer to receive fixed rates for four years, starting in three years. The cash flows of the two legs combine to form the callable swap.

9. A payer extendible swap is equal to a package of:
   a. Floating payer swap and payer swaption
   b. Floating payer swap and receiver swaption
   c. Fixed payer swap and callable swap

d. Fixed payer swap and receiver swaption

e. Fixed payer swap and payer swaption

Answer: e. The payer extendible swap is a product that extends the maturity horizon of a fixed payer swap. This is accomplished by allowing the fixed-rate payer the option to extend into a further fixed pay swap, which can only be done by adding in a payer swaption.

10. If a bank has sold an investor a callable asset swap package it will exercise against the investor when:

a. Credit spreads have widened beyond the strike

b. Interest rates have exceeded a fixed level

c. Credit spreads have tightened inside the strike

d. Interest rates have fallen below a fixed level

e. None of the above

Answer: c. The bank will call the package when there is an inherent gain on the credit-risky bond; this occurs when spreads tighten within the strike price related to the package.

CHAPTER 6 EXERCISES

1. Which of the following is/are true?

a. Selling a put is a bullish strategy

b. Buying a call is a bullish strategy

c. Selling a call is a bearish strategy

d. Buying a put is bearish strategy

e. All of the above are true

Answer: e. To capitalize on a bullish market an institution can buy a call (and gain the upside of the market) or sell a put (preserving premium); to capitalize on a bearish market it can sell a call (preserving premium) or buy a put (and gain the downside of the market).

2. What is the maximum net profit for a €/$ FX bull spread with a long at-the-money call of 1.20, a short call of 1.25, and a net premium of 0.005?

a. 0.045

b. 0.05

c. 0.055

d. 0.035

e. None of the above

Answer: a. The maximum profit that can be earned on a bull spread is the differential between the long and short strikes, less the cost of acquiring the spread. In this case it is equal to 1.25 – 1.20 – 0.005, or 0.045.

3. Which of the following is not a volatility strategy?
   a. Straddle
   b. Strangle
   c. Calendar spread
   d. Call spread
   e. Condor

Answer: d. The call spread, which involves the purchase and sale of calls at different strikes, seeks to take advantage of changes in market prices (within a limited range), rather than changes in volatility.

4. Which of the following can be used to create a long Nikkei straddle?
   a. Buy 16,000 call, sell 18,000 put
   b. Sell 16,000 call, buy 18,000 put
   c. Buy 16,000 call, sell 16,000 put
   d. Sell 18,000 call, buy 16,000 put
   e. Buy 18,000 call, sell 16,000 put

Answer: c. A straddle is created only by buying puts and calls with the same strike, in this case at 16,000. If the strikes are not matched, a straddle does not result.

5. A long butterfly is comprised of:
   a. A short call spread and a long strangle
   b. A long call spread and a short strangle
   c. A long straddle and a long strangle
   d. A long straddle and a short strangle
   e. A short straddle and a long strangle

Answer: e. A long butterfly, which is similar to a short straddle without the downside wings, is created by overlaying a long strangle on top of the short straddle. The long strangle neutralizes the straddle's downside wings.

6. The short butterfly is:
   a. Cheaper than a long straddle
   b. Provides less upside than a long straddle
   c. Is more expansive than a long straddle
   d. a and b
   e. b and c

   Answer: d. A short butterfly provides less upside profit potential than a long straddle as a result of the embedded short strangle. Since the upside profit is removed, it is cheaper than a straddle.

7. Which strategy would be taken to capitalize on increasing volatility?
   a. Long call spread
   b. Short straddle
   c. Long strangle
   d. Short put spread
   e. Short strangle

   Answer: c. To take advantage of a rise in volatility an institution could purchase a strangle (long call, long put, different strikes). The short straddle and strangle seek a quiet market, while the call and put spreads are focused on market direction rather than volatility.

CHAPTER 7 EXERCISES

1. Speculative positions can be created by
   a. Selling a strangle
   b. Buying a straddle
   c. Buying a power call
   d. Selling a put spread
   e. All of the above

   Answer: e. A speculative position is established through any position that does not have an underlying offsetting exposure. Each of the strategies noted can be used to express bullish or bearish views on market direction or volatiliy.

2. An up-and-out call can be a benefit to speculators because:
   a. It is cheaper than a vanilla option
   b. It allows crystallization of a very defined market view
   c. It can be applied across asset classes
   d. All of the above
   e. None of the above

   Answer: d. A speculator can use an up-and-out call to express a specific market view in any asset class, and can do so at a cheaper price (and with more precise results) than with a vanilla option.

3. The maximum payoff to a speculator on a down-and-in put struck at 1,000, with a barrier of 900 and a terminal price of 750 is:
   a. 250
   b. 100
   c. 150
   d. 350
   e. None of the above

   Answer: a. A down-and-in put pays off only if the barrier is triggered and the contract has intrinsic value. In this case a terminal price of 750 triggers the barrier (900), and the strike of 1,000 generates intrinsic value (1,000 – 750).

4. If a company has a foreign currency payable that is unhedged its liability will
   a. Increase if the foreign currency increases
   b. Decrease if the foreign currency increases
   c. Increase if the foreign currency remains unchanged
   d. Depend on market volatility
   e. None of the above

   Answer: a. An unhedged foreign currency liability increases if the foreign currency value increases versus the domestic currency. This occurs because the translation of the foreign currency liability back into the domestic currency is done at a less favorable exchange rate.

5. To hedge a foreign currency receivable exposure a company can
   a. Sell a foreign currency forward
   b. Buy a foreign currency put option
   c. Buy a domestic currency call option
   d. All of the above
   e. None of the above

   Answer: d. The foreign currency receivable needs to be protected against a strengthening of the domestic currency versus the foreign currency; this can be accomplished by selling the foreign currency forward, buying a foreign currency put, or buying a domestic currency call. Each solution produces a gain to offset a loss on the receivable.

6. A 75% participating forward is created through a package of:
   a. 25% forward, 75% option
   b. 75% forward, 25% option
   c. 50% forward, 50% option
   d. 10% forward, 90% option
   e. 100% forward

   Answer: a. The 75% participating forward provides 75% of the gains of a normal option, meaning the balance comes from the forward position; in exchange for giving up a portion of the gain the cost of the hedge strategy declines commensurately.

7. Consider the following collar transaction:
   Long call struck at 100, premium of 3
   Short put struck at 95, premium of 2
   If the price of the underlying moves to 105, the net P&L on the collar is:
   a. 3
   b. 4
   c. 5
   d. 2
   e. 1

   Answer: b. At a price of 105 the long call has 5 points of intrinsic value, the put is worthless, and the net premium paid is equal to 1 (e.g., 2 − 3).

8. Given the transaction details in 7, what is the net P&L if the price of the underlying moves to 91?

   a. – 2
   b. – 1
   c. 0
   d. – 3
   e. 3

   Answer: d. At a price of 91 the long call is worthless, the short put generates a liability of –4, and the net premium received amounts to 1 (e.g., 3 –2).

9. If a company is hedging a $10m 12-month interest-rate risk at 5% through the purchase of a cap that costs $62,000, what is the maximum all-in funding cost?

   a. 5%
   b. 5.26%
   c. 5.62%
   d. 5.72%
   e. None of the above

   Answer: c. The maximum cost the firm faces is equal to the 5% cap strike and the 62 bps premium paid for the contract (e.g., $62,000/$10m).

10. A company might choose to hedge with a collar to:
   a. Reduce its hedge cost
   b. Create more upside
   c. Create more downside
   d. All of the above
   e. None of the above

   Answer: a. The collar is a common strategy for hedgers who seek to reduce costs through the sale of an opposing option. Though it provides a floor on the hedge benefits that can be achieved, it results in a lower premium payable.

CHAPTER 8 EXERCISES

1. The one-year forward price of an asset is 100. The forward price in one year will be either 85 or 115, as shown below:

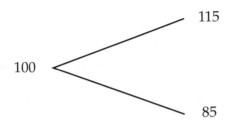

    12M Forward Price   Spot price in 12 months

a. What is the correct hedge of a short put struck at 95 in terms of amount and position (e.g., purchase or sale)?

Answer: The hedge of a short put is to sell the underlying asset. The amount is calculated using the following formula:

$$\text{Hedge}_{\text{Put}} = \frac{\text{Down} - \text{Strike}}{\text{Up} - \text{Down}}$$

$$\text{Hedge}_{\text{Put}} = \frac{85 - 95}{115 - 85} = \frac{-10}{30} = -0.3333 = -33.33\%$$

b. What is the price of the put struck at 95 if the one-year interest rate is 5%?

Answer: The value of the put can be calculated by comparing the P&L for either the Up move or the Down move (or both). This is shown as:

Case		Put	Hedge
Up	P&L =	0	Hedge × (Up − Forward)
Down	P&L =	(Down − Strike)	+ Hedge × (Down − Forward)

Case		Put	Hedge	All-In
Up	1.6000	0	− 33% × (115 − 100) = − 5	− 5
	1.5000			
Down	1.4000	(85 − 95) = − 10	− 33% × (85 − 100) = + 5	− 5

The option seller will lose 5 in either case. To bring his P&L back to zero in both cases, the option writer needs to have 5 of premium at the end of the year. To compute the premium paid up-front, the one-year future value must be discounted back to present value terms using the 5% discount rate:

$$\frac{5}{1+5\%} = 4.761905$$

This result can also be calculated on a financial calculator or spreadsheet:

	TVM Key	Value
1) Price of the option in one year	FV	5
2) Number of periods	N	1
3) Interim payments	PMT	0
4) Interest rate	i	5
5) Price of the option today	PV	4.761905

2. What is the relationship between option premium, intrinsic value, and time value?
   a. Option premium + Intrinsic value = Time value
   b. Option premium = Intrinsic value + Time value
   c. Option premium + Time value = Intrinsic value
   d. Option premium < Intrinsic value + Time value
   e. None of the above

   Answer: b. Option premium is always comprised of intrinsic value and time value. Though intrinsic value may equal 0 if the option is struck at- or out-of-money, it still forms part of the total option premium. Time value is always positive until expiry.

3. What is the intrinsic value of a put option on a one-year forward £/$ exchange rate with a strike of $1.5000, premium of $0.0765, and a market forward rate of $1.5200?
   a. 0
   b. 0.02
   c. −0.02
   d. 0.0765
   e. None of the above

Answer: a. The put gives the holder the right to sell at $1.50, but the current forward rate is $1.52, a rate higher than the option's strike price. This means that intrinsic value is equal to 0.

4. What happens to time value as an option approaches expiration (other factors remaining constant)?
   a. Time value increases, but only for out-of-the-money options
   b. Time value is constant for in-the-money options
   c. Time value increases for in-the-money options
   d. Time value declines for all options
   e. None of the above

   Answer: d. Time value represents the potential for the option to move (further) into the money. As expiry draws near the opportunity for volatility to move the price steadily reduces, until it reaches 0 at expiry.

5. Which of the following is/are true for in-the-money options?
   a. Calls: market price > strike price, puts: market price < strike price
   b. Calls: market price < strike price, puts: market price > strike price
   c. Calls: market price > strike price, puts: market price > strike price
   d. Calls: market price < strike price, puts: market price < strike price
   e. None of the above

   Answer: a. A call is in-the-money when the market price exceeds the strike price; at any point below that the option has no intrinsic value. Conversely, a put is in-the-money when the market price is below the strike price.

6. Which of the following is/are true for out-of-the-money options?
   a. Calls: market price > strike price, puts: market price < strike price
   b. Calls: market price < strike price, puts: market price > strike price

   c. Calls: market price > strike price, puts: market price > strike price
   d. Calls: market price < strike price, puts: market price < strike price
   e. None of the above

   Answer: b. A call is out-of-the money when the market price is below the strike price; at any point above that the option has intrinsic value. Conversely, a put is out-of-the-money when the market price is above the strike price.

7. Consider the following positions:
   Long call, strike 100, current asset price 101
   Long put, strike 99, current asset price 101
   Time value of call: 1
   Time value of put: 1
   Which of the following is/are true?
   a. Call intrinsic value = 1, time value = 1, option price = 2
   b. Put intrinsic value = – 1, time value = 1, option price = 0
   c. Call intrinsic value = – 1, time value = 1, option price = 0
   d. b and c are true
   e. None are true

   Answer: a. The call has intrinsic value of 1, which is the difference between the strike of 100 and the current asset price of 101; added to this is time value of 1, which yields an option price of 2. The put and call in the other responses are shown as negative; since an option is an asymmetric contract, it cannot have negative intrinsic value, only 0 intrinsic value.

8. Which of the following is not an input into the pricing of a currency option?
   a. Domestic interest rate
   b. Spot rate
   c. Volatility
   d. Dividends
   e. Time to expiry

   Answer: d. While dividends form part of the option valuation process, they are only applicable to stock and index contracts, and not currency contracts (which do not pay any dividends).

9. If the strike price of a call option on gold is increased, the value of the option will:
   a. Increase
   b. Decrease
   c. Remain the same
   d. Depends on the volatility of gold
   e. None of the above

   Answer: b. Since the call option conveys the right to buy gold at a specific price, raising that price reduces the potential profit of the option; accordingly, its value will decline.

10. Rising volatility increases the value of:
    a. Call options
    b. Put options
    c. Call and put options
    d. Depends on the strike price
    e. None of the above

    Answer: c. An increase in volatility means that the likelihood of an option, whether put or call, stands a greater chance of moving in-the-money (or further in-the-money). As a result, the value of the option increases.

11. As dividends are increased on a stock:
    a. Call prices decrease and put prices increase
    b. Call prices increase and put prices decrease
    c. Call prices and put prices decrease
    d. Call prices and put prices increase
    e. None of the above

    Answer: a. Dividends reduce the stock price on the ex-dividend date, which lower the value of a call and increases the value of a put.

CHAPTER 9 EXERCISES

1. Put-call parity in the Black-Scholes pricing framework indicates that:
   a. $C - P = X - S(\exp(-rt))$
   b. $C - P = S(\exp(-rt)) - X$
   c. $C + S(\exp(-rt)) = X - P$

d. $C - S(\exp(- rt)) = P - X$

e. None of the above

Answer: b. Put-call parity indicates that the value of a call less the value of a put is precisely equal to the discounted value of the asset less the strike.

2. The natural log of the daily returns of an asset price that trades at 47 on day one and 51 on day two is equal to:

   a. 3.75
   b. 3.65
   c. 3.85
   d. 3.95
   e. 4.05

Answer: c. The computation is simply LN(51/47), which yields a net result of 3.85.

3. Given asset volatility of 25% and a half-year time step, what is the upward move of an asset under the binomial framework?

   a. 118.34
   b. 117.89
   c. 123.32
   d. 119.26
   e. None of the above

Answer: d. Under the binomial framework the upward move of the asset is computed as $u = \exp(0.25 * \sqrt{0.5})$, or 119.26.

4. Given spot prices today of $1,000, 25% asset volatility, two standard deviation statistical measurement, and a time period of two years, what is the expected spot price in two years?

   a. 1,982
   b. 1,783
   c. 2,023
   d. 2,301
   e. 2,454

*Answer: c. Under the binomial framework the spot asset price in two years is computed as $\$1,000 * \exp(2 * 0.25 * \sqrt{2})$.*

5. A disadvantage of the geometric Brownian motion for interest rates is that:
   a. It allows for negative rates
   b. Rates do not mean revert
   c. The volatility of rates is constant across maturity
   d. All of the above
   e. None of the above

   Answer: d. The standard GBM, a one-factor process, is not generally suitable for interest rate modeling as it allows for negative rates and does not account for mean reversion or volatility differentiation.

6. Under the Black-Scholes framework the put price can be regarded intuitively as:
   a. (costs * weight of costs) – (benefits * weight of benefits)
   b. (costs * weight of costs) + (benefits * weight of benefits)
   c. (costs + benefits) * weight of benefits
   d. (costs – benefits) * weight of benefits
   e. None of the above

   Answer: a. The payoff of a put is equal to the strike less the market price, or cost-benefits. Under the Black-Scholes framework the weights (or probabilities) are inserted into the process to generate a value estimate.

7. Which of the following is/are true?
   a. Swaptions can be priced using a Black-Scholes extension
   b. A two-factor interest rate model is more difficult to calibrate than a one-factor model
   c. The most accurate interest rate models include mean reversion
   d. All of the above
   e. None of the above

   Answer: d. Though many pricing models can be used to generate swaption values, the Black-Scholes model can also be extended to serve the same purpose. Two-factor models, while more accurate than one-factor models, can also be more time-consuming to calibrate. Since historical data suggests that interest rates revert to some mean level over time, the most accurate models allow for some degree of reversion.

CHAPTER 10 EXERCISES

1. A bank has sold a €/$, 10 million € put with a delta of 45%. The position can be hedged by:
   a. Buying € 4.5 million against $ spot
   b. Selling € 4.5 million against $ spot
   c. Buying € 5.5 million against $ spot
   d. Selling € 5.5 million against $ spot
   e. None of the above

   Answer: b. If the buyer of the put exercises this option, the buyer will sell €10 million to the bank. The bank therefore delta hedges 45% by selling €4.5 million today in anticipation of possible exercise.

2. An option book manager is worried about imminent changes in currency volatility. Which tool might this manager use to measure this exposure in the trading book?
   a. Vega
   b. Theta
   c. Phi
   d. Gamma
   e. Rho

   Answer: a. Vega is the Greek measurement tool used to measure an option's sensitivity to changes in volatility. It is usually expressed as the change in option price for a 1.00% change in implied market volatility.

3. The sensitivity of an option's price to changes in spot is at its highest when the option is:
   a. At-the-money
   b. Out-of-the-money
   c. In-the-money
   d. Six months to expiry
   e. None of the above

   Answer: a. Because very small moves in spot can mean that an at-the-money option could go into the money, delta, gamma and vega sensitivities to the spot change are at their greatest for at-the-money options. Out- and in-the-money options display much lower sensitivities.

4. Delta measures the sensitivity of an option's price with regard to a change in:
   a. Time
   b. Volatility
   c. Rates
   d. Underlying asset
   e. None of the above

Answer: d. Delta measures the change in the option's price for a small change in the reference asset price. It can be further described as the slope of the line tangent to the payoff function.

5. Given an underlying asset of $100 and a strike price of $100, the delta of a long call is approximately equal to:
   a. -0.25
   b. $+0.25$
   c. -0.50
   d. $+0.50$
   e. $+0.10$

Answer: d. The long call option that is at-the-money has an approximately equal chance of ending in- or out-of-the-money, suggesting a delta of 50%; since the option gains in value as the asset price increases, if the delta is positive, not negative.

6. The proper sequence by which to rebalance an option portfolio is:
   a. Vega, gamma, delta
   b. Delta, gamma, vega
   c. Vega, delta, gamma
   d. It does not matter
   e. None of the above

Answer: a. Vega and gamma must be hedged before delta, because vega and gamma can be hedged only with other options (nonlinear instruments), while delta can be hedged with options or linear instruments. Since the addition of nonlinear instruments will also impact delta, delta must be managed as the final step.

7. Given the following positions:
   Long call + $100,000 delta
   Long put − $250,000 delta
   Short call − $100,000 delta
   The necessary hedge to neutralize delta is to:
   a. Buy $250,000
   b. Sell $250,000
   c. Buy $100,000
   d. Sell $100,000
   e. None of the above

   Answer: a. In order to neutralize the portfolio delta of −$250,000, the correct hedge is to repurchase $250,000. This will yield a net portfolio delta of 0.

8. Which of the following is/are true?
   a. At-the-money options have maximum gamma
   b. Out-of-the-money options have minimum gamma
   c. In-the-money options have minimum gamma
   d. All of the above
   e. None of the above

   Answer: d. Gamma is maximized for at-the-money options as delta is most sensitive to changes in the underlying at this point. When an option is well in- or out-of-the-money, delta is relatively insensitive to changes in the underlying, meaning gamma is low.

9. The inclusion of a barrier option in a portfolio:
   a. Always creates greater delta and gamma instability
   b. May create greater delta and gamma instability
   c. Never creates greater delta and gamma instability
   d. Creates the same delta and gamma instability
   e. None of the above

   Answer: b. A barrier option can create greater delta and gamma instability in a portfolio, though only if the market price of the underlying asset is approaching a sensitive barrier point. As the price moves away from the barrier, instability is no greater than it is for a vanilla options portfolio.

CHAPTER 11 EXERCISES

1. The credit risk exposure of an option contract is influenced by:
   a. Volatility
   b. Time
   c. Current intrinsic value
   d. All of the above
   e. None of the above

   Answer: d. The amount of credit risk in an option is a direct function of its value: the greater the value, the greater the potential risk. Volatility, time, and current intrinsic value all have a bearing on the value of an option and, by extension, its degree of risk.

2. Credit risk limits are typically established to:
   a. Control the maximum amount of counterparty losses
   b. Eliminate all credit losses
   c. Reduce gamma exposure
   d. All of the above
   e. None of the above

   Answer: a. Credit risk limits are created to control counterparty losses, not to eliminate all credit losses (which is a practical impossibility for a business that seeks to generate profit). Credit risk limits are not used to control gamma exposure, which is a market risk parameter.

3. Credit risk appears with short options:
   a. Never
   b. Always
   c. With select compound and currency options
   d. When combined with long options
   e. None of the above

   Answer: c. Credit risk does not appear with short option positions as the buyer is looking to the seller for performance, and not vice versa. However, two exceptions exist—certain compound options can lead to exercise against the seller, forcing the seller to become long on option, and currency options, which lead to delivery risk of currencies.

4. Which of the following is not a form of market risk?
    a. Delta risk
    b. Sovereign risk
    c. Basis risk
    d. Theta risk
    e. Gamma risk

Answer: b. Sovereign risk, which is the risk that a sovereign nation will impose capital or exchange controls, is a form of credit risk, not market risk. All others are market risks.

5. Which of the following form part of the conventional risk management process?
    a. Risk monitoring
    b. Risk identification
    c. Risk quantification
    d. Definition of tolerance
    e. All of the above

Answer: e. The standard risk management process begins with the definition of a risk tolerance (and philosophy). It is then followed by identification, quantification, management, and reporting. If any steps are lacking, the process may be flawed and inadequate in the control of risks.

6. FAS 133 accounting rules allow options (and other derivatives) to be accounted for as:
    a. Speculative (no hedge) position
    b. Currency hedge
    c. Cash flow hedge
    d. Fair value hedge
    e. All of the above

Answer: e. FAS 133 specifically permits an institution to treat an option position as a speculative position, or a currency, cash flow, or fair value hedge position; those classified as hedges must be properly documented.

7. Which of the following is/are not considered part of the regulatory risk framework?

   a. General market risk
   b. Specific market risk
   c. Detailed market risk
   d. Counterparty credit risk
   e. All are part of the regulatory framework

   Answer: c. Detailed market risk is not part of the regulatory risk framework. Capital charges are allocated on the basis of general and specific market risk and counterparty credit risk.

8. Which of the following is/are not part of the ISDA framework?

   a. Master Agreement
   b. Definitions
   c. Credit Support Documents
   d. Confirmations
   e. Attachments

   Answer: e. Attachments are not part of the ISDA frameworks, which is based on the Master Agreement (Schedule and Printed Form), Definitions, Confirmations, and Credit Support Documents.

SELECTED REFERENCES

Acharya, V, S Das, and R Sundrama, "Pricing Credit Derivatives with Rating Transitions," *Financial Analysts Journal*, May/June 2002, Vol. 58, p. 28.

Banks, E, 2006, *Synthetic and Structured Assets*, London: John Wiley and Sons.

Banks, E, 2004, *Alternative Risk Transfer*, London: John Wiley and Sons.

Banks, E, 2004, *The Credit Risk of Complex Derivatives*, 3d edition, London: Palgrave.

Banks, E, and R Dunn 2004, *Practical Risk Management*, London: John Wiley and Sons.

Black, F, and M Scholes 1973, "The Pricing of Options and Corporate Liabilities," *Journal of Political Economy*, 81, May–June.

Bodie, Z, A Kane and A Marcus, 2005, *Investments*, 6th edition, New York: McGraw-Hill Irwin.

Brennan, M, and E Schwartz 1980, "Analyzing Convertible Bonds," *Journal of Financial and Quantitative Analysis*, 15, pp. 907–929.

Chew, D, 1992, "The Use of Hybrid Debt in Managing Corporate Risk," *Journal of Applied Corporate Finance*, Winter.

Choudhry, M, 2004, *Structured Credit Products*, London: John Wiley and Sons.

Das, S, 2002, *Credit Derivatives and Credit Linked Notes*, 2d edition, Singapore: John Wiley and Sons.

Das, S, 1996, *Structured Notes and Derivative-Embedded Securities*, London: Euromoney.

Das, S, 1994, *Swaps and Financial Derivatives*, 2d edition, Sydney: Law Book Company.

Fabozzi, F, ed, 1993, *Bond Markets*, 2d edition, Englewood Cliffs, NJ: Prentice Hall.

Fabozzi, F, ed, 1993, *The Handbook of Mortgage Backed Securities*, 2d edition, Chicago: Probus.

Haug, E, 1997, *The Complete Guide to Option Pricing Formulas*, New York: McGraw-Hill.

Higham, D, 2004, *An Introduction to Financial Option Valuation*, Cambridge: Cambridge University Press.

Kolb, R, and J Overdahl 2002, *Financial Derivatives*, 3d edition, New York: John Wiley and Sons.

McDonald, R, 2003, *Derivatives Markets*, Boston: Addison Wesley.

McLeish, D, 2005, *Monte Carlo Simulation and Finance*, New York: John Wiley and Sons.

Nelken, I, 1999, *Implementing Credit Derivatives*, New Jersey: Irwin.

Ong, M, 1999, *Internal Credit Risk Models*, London: Risk Books.

Rebonato, R, 2004, *Volatility and Correlation*, 2d edition, New York: John Wiley and Sons.

Redmayne, J, 1993, *Convertibles*, London: Euromoney.

Smithson, C, 1999, *Managing Financial Risk*, 3d edition, New York: McGraw-Hill.

Taleb, N, 1997, *Dynamic Hedging*, New York: John Wiley and Sons.

Tavakoli, J, 1998, *Credit Derivatives*, New York: John Wiley and Sons.

Zubulake, L, 1991, *Guide to Convertible Securities Worldwide*, New York: John Wiley and Sons.

INDEX

About the Authors

Erik Banks is chief risk officer at a multistrategy hedge fund and has been active in the banking sector for 20 years. Erik has held senior risk management positions at Merrill Lynch, XL Capital, and Citibank in New York, Tokyo, London, and Hong Kong, and has written 20 books on derivatives, risk, emerging markets, and merchant banking.

Paul Siegel is Chief Executive Officer of The Globecon Group, a specialized banking and financial services professional development, conference, and publishing firm operating in the capital markets, credit, risk, corporate finance, and wealth management markets. Paul holds a bachelor's degree in economics and a master's degree in business from the University of Pennsylvania and New York University, respectively. He lives in the New York area with his wife, Helen, and their two amazing children, Lexy and Sam.